S0-BLE-566

FORTUNE'S WHEEL

ELIZABETH A. CAMPBELL

FORTUNE'S WHEEL

Dickens and the Iconography of Women's Time

OHIO UNIVERSITY PRESS • ATHENS

Ohio University Press, Athens, Ohio 45701

Ohio University Press books are printed on acid-free paper ™

11 10 09 08 07 06 05 04 03 5 4 3 2 1

Library of Congress Cataloging-in-Publication Data

Campbell, Elizabeth A., 1945-
Fortune's wheel : Dickens and the iconography of women's time / Elizabeth A. Campbell.
p. cm.
ISBN 0-8214-1514-X (alk. paper)
1. Dickens, Charles, 1812-1870—Criticism and interpretation. 2. Fate and fatalism in literature. 3. Tragic, The, in literature. 4. Fortune in literature. 5. Wheels in literature. 6. Cycles in literature. 7. Women in literature. 8. Time in literature. I. Title.

PR4592.F38C36 2003
823'.8—dc21

2003049891

To Pauline in memory of J.T.

CONTENTS

ILLUSTRATIONS

Following page 155:

ACKNOWLEDGMENTS

I wish to thank the Center for the Humanities at Oregon State University for funding a project on "Women's Time" eleven years ago that became the nucleus of this book. The fellows and especially the director, the late Peter Copek (a friend and Dickensian), were instrumental in helping me form my ideas and giving me support, as have been numerous of my colleagues in the Department of English at Oregon State, in particular Tracy Daugherty and Rich Daniels, who read portions of the manuscript and offered helpful advice; Heidi Brayman Hackel, who has been teaching me much about Renaissance literature; and Marjorie Sandor and Linc Kesler, for their much appreciated encouragement over the long haul. I want to thank the Oregon State University Valley Library for funding a trip to the Bodleian and British Libraries, which was invaluable; and the Oregon State University English Department for funding to defray production expenses. I am most grateful to Professor Michael Steig for his expertise on Dickens's iconography. His *Dickens and Phiz* has been indispensable, as have been his comments on my manuscript. Anita Sullivan and Adelheid Fischer have listened patiently and responded in kind over the years as my ideas developed. Finally I would like to thank my husband, Ted Leeson, for his Herculean labors throughout; he has shouldered the wheel in more ways than I can name, and I could not have written this book without him.

INTRODUCTION

In this round world of many circles within circles, do
we make a weary journey from the high grade to
the low, to find at last that they lie close together, that
the two extremes touch, and that our journey's end
is but our starting-place?

—CHARLES DICKENS, *Dombey and Son*

Of the many sweeping changes the Industrial Revolution brought to England, one obvious change whose importance has often been overlooked was the reinvention of the wheel in Victorian iconography. The phrase "wheels of industry" was no empty metaphor, for the great technological advances of the period, like the traditional mechanisms that had provided motion and power for centuries, had everything to do with wheels. Throughout the nineteenth century waterwheels and windmills continued to be conspicuous—and increasingly efficient—features of the British landscape, serving as crucial sources of power for manufacturing as well as for mining and milling grain.[1] Carlyle's name for his representative Captain of Industry, "Plugson of Undershot," which recalls the wooden undershot waterwheels most common in England from the Middle Ages until the eighteenth century, attests to the ongoing importance of this method for driving machines in the textile industry during the early Victorian period.[2] Wheeled transportation also improved, with sophisticated engineering of bridges and roads and technological advances in processing iron, making swift and more frequent travel in well-designed mail coaches and private carriages a reality for more people of every rank. It is no wonder that in the nineteenth-century novel, the phrase "the sound of wheels" is fraught with significance, for the arrival of a carriage was commonplace enough to serve as a credible plot device, while still dramatic enough to communicate a sense of excitement, urgency, or dread.

But the prime mover of the Industrial Revolution was the steam engine, which became adaptable to a broadening range of industrial applications after the late eighteenth century, when James Watt made steam-powered rotary action possible with his groundbreaking "sun and planet" gear system, consisting of a wheel circling another wheel to turn a giant flywheel, which moved a beam connected to the engine's piston.[3] These are the "intricate wheels" of factory work that William Blake describes, with remarkable accuracy, in *The Four Zoas:*

> Wheel without wheel,
> To perplex youth in their outgoings & to bind to labours
> Of day and night the myriads of Eternity, that they might file
> And polish brass & iron hour after hour, . . .[4]

Even more astonishing were the steam-powered wheels of the trains, which revolutionized travel and transportation, as well as the English landscape and culture, for all time. The history of the locomotive begins in the mining industry at the turn of the nineteenth century, when Richard Trevithick's compact high-pressure engine made portable steam power practicable. The locomotive he designed for hauling coal from the Welsh mines inspired further improvements that eventually led to the celebrated *Rocket,* built by George Stephenson and son, and then to the opening of the Liverpool and Manchester Railway on September 15, 1830. The Railway Age had begun.[5] By 1872, as Gustave Doré's "Ludgate Hill" reveals, Victorian London—and by implication, the modern city—had come to be defined by its wheeled conveyances, whether horse-drawn or steam-powered (plate 1).[6]

This familiar illustration, taken from the heart of Dickens's city and depicting a jam in Fleet Street at Ludgate Circus of omnibuses, hansoms, carts, wagons, and people hemming in a flock of sheep, could well have been intended as both a celebration and parody of progress in the new industrial age. Above the crush of animals and old-fashioned vehicles a train steams by, but the Escher-like bridge on which it travels seems to terminate at the wall of a nearby building. St. Paul's rises majestically in the background on the left, but the engine's trail of smoke directs the viewer's attention to the building on the opposite side, where an advertisement for the London, Chatham, and Dover Railway agents Partington and Company reasserts the ascendancy of steam-powered locomotion in Victorian England's hierarchy of values. Indeed, in the first half of the century, the wheels of trains had already been inserted into biblical typology. As John Francis noted in *A History of the English Railway* (1851), the British obsession with the new railway system during the mid-1840s caused ministers to reinterpret Ezekiel's vision as an apocalyptic prophecy of the nineteenth-century changes brought about by steam locomotion, moving swiftly and inexorably to the farthest corners of England on "the chariot wheels of the Fire King."[7]

If the railway elicited a range of responses from enthusiasm to fear, the many wheels on display at the Great Exhibition in 1851 and recorded in the official catalogue attest to their inextricable association with midcentury faith in "the progress of the human race." They were the means to the end that the exhibition promoted, according to its royal patron, Prince Albert, who proclaimed, "we are accomplishing the will of the great and blessed God."[8] In the extensive Machinery in Motion department, gears, wheels, and rollers of every size turned in the manufacture of textiles and many other products, while vehicles and wheeled implements of all descriptions filled the carriage court, the locomotive exhibit, and the agricultural machinery section inside and outside the Crystal Palace. These included not only Watt's steam engine, McCormick's reaper, and a carriage fire engine built by Moses Merryweather, called the "Paxton" after the Crystal Palace's designer, but also phaetons, barouches, broughams, and Bath chairs.[9] As these examples suggest, the industrial world was quite literally a world on wheels, and it is no wonder that they move from such particular, metonymic examples to the controlling metaphor in the economic theory of the period. Adam Smith had defined "[t]he great wheel of circulation" in *The Wealth of Nations* as being "different from the goods that are circulated by means of it," thereby establishing a trade-cycle theory advanced by (among others) Frederick Engels, in *The Condition of the Working Class of England.* In chapter 4 ("Competition") of Engels's work, the full range of literal and tropic meanings occur: wheels serve as a motif to denote the new industrial age, characterized by "a great deal of wheeled traffic"; "the wheels of industry" metaphorically stand for the new, steam-powered "factory wheels"; and the metonymical use of the above examples underscores Engels's theory of the English industrial trade cycle as "a continuous series of cycles of boom and slump."[10] The wheel thus suggested common terms for the newly created industrial rhythm of life—as diurnal "rounds" of activity and movement between the public and private "spheres." In short, the wheels and cycles of industry defined a new economic rule of life that affected nineteenth-century time more immediately than the cycles of nature—the turn of the seasons or the wheel of the stars—creating a new order of time and being that couched "felt" time almost entirely in economic terms. And even though, as E. P. Thompson explains, "violence was done to *human* nature" by way of the new capitalist values that promoted a "violent technological differentiation between work and life,"[11] the official narrative of the Victorian era at midcentury was one of self-congratulation and improvement. There was a sense that England's exalted position as the first industrial nation was part of a divine plan, the workings of a special national providence. The iron wheels of the Victorians, therefore, carried astonishingly heavy baggage—actual as well as philosophical, religious, economic, political, and historical; and these wheels—both real and symbolic—revolved at hitherto unforeseeable speeds to become major tropes for power, modernity, and progress.

For a new technological age obsessed with wheels and wealth, the iconographic tradition of Fortune's wheel, so richly suggestive to preindustrial Europe from the late classical period to the eighteenth century, would seem to be a natural source of imagery; but certain elements in the goddess's checkered past must have rendered the icon unacceptable to the morally earnest Victorians. The personification of chance or luck, Fortune by definition embodies uncertainty, and this quality marred her reputation from late Roman times, causing even the society that gave her birth to label her a strumpet or whore. As most famously articulated by the sixth-century Roman politician and philosopher Boethius, Fortune symbolizes the mutability inherent in all human affairs, which is suggested by the wheel she spins; and it was as a cautionary tale about the consequences of worshipping Fortune that the icon found its way into the medieval church. But because the dangers inherent in pursuing fortune could never be separated from its desirability, the goddess demonstrated remarkable staying power through the Renaissance, when Fortune's wheel became one of the most ubiquitous and celebrated emblems in literature and art.[12] With the ascendancy of the iconoclastic and strictly conscienced Puritans in the next century, however, Fortune's reputation suffered, not only because of her pagan origins and her worldly—even reprobate—character, but also because "fortune," no longer considered "chance," was attributed to God's providential design and direct involvement in human affairs.[13] Puritanism, therefore, dealt Fortune a blow from which she never fully recovered; and even though the mania for speculation and riches in the more secular and sophisticated eighteenth century revived considerable interest in both the idea and the icon, the goddess emerges as an ironic or comic figure, no longer to be taken seriously after the Industrial Revolution—certainly not among the mid-Victorian proponents of national and historical progress. Thus it was left for the genius of Charles Dickens to retrieve and transform, renew and revitalize, Fortune's wheel for the Victorian period. Indeed, Fortune is the only representative of the classical pantheon who serves, deftly, to personify Dickens's world.[14] Nevertheless, critics have generally taken the presence of Fortune on the cover wrappers of two major novels (*Nicholas Nickleby* and Dickens's signature novel, *David Copperfield*) for granted, as they have the increasingly significant and formidable role that wheel imagery plays in the midcentury novels. I wish to show that Dickens's Fortune and wheel imagery are not separable motifs, but come together dramatically to offer a commentary about "fortune" in the economic sense and about Dickens's beliefs concerning gender and time in the Victorian era.

No doubt the most immediate influence on Dickens's iconography of Fortune's wheel were the graphic and literary images of the goddess found in the works of Hogarth and Fielding, which mark her last grand appearances before the Industrial Revolution. In early engravings from the 1720s like *Benefit Ticket for Spiller, The South Sea Scheme,* and *The Lottery,* Hogarth parodied the emblematic tradition by depicting Fortune ironically and her wheel as an Ixionic rack or an enormous merry-go-round of chance and speculation. Fielding continues this ironic trend by appropriating Shakespeare's and Machiavelli's Fortune, turning her into the playful goddess who sports with the title character throughout *Tom Jones* but who reigns supreme in London when Tom arrives there in the unlucky book 13. We know that Hogarth's and Fielding's works were still a living part of Victorian popular culture, and their influence on Dickens is pervasive. But Dickens was also keenly responsive to folkloric and oral traditions, and what remains of ephemeral literature—as recorded in the broadsides, chapbooks, penny merriments, and almanacs that saturated London and the countryside from the English Civil Wars well into the nineteenth century—indicates that Fortune and her wheel remained alive and well and living in England among the poor. Chapbook works instructing readers in the art of divination (like *Mother Shipton's Wheel of Fortune*) or "histories" (like that of Fortunatus) recycled Fortune's wheel for the entertainment of the lower classes.[15] The popularity of these works is not surprising. For those people at the bottom of the social order, the idea of Fortune's inevitable, if unpredictable, turning of her wheel offered the only traditionally sanctioned model that seemed to promise improvement for their unfortunate, impoverished condition. The rival model—the Christian providential one—had by the mid-nineteenth century been so completely appropriated by the middle classes as a rationalization and justification of their successes that "providence" and "progress" (both construing history as a rising, linear projectile rather than a series of cycles) were practically synonymous terms.[16] Thus poverty and hardship were increasingly equated with moral disability—forcing the more ambitious and the most frustrated among the poor to put even more faith in the sudden appearance of the goddess Fortune. These two iconographic traditions—the middle-class and the ephemeral—continue in Dickens's works most obviously in the Phiz-illustrated cover-wrapper Fortunes: the blind goddess with her cornucopia and wheel who graces the top of the *Nickleby* wrapper recalls the emblematic tradition that culminated with Hogarth's engravings, whereas the aged, grotesque Fortuna who holds the same position on the *Copperfield* wrapper reflects the influence of street literature. Moreover, these two designs suggest the two aspects of the goddess that appear in various permutations as Fortune's avatars in the novels: the youthful, sexually attractive Fortune who embodies the hero's desires, and the Fortune as ancient and deadly sorceress who embodies the hero's fears, reminding him of his vulnerability and mortality. The most obvious examples of these pairs are Mrs. Skewton and Edith Granger (with their doubles Mrs. Brown and Alice Marwood) in *Dombey and Son* and Miss Havisham and Estella in *Great Expectations;* but I argue that Lady Dedlock and Esther Summerson in *Bleak House* and Amy Dorrit and Mrs. Clennam in *Little Dorrit* are also exciting innovations on this pattern. They serve as commentary on Dickens's vision of the world becoming Fortune's—and women's—sphere. Thus what may have begun as illustration seems to have evolved quickly into narrative imagery and, finally, into controlling idea, for the great structural principle that becomes operative in Dickens's novels at midcentury is one of circularity, identifiable with Fortune's wheel.

My purpose in this study is to trace this revolution in Dickens's iconography of the wheel, from the "wheel of Time" rolling to its providential conclusion at the end of *Pictures from Italy* to the more fatal images of the "Wheel of Chancery" and the "whirling wheel of life" that inform *Bleak House* and *Little Dorrit.* As the wheel came more and more to be employed as an official symbol for British industrial and economic progress, Dickens reacted like Barrett Browning in "The Cry of the Children," increasingly using wheel imagery as a symbol for punishment and oppression of the innocent and the victimized. Ultimately, Dickens's imagery suggests that the industrial wheel and Fortune's wheel conjoin to become a tragic symbol of fate. In the words of R. Rupert Roopnaraine, describing Dickens's vision in *Little Dorrit,* "The 'whirling wheel of life,' with its implications of a detached, cynical fate and of a mechanical rotation of life's events and experiences, becomes the symbol of utter, irreversible futility. Human lives, trapped on a great cosmic roulette wheel spun by a wanton fate, fall victim to fortuitousness and contingency."[17] Although Roopnaraine does not identify it as such, this is the wheel of Fortune as Boethius described it. Moreover, Dickens's Fortune, like Boethius's and especially Machiavelli's, is emphatically a woman: that is, in conjunction with the controlling wheel imagery there emerges a vision of the historical moment as one in which women, for good or ill, are the prime movers and decisive agents in the affairs of the world, so that Fortune's wheel becomes a complex emblem of emasculation and incarceration, associated with feminine fatality and temporality. Edward Burne-Jones's several versions of the *Wheel of Fortune,* begun in 1871, might serve as an iconographical model for Dickens's final conception of Fortune's wheel, as a symbol for man's fate in the hands of a more powerful feminine principle.

Through Dickens's imagery the industrial wheel comes full circle into an emblem of fate and of "women's time," as Julia Kristeva has described it. That is, rather than envisioning time as history, moving in a linear fashion (the temporality traditionally associated with men), Dickens's narratives give priority to time's cyclicality, to the representation of time as a space that emphasizes at once repetition and eternal return—movements inherent in the turning of a wheel. Dickens, like his contemporaries, was obsessed with time and offers many patterns of temporality in his novels; but circularity comes to predominate after midcentury.[18] This cyclical and monumental time, Kristeva explains, is associated with female subjectivity because of women's intrinsic connection to the biological rhythms of life by way of maternal functions: women's bodies, through the processes necessary for reproduction—menstruation and gestation—register the repetitive rhythms of nature more obviously than men's.[19] This way of conceiving time also applies to the rhythm of an earlier historical moment when an agrarian culture lived in closer harmony with the seasons and cycles of nature, generations moving from birth to death—from beginnings to endings—within the larger circle of the cosmos. Thus medieval preachers used the iconographic Fortune's wheel as an exemplum for "women's time," according to this definition, to represent "the inevitable round of existence for every mortal human being, the successive stages of man's tragic journey upon earth from cradle to grave."[20] Similarly, Dickens's final conception of Fortune's wheel returns to this vision, which brings the temporalities of Fortune and Nature together.

The revolution in Dickens's wheel imagery—from a sign for linear progress to a tragic emblem of fate and female power—develops most visibly in those novels devoted to a serious consideration of "women's time," defined in various ways that are all implied by Kristeva's discussion. First, Dickens's narratives begin to turn from the picaresque to the domestic after he becomes a father several times over, and thus becomes intimately involved in the cycles of maternal reproduction that rivaled his own fecund writerly production. It is probably no coincidence that the inimitable nurse and midwife Sairey Gamp, who presides over "a lying-in or laying out with equal zest and relish" (and who complains about the untoward effects on gestation of steam-engines, calling them a "man's inwention"), appears in Dickens's fiction during this period (*MC,* 313). Second, this new focus on domesticity inevitably engages Dickens's imagination with a consideration of women's sphere and its proper limits: with a historical moment when a "female sensibility" became a matter of public discourse that included the introduction of gendered conceptions of time.[21] And third, Dickens's abiding fascination with the female in the roles of daughter, sister, companion, lover, mother, and destroyer informs his mature novels to such an extent that women literally take control in and of his narratives, so that these novels can be said to be written under the influence of women's time. I therefore trace Dickens's development of female characters and his new sensitivity to women's concerns from the 1840s to the mid-1850s, when women's time was clearly a focus of his art. Thus the bulk of this study will be a close consideration of Dickens's "women's" novels, the three works that seem to have been written with a female audience and/or women's concerns particularly in mind: *Dombey and Son, Bleak House,* and *Little Dorrit.* The final chapter, on *Great Expectations,* shows the results of these deliberations on women and time: the theme seriously explored in *Little Dorrit* of a world governed by women is parodied rather bitterly here, thereby suggesting that the era of "men's time" is over and that women have gained full control in both the public and private spheres. Appropriately, avatars of the goddess Fortune are most noticeably present in these four works, which also use the wheel as a local motif and a controlling metaphor to symbolize the relentless cyclicality of existence that had come to characterize Dickens's world.

ABBREVIATIONS

For page references to Dickens's novels and travel writings throughout this book I have used the Oxford Illustrated Dickens, with the following title abbreviations:

BL	*Bleak House*
CHE	*A Child's History of England*
DS	*Dombey and Son*
DC	*David Copperfield*
GE	*Great Expectations*
HT	*Hard Times*
LD	*Little Dorrit*
MC	*Martin Chuzzlewit*
MHC	*Master Humphrey's Clock*
NN	*Nicholas Nickleby*
OCS	*The Old Curiosity Shop*
OMF	*Our Mutual Friend*
OT	*Oliver Twist*
PI	*Pictures from Italy*
PP	*Pickwick Papers*
SB	*Sketches by Boz*
TTC	*A Tale of Two Cities*
UT	*The Uncommercial Traveller and Reprinted Pieces*

THE WORLD OF FORTUNE

1

You have put yourself in Fortune's power; now you must be content with the ways of your mistress. If you try to stop the force of her turning wheel, you are the most foolish man alive. If it should stop turning, it would cease to be Fortune's wheel.

—LADY PHILOSOPHY TO BOETHIUS, *The Consolation of Philosophy*

Two Cover Wrappers

When *Nicholas Nickleby* began serial publication on March 31, 1838, Dickens had completed only the opening number of this, his third novel. His illustrator, Hablot K. Browne, whose task it was to design the cover wrapper that would appear on each of the novel's nineteen monthly installments, was therefore faced with, as Michael Steig says, "the most iconographically interesting challenge" of his career.[1] Since the cover had to be suitable for a narrative whose particulars had not yet been created, Browne's design needed to be generic—that is, conventional enough to bear some thematic resemblance to Dickens's story as it unfolded. Given this requirement, the wrapper that "Phiz" fashioned would prove to be thematically appropriate not just for this first number or even the rest of *Nicholas Nickleby,* but for almost all of Dickens's subsequent novels as well. The predominating scene at the top of the design suggests a traditional allegorical story familiar enough to be grasped by a majority of nineteenth-century viewers, even those who were barely literate (plate 2).[2]

At the top of the cover and slightly right of center, a blindfolded woman bends over to the left, pointing a rod or wand toward a young man, who leans against a rock and holds his head. To the left of the woman is a wheel, and to her right a cornucopia, from which bags of money seem to be flowing. Farther to the right is a person, probably a woman, in a clearly haggard condition, with hair flying about wildly and clothes—or what remains of them—in rags. Of these three human figures, the only one identifiable by name (and positively identifiable by gender) is the blindfolded woman who occupies the highest position in the design. She is, of course, Fortune, described by Howard Patch as the only exclusively Roman deity "to have survived the fall of ancient Rome."[3] Her dress suggests her classical origins, just as her youthful figure reveals her desirability. Of the two accoutrements that flank Fortune in this scene, only the cornucopia is visually self-explanatory: it seems to have poured forth its plenty just before the scene was captured, indicating that when the distraught young man feels the prick of the wand, he will turn around and find good fortune. (Misfortune is indicated by the haggard figure at the right.) The wheel, on the other hand, which looks rather ordinary, like one made for a cart or a horse-drawn wagon, has no obvious narrative function here; but its unobtrusiveness conceals the wheel's far greater symbolic value, the significance of which is one of the major concerns of this study.

By itself, this top scene of Browne's cover wrapper metaphorically and quite conventionally symbolizes the nineteenth-century world that Dickens inhabited and represented in his novels. As Stephen Wall described it over thirty years ago, this is a world "largely governed by fortune, in the modern, economic sense of the word."[4] But the personification of Fortune as a female deity, one credited in this design with control over human affairs, should not be taken for granted—as most Dickens critics have done. As W. J. T. Mitchell argues, iconographic conventions, however familiar or innocent they may appear to be, are laden with social, cultural, and political—that is to say, ideological—value.[5] Erwin Panofsky explains in *Studies in Iconology* that symbols or icons stay alive if their meaning can somehow be adapted to current cultural and social concerns; consequently their histories are often highly complex, and the historical moment—as well as the local context—must be considered as the best guide to interpretation.[6] Nevertheless, the ability of an icon to withstand the test of time is an indication of a rich, if varied, heritage, one whose implications are worth exploring. Since Dickens more than any other artist insured the survival of Fortune through the mid-nineteenth century, a study of his novels during this period provides the crucial grounding for what happens to the goddess and the iconographic wheel in the Victorian era. Briefly, Dickens's representation of Fortune and his wheel imagery conjoin over the course of his career to reveal an actual revolution in his thinking about historical time: from faith in a linear, progressive, "masculine" time to a belief in a more fatalistic, cyclical time that could be construed—in several distinct, but related, ways—as "feminine." As the industrial wheel in official iconography during this period became more and more a symbol for Victorian progress, Dickens counters this movement by returning the wheel to its earlier significance as a symbol—essentially a tragic one—for the cyclicality of existence and a geometric visualization of man's fate.

Both Dickens and Browne continue a long iconographic tradition that conflates Fortune and Time.[7] But their great contribution to this tradition was to reveal how the iconographic Fortune's wheel conveys a timely historical message about women's power and potentiality. That is, Browne's and particularly Dickens's implementation of this icon coincides with the moment in history—the nineteenth century—when the topic of gender became an obsession in public discourse. Male and female writers alike attempted to specify the essences of gender and to prescribe the rights and duties of both sexes. Moreover, an incipient women's movement launched its investigation of what it means to be female and of how gender affects all relationships, extending beyond the private and domestic and into the public sphere. Much attention was being focused on what constituted the "female sensibility," and toward the latter part of the century the New Woman had emerged, quite self-consciously creating an imposing space for the female gender in history. And this double way of apprehending "women's time"—as a cyclical calibration of time associated with motherhood, repetition, and reproduction and as a space or an opening in history in which women find themselves and even take control—is registered in Dickens's iconography.[8]

Thus Dickens's particular way of fusing ideas about fortune (meaning both wealth and chance) with sexuality and temporality in the image of Fortune's wheel was unprecedented and indeed probably impossible before the nineteenth century. As depicted in the iconography of Dickens's novels—via the illustrations and through textual imagery and structure—Fortune's power over temporal affairs suggests both the high value placed on wealth and prosperity in Victorian society and the increasing symbolic (and often real) power of women in nineteenth-century England. Dickens's representations of Fortune and his iconographic use of the wheel register his growing belief in a theory that Havelock Ellis would posit at the end of the century in his assessment of gender roles through history—that civilization charts the widening sphere of what were originally female industries, so that industrialization and feminization are synonymous. In Ellis's words from *Man and Woman:* "our phase of civilization has been industrial, that is to say, feminine, in character, for the development of the industries belonged primitively to women, and they tend to make men like women. . . . While the women remain as 'womanly' as ever, the men have become less 'manly.'"[9] Dickens's appropriation of Fortune and her wheel records a male artist's evolving consciousness of a world that to his mind is becoming increasingly feminized, a world in which female authority, by the latter half of the century, comes into its own and in some cases gains ascendancy.[10] Not surprisingly, this change in Dickens's thinking becomes most apparent through the course of those mid-career novels that have as their primary focus a female protagonist. This study therefore considers in greatest detail the way Dickens employs Fortune and wheel imagery in what we might call his three "female" novels: *Dombey and Son, Bleak House,* and *Little Dorrit,* where the world that Amy and Arthur go "quietly down into" on that fall morning at the novel's conclusion is without question a world governed by Fortune.

It is now widely accepted that Victorian novelists in general, and Dickens in particular, "strove for the illusion of a complete world" as a method of satisfying an aesthetic centered in realism.[11] J. Hillis Miller's more specific definition of "the world of Dickens' novels" as one whose "totality" finds its "concrete embodiment" in "the great modern commercial city"—particularly London—underscores the fact that Fortune's world and Dickens's world are one and the same.[12] This conjunction is not surprising: the task of representing anything so incomprehensibly vast and complex as the modern city of course requires dependence on convention—and Fortune's earliest connection, with the great urban commercial and financial center of Rome, makes her a likely candidate for iconographic appropriation by nineteenth-century London.[13] But Fortune's association with both superstition and risk seems to have dictated that—except for the major exception of Dickens—she not be taken too seriously in literary and artistic imagery until the last third of the century, when she reappears as the epitome of the "monumental heroic female" in Edward Burne-Jones's six versions of "The Wheel of Fortune," which he began in 1871.[14]

One conventional way of representing the city among Victorian artists, including Dickens, was to draw images more directly from the Christian, especially the Puritan, tradition, as Alexander Welsh has most effectively demonstrated. According to Welsh, the metaphor inherited and employed by Dickens was the "Christian tradition of two cities," which "supposed that the earthly city must contain its own antithesis"—namely, the celestial city of John's *Revelation.*[15] But Dickens's novels could convey a truth about modern urban existence by incorporating antithesis without recourse to New Testament exegesis: a streetwise but theologically ignorant nineteenth-century Londoner did not need a knowledge of Christian typology to apprehend the city's antithetical qualities. The most visible of these, wealth and poverty, must have been as immediately obvious to even the most casual observer as they were to the more discerning Disraeli, whose concept of the two nations, the rich and the poor, was quickly embraced as a truth by his contemporaries. The sight of such polarized economic situations—in any century—tends to call attention to the temporal at the expense of things eternal.

The top scene of the *Nickleby* cover wrapper thus illustrates what subsequent novels bear out: because Dickens's world is ruled by "fortune" in the economic sense, this world partakes of the randomness, chance, unpredictability, blindness, and even the fickleness that have traditionally characterized Fortune, the goddess who presides over worldly riches and prosperity. Fortune's world also operates by the economic principle of supply and demand, which is a law of antithesis: this world includes both prosperity and adversity, for these very terms accrue meaning only in their relation to one another. This inclusive conception of fortune is accurately symbolized by the wheel, whose circular shape signifies closure and whose function of turning suggests the possibility (indeed, the inevitability) of reversal. In other words, the iconographic wheel of Fortune symbolizes the belief that, since there is a fixed supply of "good" fortune, one person's success necessitates someone else's failure. This principle, writ large, underscores the nineteenth-century theory of trade cycles, as advanced by Engels in the mid-1840s, a few years after the publication of *Nicholas Nickleby.*

From the viewer's perspective (and according to a familiar emblematic pattern that Browne would employ in later cover designs), the left side of the *Nickleby* cover illustrates good fortune, while ill fortune is depicted on the right. Here, this division is made explicit by the facial expressions of the two comical figures on stilts who hold up the cover's top scene. Interestingly, the gender of these two rustics can be easily distinguished, and Browne's assignment of the unfortunate right side to a weeping woman may be an acknowledgment (although probably an unconscious one) of the typically mournful role of the female in Dickens's comedy up to this point in the novelist's career. Interestingly, this woman wears a conspicuous ornament or medallion of some sort around her neck. It may be worth recalling (with thanks to J. Hillis Miller) that Browne had similarly placed a watch on a chain around Pickwick's neck as a focal center in "plate after plate" of *Pickwick Papers* to call attention to the hero's "globular white stomach"—with both watch and stomach serving as visual puns to indicate Pickwick's sunlike radiance.[16] If the sun imagery of Pickwick suggests what Steven Marcus termed the "thoroughly masculine world" of Dickens's first novel,[17] then this woman's ornament could be intended to convey a more reflectively mournful "female" world, perhaps to be associated with the crescent moon between the woman's stilts in the lower right-hand corner of the design.

Whereas Browne's scene at the top conveys a somewhat static, but nevertheless self-explanatory, allegory about a world dominated by Fortune, his bottom scene suggests a conventional, but more cryptic, narrative. At bottom center a man wearing contemporary nineteenth-century dress slogs through still water, perhaps a swamp. Like a caricature of a pilgrim, this man has a staff to help him keep balance; and even though he seems, according to the larger scheme of the design, to be headed in the direction of good fortune—toward the design's happier left side—he looks miserable, with his scarf about his ears, perhaps to muffle the taunts of the odd creatures holding lanterns in front and back of him. The whole scene suggests that this man is on a journey; but having lost his way, he is stuck in a slough of despond. The "right" direction could be toward the huge spire off in the distance at the man's back and to his right. In any case, this structure, which looks like both a church and a lighthouse, seems intended to suggest an unheeded source of illumination for the man, who is being misled by "will-o'-the-wisps" through a "swamp of materialism."[18]

Taken together, the top and bottom scenes suggest a secularized, Victorian version of a traditional narrative about "the pilgrimage of life," as Samuel C. Chew calls it in his splendid study of Renaissance iconography by that title. Just as the top scene makes explicit the role of Fortune in this story, so the lower scene recalls and parodies the originally religious purpose of this pilgrimage. Chew describes the pattern of this traditional narrative, couched in Christian terms, as follows: "Man, having through Sin forfeited the boon of immortality, passes into the World of Time, governed under God's ordinance by Fortune. A free agent, he may choose either of the Two Paths. If he chooses aright there are perils along the strait and narrow way, but clad in the armor of St. Paul he will be able to withstand the assaults of the Infernal Trinity, and though the Deadly Sins assail him a great company of Virtues counsel and protect him. Death awaits him at the Journey's End, but beyond Death is the Celestial City."[19] The religious journey described in this passage is archetypal: it is the linear "progress" of the Christian pilgrim as recorded in religious literature and ecclesiastical iconography, as portrayed in the seventeenth century in Bunyan's *Pilgrim's Progress,* and as secularized and parodied in the eighteenth century by Hogarth.[20] According to the terms of this archetype, "progress" results from choosing the "right" path and then keeping to its "strait and narrow way," thereby avoiding the temptations and pitfalls of "the World of Time, governed . . . by Fortune." Although both Time and

Fortune are "under God's ordinance," they seem to be the enemy of "Man," for his goal is not to attend to their World, but to stick to the "strait and narrow way" so as to get to the "Celestial City" as quickly as possible. Thus, despite the strictures and difficulties of the Christian pilgrimage, the right path is nevertheless posited in this narrative as linear progress. The second of the "Two Paths"—the one presumably depicted in the bottom scene of the *Nickleby* cover—must by implication be circuitous. In other words, embracing the temporal world puts one completely in Fortune's power, subject to the turns effected by her wheel.

Because he is seeking Fortune, the muffled man on the *Nickleby* cover is committed to a circuitous journey. Although he is headed toward Fortune's favorable side, he is clearly lost, in the terms of the Christian pilgrimage. Were his fortune to rise (in a literal reading of the design), he would proceed clockwise around the left side to the moneybags; but for him, this is the farthest distance between the two points. Moreover, the "right" path to the Celestial City—as represented here by the spire—is clearly in the opposite direction. The young man and the woman in the top scene are equally stuck in the world of Fortune, but the man's fortune, at least, promises to take an immediate turn for the better. Browne's decision to illustrate a secular pilgrimage of life through the world of time governed by Fortune was no doubt inspired by Dickens's full title: *The Life and Adventures of Nicholas Nickleby, Containing a Faithful Account of Fortunes, Misfortunes, Uprisings, Downfallings, and Complete Career of the Nickleby Family.* And this cover must have met with Dickens's satisfaction, for a variation on its theme also serves for the monthly wrapper of *David Copperfield* eleven years later (plate 3).

In the *Copperfield* design, the "world" holds a position at dead center, with a cherubic and apparently pensive baby, no doubt representing the young David, perched above it on the "er" of the word "Copperfield" in the title. Moving around this world in a clockwise direction are human figures, who, as the variation in ages suggests, represent the pilgrimage of life, now depicted as a cyclical journey from cradle to grave. Infancy is at the bottom; youth and the "prime" of life move upward on the left; while on the right several figures illustrate the headlong fall and the tottering into old age and the grave. The grave is at the bottom and separated from the cradle, and thus from the renewal of life, by a tree (which is, like the cross that derives from it, the Christian symbol for life, death, and generation—as in family genealogies). The movement up or down on either side of the design is accomplished by a stairway, a familiar iconographic device that symbolizes the pilgrimage when it is conflated with the topos of the "ages of man," as it is here.[21] And at the very top—in a position of importance equivalent to the one she occupies in the *Nickleby* design—is a comically grotesque Fortune, transmogrified into something like a Victorian bag lady, who holds what appear to be a crown and a purse in one hand and a medal of honor in the other. These accessories, like the ones hanging from a belt around her waist, help to identify this rather frightening woman as Fortune. Her wheel, as unobtrusive but necessarily present here as in the *Nickleby* wrapper, is now located to the viewer's right. The implied movement of the figures around the periphery of the design suggests that the stairway also represents the wheel of Fortune, since the goddess's position indicates that she holds sway over the cycle of life and time presented here. If this is the case, then the pilgrimage of life no longer offers the pilgrim a choice of direction: as the design shows, there is only the one path, a cycle of life framing the design and rounding it into not only a wheel, but a clock.

The *Copperfield* cover asserts, on the one hand, that when economic materialism defines reality, humanity is necessarily subjugated to Fortune; and on the other hand, it asserts one version of cyclical time, the biological cycle of birth, aging, and death. In this case, however, Fortune is no longer represented as a desirable woman; instead, her cronelike appearance serves as a reminder of a tradition that portrays Fortune as a terrifying goddess who presides over the inevitable movement of human life toward death. With this power over human destiny, Fortune becomes a sort of composite deity, combining the somber attributes of the Fates with the capriciousness of Lady Luck—a fearful and ultimately deadly combination. This version of Fortune dates from the Middle Ages, as evidenced by medieval lyrics and illuminations that represent life and/or fate as a wheel of Fortune turned by the goddess. In this tradition, Fortune not only takes over the function of the Fates; she challenges the authority of that grand patriarch of iconography, Father Time himself.[22]

The Fortune of *Nicholas Nickleby* featured on the cover wrapper and shadowily figured in the novel is the classical deity who reached her apogee in the Renaissance, both as the ubiquitous, versatile goddess of Renaissance literature and probably the most popular personage of the Renaissance pictorial tradition, if the emblem books that were the fashion during the period can be taken as evidence. As outlined later in this chapter, this Fortune finds her way into the popular, but urbane and sophisticated, tradition that culminated in the eighteenth century in the works of Hogarth and Fielding. She takes many forms, but in her most desirable and familiar mode, as she is presented here, she is identifiable with Lady Luck or Opportunity. This "Renaissance" Fortune to some extent suffers the fate, described by E. H. Gombrich, that awaited most "allegorical imagery" in the iconographical tradition after the eighteenth century: "The phrase of the 'bloodless' abstraction was no empty metaphor. Artists began to think that the more generalized was the concept they had to symbolize the paler and more etiolated should be the image. Thus the visual symbols of invisible entities became more shadowy every day. Even in the nineteenth century they continued to parade their emblems on the corners of monuments and on the pediments of museums and stock-exchanges—but they had acquired the faculty of making themselves as invisible as the abstractions they were supposed to symbolize."[23] Fortune, however, has the advantage over other abstractions—for example, Truth, Justice, or even Providence—of being more inextricably connected to material reality, and so can be more easily fleshed out in visible and identifiable form. In a move adapted from both the visual, iconographical and the narrative traditions reflected in the works of Hogarth and Fielding, Dickens frequently bodies forth the generalized concept of fortune via individual characters, both male and female; but certain females especially become incarnations or avatars of the goddess herself. Dickens uses this method of displacement to create Dora Spenlow, Edith Dombey, Lady Dedlock, Mrs. Merdle, and Estella, who are all obvious incarnations of the *Nickleby* Fortune, goddess figures who, in their respective novels, have the power—associated with class or wealth as well as beauty—to enslave admirers and to bestow favor on those they choose. Local personifications of the goddess Fortune appear in the works of other novelists, of course: Blanche Ingram in *Jane Eyre,* for example, is a type of the marriageable, if rather bland, "fortune" who often appears in the Victorian novel—frequently as a foil for the heroine. Thackeray's incorrigible Becky Sharpe, notorious for her fortune-hunting and gambling, personifies "fortune" in the form of ruthless opportunism, rivaling Estella as the Victorian epitome of the desirable but heartless mistress.[24] Nowhere, however, is the type of the desirable Fortune so familiar and identifiable as in the novels of Dickens.

The *Copperfield* Fortune on the one hand adumbrates the somber change that took place in Dickens's textual imagery regarding Fortune, and on the other hand visually draws from the tradition of street literature—a tradition that accepted Fortune's reality while having no pretensions to the tragic high seriousness with which Dickens ultimately endows the goddess's image. Browne's rendering of Fortune in this case resembles most closely those fortune-tellers, like Mother Bunch and Mother Shipton, who presided over chapbook prognostication, and who began appearing—in various permutations—in Dickens's novels from about this period. Whereas the *Nickleby* Fortune's sexual attractiveness communicates the desirability of what the goddess has to bestow, the *Copperfield* Fortune's grotesque appearance functions in a similar fashion to convey a contrary message—one about Fortune's association with fate and death. The immediate inspiration for this fatal Fortune could easily have been two linked characters from *Dombey and Son,* Mrs. Brown and Mrs. Skewton, both of whom are associated with grim fortune in the novel. Depicting the *Copperfield* goddess as a chapbook fortune-teller—probably prompted by Dickens's implicit fusion of fortune and fortune-telling via character in the preceding novel—is evidently Browne's innovation. Dickens (following a pattern that is typical of their collaboration) appropriates Browne's innovation for later works. Thus the *Copperfield* Fortune finds incarnation at the beginning of *David Copperfield* in Betsey Trotwood, who seems intended to be a comically benign example of the fatal goddess, a cross between a fortune-teller and fairy godmother. But the prime examples of horrific fortune are Mrs. Skewton, Mrs. Clennam, and Miss Havisham, those grotesque, inexorable crones who are moved about in their wheeled chairs, who wield a fatal power associated with class or wealth, and whose appearance is a reminder that Fortune can be old, impoverished, ugly, cruel, and/or deadly as well as young, rich, beautiful, sexy, and/or good. As will be discussed later, Esther Summerson in *Bleak House* serves as the pivotal figure between these two types of the goddess: the desirable female who symbolizes prosperity and romance, and the terrifying female whose image is a memento mori, a forecast of adversity and death.

The Speculator's Goddess

Using the formal qualities of nineteenth-century literature as evidence, most critics concerned with assessing Victorian belief—particularly at midcentury—have categorized it as providential.[25] The novels of this period and the other records we have of Victorian discourse give lip service, at least, to faith in a purposive universe operating to fulfill a religious destiny—in great things and small, in individual lives and history in general. The prosperity that came to large numbers of people with the Industrial Revolution perhaps created the Victorian need to reconcile worldly success with otherworldly reward. In any case, by midcentury the resourceful Victorians had successfully completed a task begun by the Puritans in the seventeenth century: the fusion of the religious and the economic on empirical grounds. It could now be said that divine providence was *visibly* at work in history because evident in a growing market economy and a rising middle class. Progress—production and profit—could thus be rationalized as part of a divine plan that grants the Elect a continuum of rewards beginning in the here and now and extending to the hereafter.

If one were to chart the ideal course of an individual life that fulfilled this providential plan, the resulting figure would be linear, just as a line moving onward and upward graphs a notion of general historical progress, a collective improvement in the quality of lives on the temporal side of paradise.[26] As Jerome Buckley observes in *The Triumph of Time,* the idea of the "future" as being by definition a better time to come was a Victorian invention, first recorded in 1852.[27] Moreover, the sense of linear, historical time was corroborated by the scientific discoveries of the age. As Loren Eiseley argues, it was during "Darwin's Century" that "man was adjusting himself, not just to time in unlimited quantities, but rather *to complete his-*

toricity, to the emergence of the endlessly new."[28] Although scientific advances would, before the century's turn, ultimately separate the linear and historical from the idea of progress, nineteenth-century Christianity, technology, and economics all worked together to erode belief in a much older—both pagan and medieval—conception of time as cyclical.[29]

During the nineteenth century these two temporalities—the linear, historical as opposed to the cyclical—also became implicitly associated with gender. Perhaps never since Adam's curse had labor been divided so absolutely by sex as it was among the new Victorian genteel. In the families that represented the urban monied interest, the male was responsible for production and profit, those aspects of the culture associated with the new historical consciousness of linear time; the female's duties had to do with reproduction, the labors of bearing and rearing children. The maternal function thus tied women more closely to an older temporal order, that of nature and its laws, thereby accounting for one association of cyclicality with "women's time."[30] And despite the Victorian emphasis on the sanctity of the home, the designated "woman's sphere," cultural values were located with economic value in the marketplace. Prince Albert's words launching the Great Exhibition of 1851 articulate the mid-Victorian teleology that fused patriotism and patriarchy, piety and production, by glorifying industry and technology as manifestations of God's providence: "The progress of the human race, resulting from the common labour of all men, ought to be the final object of the exertion of each individual. In promoting that end, we are accomplishing the will of the great and blessed God."[31] The "common labour of all men" may ultimately contribute to the general improvement of the race, but it does not necessarily better the life of the common laborer, with whom the collective phrase should not be confused. And women are left out of this triumphal march toward the future altogether. The conflation of religion and economics served to sanctify men's time when directed toward labor and profit, and it inevitably devalued the time of those whose work was exchanged for low wages or no wages at all: the working class and the poor of both sexes, and almost all women regardless of class.

In a nation that chose to view its official economic destiny as under God's providential care, Fortune—that fickle goddess of chance, the unforeseen and unpredictable, and sheer, unholy luck—seemed destined to disappear as an icon of the Victorian genteel. For one thing, the idea of reversal—so essential to the traditional representation of the goddess—was anathema to the Victorian economically Elect. As V. S. Pritchett puts it, Fortune, "the speculator's goddess" who had held such a prominent place in Western literature into the eighteenth century, lost stature in the nineteenth, when investment succeeded speculation as the socially sanctioned means of accumulating wealth.[32] To be sure, the preoccupation with fortune as a concept was perhaps greater than ever, but the need to justify the prevailing mood of materialism on religious grounds required some adjustment in terminology and representation. The glorification of a pagan female deity, however metaphorical her existence, smacked of retrogression and sacrilege, as well as a lack of gentility. Nevertheless, the fascination with Fortune continued to flourish among the "lower orders" and marginal groups, evidenced by the cheap street literature of the day.[33] The goddess makes a spectacular appearance in the popular *History of Fortunatus*; and many versions of a traditional chapbook titled *The World Turned Upside Down* entertained children and the lower classes with depictions of a topsy-turvy world in which fortunes are reversed—a fantasy world of revolution.[34] Moreover, *Zadkiel's Almanac,* debunked in Dickens's *Household Words,* and ephemera like *The Compleat Fortune-Teller, The Old Egyptian Fortune-Teller's Last Legacy,* and *Mother Shipton's Wheel of Fortune* instructed readers in predicting the future under the guise of the science of astrology and the art of divination. These works, which celebrate Fortune's power to redirect events and change the order of things, are the last vestiges of a rustic, uneducated peasantry and of an earlier historical moment: they are evidence of a simpler culture that had by the nineteenth century all but disappeared among the better-educated English middle class. For example, Hardy records in *Tess of the d'Urbervilles* that Tess's mother, Joan Durbeyfield, who still puts faith in a dog-eared copy of *The Compleat Fortune-Teller,* is a living representative of an earlier historical time: "Between the mother, with her fast-perishing lumber of superstitions, folklore, dialect, and orally transmitted ballads, and the daughter, with her trained National teachings and Standard knowledge under an infinitely Revised Code, there was a gap of two hundred years as ordinarily understood. When they were together the Jacobean and the Victorian ages were juxtaposed."[35] Hardy's observation reveals that during the Victorian period people still put stock in fortune-telling, thereby keeping an archaic belief system extant in an increasingly scientific age. If no one actually believed in Fortune as a living goddess, some people still thought it possible to predict the future, and many more evidently engaged in fantasies about fortunes sought and found: to do so was less a sign of ignorance than a form of psychic preservation, since it seemed increasingly clear that the old Christian dogma of rewards in heaven for labor and hardship on earth was probably no better than a superstition. In any event, heavily illustrated cheap publications like those mentioned above kept the image of Fortune and her wheel alive among the lower classes, suggesting that there was some kind of faith in her existence that possibly exceeded the merely metaphorical. After all, if the two nations of England had been created according to a divine plan, then the nation of poverty—already damned—had nothing to lose in worshiping a pagan goddess. The poor could always hope, and the off chance, the long shot, the unsuspected glitch in the providential order were the thrilling, if infrequent, manifestations of Fortune's power. Under-mining the values of the dominant class is always a pleasure for those who have been denied its rights and privileges, and fantasies about Fortune smiling on the needy undoubtedly provided a satisfaction that reached to the depths of a spiritual as well as a political unconscious.[36]

But as the *Nickleby* and the *Copperfield* cover wrappers should lead us to expect, Dickens, more than any other major British artist through the mid-Victorian period, helped to keep Fortune alive as well. Moreover, both the goddess in her own person and the imagery related to her undergo revealing metamorphoses over the novelist's career, changes that signal not only Dickens's increasing identification with the lower classes, but also his growing skepticism about Britain's destiny, male superiority, and a providential order, whether national or universal. Dickens's basic narrative pattern with regard to Fortune is an adaptation of Fielding's pattern in *Tom Jones*. The hero who seeks his fortune inevitably finds it embodied in a sexually desirable woman, whose function—inadvertently or not—is to teach the hero a lesson. Thus Fortune forms the youthful fantasy that the hero must review, revise, and/or give up before he can come of age as a true gentleman and secure a good wife as reward and consolation. The providential closure seems to align Dickens with the dominant cultural belief in a middle-class ideology, with Christianity and a progressively linear sense of history. But Fortune's control of the plot—a control that increases over the course of the novelist's career—reveals a countertendency in Dickens's writing: his desire to liberate himself from the strictures of class ideology, to express a working-class view of time and history as a cyclical "whirling wheel of toil,"[37] to admit to his own affair with Fortune as the personification of the material world, and, ultimately, to affirm his acceptance of a fatalistic belief in the inevitability of Fortune's reversals.

This pattern has variations, of course, but the paradigm is *David Copperfield.* The well-heeled and irresistible but childlike Dora Spenlow, as the incarnation of all young David's dreams, becomes the embodiment of his fortune. In chapter 26, appropriately entitled "I fall into Captivity," David describes the sudden, dramatic change that takes place in his life on their first meeting:

> All was over in a moment. I had fulfilled my destiny. I was a captive and a slave. I loved Dora Spenlow to distraction!
>
> She was more than human to me. She was a Fairy, a Sylph, I don't know what she was—anything that no one ever saw, and everything that everybody ever wanted. I was swallowed up in an abyss of love in an instant. There was no pausing on the brink; no looking down, or looking back; I was gone, headlong, before I had sense to say a word to her.
>
> . . . There was nothing worth mentioning in the material world, but Dora Spenlow, to be astonished about. (*DC,* 390)[38]

This description precisely defines Dora's function in the novel as the avatar of Fortune. Her first name (meaning "gift") calls attention to Fortune's role as donor, and her last name suggests Fortune's association with the wheel that will cause a turn (first up and then down) in the hero's fate.[39] As we might expect, therefore, the fantasy of possessing Dora proves to be better than the possession: like Fortune, Dora epitomizes disruption and disorder, so that Dora's death releases David from a life of exasperation and bad housekeeping. In contrast, Agnes Wickfield is the mature, sober David's providential reward for the getting of wisdom. The novel's conclusion is Agnes's apotheosis, as David recollects her Christlike gesture that signaled Dora's death: "O Agnes, O my soul, so may thy face be by me when I close my life indeed; so may I, when realities are melting from me like the shadows which I now dismiss, still find thee near me, pointing upward!" (*DC*, 877).[40] Agnes's gesture signifies the progressively linear, providential movement of the genteel from earth upward to heaven that David's marriage to Agnes symbolizes.

Although David idealizes both women, only Dora's image changes—by diminishing—with time. She is the capricious, ephemeral creature that David desires, almost loses, gains, and finally loses—for good, as it were; whereas Agnes is noted for her steadiness of character, her constancy in love, and her continual "dear presence" (*DC*, 877). David's vision of Agnes and his love for her transcend temporality, as the novel's conclusion, quoted above, suggests. But the author's interest through the course of the narrative has been on things temporal rather than eternal. Thus we are left to contemplate David's second marriage, made in heaven, from a safe, blurry distance only after the novel's close. From this example alone we can reasonably conclude that the fleshing out of Fortune's plot is more compelling than the predictable, providential conclusion. As discussed in the final chapter of this study, *Great Expectations,* the novel that serves as the obverse, the upside-down version of *David Copperfield,* makes the point quite explicitly. After Dickens's faith in providence has ceased to exist, Fortune—for better or for worse—remains his mistress and his muse.

The Divine Duality of Fortune

Jean Seznec explains in *The Survival of the Pagan Gods* that the myths of the early European tradition continue through the Middle Ages and into the Renaissance and beyond, thanks to theories attempting to rationalize the origins and nature of divinity "proposed by the ancients themselves." Thus the divinity of Fortune could certainly be explained as an example of "allegorical interpretation": "the tendency, shared by Greeks and Romans alike, to personify abstractions."[41] But one "allegory" that Fortune personifies and that her wheel represents—that chance determines everything, that the world turns by an unpredictable, uncontrollable element—does not easily accommodate itself within a Christian, providential tradition. Even more than the Olympian gods, then, Fortune offended the early church fathers, who attack her divinity on moral grounds. In *City of God,* the work that reflects the official ecclesiastical word on the subject at the end of the Roman era, St. Augustine reasons Fortune away by calling attention to the inherently dual nature of the abstraction she represents: "Certainly we ought to think all the gods of either sex (if they also have sex) are only good. This says Plato; this say the other philosophers; this say all estimable rulers of the republic and the nations. How is it, then, that the goddess Fortune is sometimes good, sometimes bad?"[42] Putting tempting speculations about Fortune's having sex aside, Augustine argues that as the embodiment of a duplicity, of moral contradiction, Fortune can have no place within God's providential—supremely benevolent and rational—design. Nevertheless, according to Howard Patch, the Christian world's continued fascination with Fortune can be explained by the fact that Christianity offered no equivalent for the force or function she represented: Venus or Jove could be easily supplanted by the Christian God himself, but "chance"—as casualty or sheer luck—had no part in the new religious order, even though experience seemed to verify its existence. Indeed, the traditional Roman descriptions of Fortune, which also survived, emphasize her unchristian nature: she is characterized as "*caeca*" (invisible, random, aimless, vague, blind) and "*fragilis*" (unstable, fickle, fragile); moreover, she is a "*meretrix*" (prostitute, harlot, wench, strumpet).[43] Discrediting Fortune's position as a "divinity," therefore—as a supernatural being or presence endowed with unique and unassailable powers—presented unusual difficulties for philosophical analysis from the beginning of her history; and the ongoing debate concerning the ontological status of "fortune" inadvertently insured the goddess's iconographic survival.

The primary example of how the attempt to denounce Fortune's divinity had just the opposite effect occurs in *The Consolation of Philosophy,* the work that informed the role the goddess plays in the great classics of the Middle Ages, those of Dante, Petrarch, Boccaccio, and Chaucer (who translated *The Consolation* into English). Written from prison by the Roman politician Boethius in 524, *The Consolation* depicts the goddess pejoratively, as the personification of worldliness and mutability. Nevertheless, the almost allegorical structure of *The Consolation* lent credence to Fortune's existence in material—i.e., physical—form, helping to reify the goddess for her widespread popularity in the Middle Ages. *The Consolation* takes the form of a series of dialogues between Boethius and Lady Philosophy, who advises the author to attend to things eternal if he wishes to escape suffering and disappointment, for the temporal is subject to—indeed, is defined by—the ups and downs of fortune. To make her point, Philosophy speaks as if she were Dame Fortune, and it is this impersonation that brings the goddess and her wheel into vivid existence: "Here is the game I always play: I spin my wheel and find pleasure in raising the low to a high place and lowering those who were on top. Go up, if you like, but only on condition that you will not feel abused when my sport requires your fall."[44] By characterizing Fortune's activity as playing a game, Philosophy obviously intends to remind Boethius of the goddess's association with gambling and risk taking and of her irresponsible, treacherous, and willful nature; but the warning is also a reminder of the excitement and pleasure afforded by play and risk taking. Thus the image communicates the fact that the innate attractiveness of Fortune cannot be separated from her inherent duality.

To be sure, Fortune's dangerous attractiveness is something Boethius never loses sight of. In an attempt to reconcile Fortune's duality with a providential worldview, therefore, Philosophy offers an interesting rhetorical reversal of the terms "good" and "bad" that defines them in light of a larger moral system. She tells Boethius that, because Fortune is by nature deceitful, she is most trustworthy when she "unmasks herself, when she shows her face and reveals her true character" in times of adversity: "Good fortune deceives, adverse fortune teaches. Good fortune enslaves the minds of good men with the beauty of the specious goods which they enjoy; but bad fortune frees them by making them see the fragile nature of happiness. You will notice that good fortune is proud, insecure, ignorant of her true nature; but bad fortune is sober, self-possessed, and prudent through the experience of adversity. Finally, good fortune seduces weak men away from the true good by flattery; but misfortune often turns them around and forcibly leads them back to the true good." According to the logic of this assessment, the terms "good" and "bad," when applied to fortune, have only the most arbitrary meaning, because they reflect temporary valuations of ephemeral circumstances. To counter these terms, Philosophy posits a "true good" that transcends the temporal and thus helps to put the reversals of fortune in perspective. This "true good" is the ordering principle of the universe; it comes from God, whose divine Providence, through the workings of Fate, ultimately ensures that rewards and punishments will be meted out according to what is right. Because such is the case, Philosophy and Boethius conclude, as Philosophy says, "[t]hat all fortune is good." But in this final context Philosophy explains that "good" means "just" or "useful": "Since all fortune, whether sweet or bitter, has as its purpose the reward or trial of good men or the correction and punishment of the wicked, it must be good because it is clearly just or useful." This explanation and the rest of Philosophy's discourse on Fortune suggests that Fortune is "good" mostly in the sense that she—or it—is a necessary evil; for to be tempted by Fortune, to fall into her power and make her "your mistress," is to put yourself at the farthest remove philosophically from "virtue," the human quality that partakes of the divine and that in fact "gets its name from that virile strength which is not overcome by adversity." In other words, "fortune" has something to do with the divine plan because it tests character; but by definition it must be distinguished from virtue, and thus is certainly not a divinity. As Philosophy says, "You can make of your fortune what you will; for any fortune which seems difficult either tests virtue or corrects and punishes vice." Thus Philosophy's characterization of fortune (the abstract quality) as "good" in the latter part of *The Consolation* does not contradict her disparagement of Fortune (the goddess) as treacherous, blind, and "two-faced" at the outset. Throughout, Fortune is consistently characterized as ultimately the bringer of misery and suffering, and the "goodness" associated with the goddess must be understood to be her ability to teach a stern truth about life. According to Philosophy, "no man can ever be secure until he has been forsaken by Fortune."[45]

Through the lessons of Philosophy, Fortune first makes her transformation from an attractive to a deceitful goddess; but then she disappears from *The Consolation* except as the abstract term referring generally to sublunary affairs, local circumstances that have no real meaning or lasting effect on the wise and virtuous. In other words, Boethius ultimately agrees with St. Augustine that Fortune is the personification of an abstraction, but his vivid representation of Fortune at the beginning of *The Consolation* helped to bring the goddess not only into the literature of the Middle Ages, but into the iconography of the medieval church—presumably as a warning about the fate of those who fell into Fortune's power—and thus into the fold of Christianity, where she maintained a characteristically unstable position for the next thousand or so years.[46] Here then begins Fortune's uneasy relationship with Christianity, and her rivalry with Providence and Philosophy, who become Fortune's foils and who sometimes can be interpreted as the "other" of Fortune's faces—her "fair" or beautiful side.

There were many venues for the visual representation of Fortune in the medieval world—that is, in pictorial imagery appearing in books and manuscripts, paintings, and church interiors—just as there were many ways of conceptualizing the goddess. One of the most popular, which evidently originated with Boethius, depicted Fortune turning a wheel with any number of men (or sometimes animals) affixed to the rim. For example, the fortune of kings (and, by extension, of states) could be expressed in what Patch calls the "formula of four": four men positioned at right angles on the periphery of a wheel represent four temporal relations to kingship. The resulting image resembles a clock presided over by Fortune, with the men marking the hours of twelve, three, six, and nine. Starting at the top of the wheel and moving clockwise, the inscriptions describe the four positions in temporal terms: *regno* (I reign), *regnavi* (I reigned), *sum sine regno* (I am without reign), and *regnabo* (I will reign).[47] The formula of four suggests what might be called a law of conservation of fortune, according to which permanent success or failure is never possible, because both are part of the same closed system with a fixed amount of good and bad fortune that must be distributed. The design's symmetry communicates the inexorability of this law rather than any justice or even predictability in Fortune's actions: she may hold the wheel steady for a time or spin it swiftly, according to her whim. The image also seems to discount any notion of collective progress: the wheel turns but presumably does not roll forward—kings rise and fall at Fortune's will, but there is no other significant movement. Such designs therefore reveal no apparent connection to a providential order, but this circumstance seems not to have diminished Fortune's popularity in religious or secular art.

Through the influence of Dante, writing seven centuries after Boethius, Fortune rallied from the assault by Philosophy and recovered both her dignity and her divinity. In *The Inferno,* when the ghost of Virgil (who represents pagan philosophy) describes Fortune for Dante in the fourth circle of hell, she is clearly the prototype for the Fortune of the Renaissance pilgrimage-of-life topos: this is the Fortune identified by Samuel Chew as being ordained by God to control the world of time.[48] The goddess's realm is quite literally sublunary: Virgil explains to Dante that, just as God has set "ruling powers" over other parts of the universe, so Fortune rules "[o]ver the world's bright images." Her purpose is to manage the temporal succession of fortune, to insure that no single family, race, or nation maintains exclusive control of the earth's riches, advantage, and power for all time.[49] Unlike Boethius's goddess, however, Dante's Fortune is not merely tolerated by a providential order; she is embraced by it. Moreover, she seems to have become more powerful than her former rival, Philosophy, for Virgil tells Dante that she is beyond the ken of human wisdom:

> Against her naught avails
> Your utmost wisdom. She with foresight plans,
> Judges, and carries on her reign, as theirs
> The other powers divine.

There is no question about the divinity of Dante's Fortune or about her relation to Providence. It is now Fortune who executes the providential duties of planning, judging, and acting "with foresight." She rises to dignified heights above worldly affairs, for "she is blessed," and with this blessing fully accommodated within the Christian providential scheme. Moreover, this Fortune no longer appears treacherous or two-faced. Her mutability, instead, is communicated by the "sphere" on which she "rolls": "Amidst the other primal beings glad, / Rolls on her sphere, and in her bliss exults."[50] Dante's image of Fortune's sphere is evidence of his synthesis of the pagan and Christian traditions: in early Roman representations, the goddess stood on a sphere to indicate "a moving foundation" as a sign of the instability of fortune. When the image was necessarily flattened in two-dimensional representations, the sphere looked like a wheel, which eventually came to symbolize Fortune's direct control over human affairs.[51] Dante refers to Fortune's wheel in canto 15 ("Speed Fortune then her wheel, as likes her best"),[52] but here the sphere seems rather to suggest the world over which she has been given complete sovereignty.

The representations of the goddess by St. Augustine and Boethius on the one hand and Dante on the other establish the two major Christian medieval traditions with regard to her divinity; and although they are distinct, they often blur into one another. For example, Boethius's interpretation of a providential scheme does not recognize Fortune as a deity, but it was evidently his vivid portrayal of Dame Fortune turning her wheel that first gave the pagan goddess a place in church iconography, as a warning about her duplicity and mutability. Dante's tack was to synthesize the pagan tradition with the Christian one, so that Fortune regains her divinity while becoming part of God's providential design: as the appointed ruler of the "World of Time." This appropriation of the goddess made it possible to interpret pagan Fortune's role as unequivocally Christianized, if it also diminished her formerly uncontrollable power. Ultimately, both through this now-composite Christian tradition that either sanctioned or tolerated the goddess and through the continuation of the pagan tradition, Fortune became a ubiquitous figure in medieval religious, quasi-religious, and secular art, whether literary or pictorial. The Italian writers Petrarch and Boccaccio, who were Dante's contemporaries and survivors, and Chaucer, the English poet born a generation after Dante's death, certainly knew—and used—the two Christian versions of Fortune, just as they must have been familiar with many visual representations of the goddess. By the close of the Middle Ages, Fortune was a thoroughly popularized cultural, pictorial, and literary icon. Her face, figure, and/or her wheel could be found everywhere from cathedral frescoes—the most striking English example is Dickens's "Cloisterham," the cathedral at Rochester—to tarot cards.[53] Consequently, establishing a precise genealogy for any particular representation of Fortune—religious or secular, Christian or pagan—had already become almost impossible.[54]

Sexy Two-Faced Fortune

The fact that Dante's Fortune becomes the model for the Renaissance pilgrimage-of-life topos is not surprising, since one of the major characteristics of this humanistic epoch was its urge to accommodate Christian ideas from the Middle Ages with those of the classical past. To use Matthew Arnold's terms, the Renaissance was an epoch of Hellenism:[55] in a burst of intellectual spontaneity, Renaissance thinkers would look for their ideas anywhere—backward to the ancient philosophers and historians as well as forward through scientific investigation and exploration. The pagan and the Christian traditions of the goddess survived side by side, while new images of Fortune were introduced as well, ones drawn from forgotten sources or improvised as needed. In the most celebrated reinterpretation, that of Machiavelli, Fortune is both secularized and sexualized: to answer St. Augustine's question, this goddess does indeed have sex. Boethius provided the terms for this new sexual emphasis when he identified Fortune as his former "mistress" and asserted that resistance to her requires "virtue" defined as "virile strength"—as manliness. But what Boethius merely implied, Machiavelli accentuates: Fortune's femaleness becomes a crucial aspect of her power, not merely an effect produced at least in part by her origin as a feminine-gendered word, the Latin "*fortuna.*" Machiavelli's *The Prince,* written in 1513 while he was in exile; his *Tercets on Fortune,* written (presumably) sometime afterward; and his other writings draw to some extent on the religious tradition of Fortune established during the Middle Ages. But these works also lay out the essentials for a new secular belief in an immensely powerful, emphatically sexed, and two-faced Fortune who appears in various permutations in the plays of Shakespeare and Jonson, the essays of Francis Bacon, the emblematic tradition, and so into Hogarth, Fielding, and Dickens.

As Ernst Cassirer explains in *The Myth of the State, The Prince* was a work of political *science,* an attempt to apply universal principles of determinism and predictability to history and politics in the same way that such laws were applied to nature and the physical world. But the unpredictability of history and Machiavelli's own experience of the capriciousness of politics and politicians led him to introduce a mythical element into his theory in an attempt to account for the unaccountable. That element is Fortune.[56] After presenting the theory of statecraft that turned his name into a pejorative connoting ruthlessness and cunning, Machiavelli discusses Fortune's power, precisely dividing control of temporal matters between Fortune and men, and laying to rest—in Machiavelli's system—any notion of providential influence in human affairs. The opening paragraph of chapter 25 clearly articulates Fortune's role:

> As I am well aware, many have believed and now believe human affairs so controlled by Fortune and by God that men with their prudence cannot manage them—yes, more, that men have no recourse against the world's variations. Such believers therefore decide that they need not sweat much over man's activities but can let Chance govern them. This belief has been the more firmly held in our times by reason of the great variations in affairs that we have seen in the past and now see every day beyond all human prediction. Thinking on these variations, I myself now and then incline in some respects to their belief. Nonetheless, in order not to annul our free will, I judge it true that Fortune may be mistress of one half our actions but that even she leaves the other half, or almost, under our control.[57]

At the outset, Machiavelli puts Fortune's power before God's and ultimately dismisses God's involvement in human affairs altogether. As Cassirer asserts, Machiavelli's Fortune is absolutely secularized; she is no longer a Christian figure, but resembles instead the pagan deity of the Greeks and Romans.[58] In Machiavelli's formulation, it is man against goddess: a mortal male unassisted by the Christian God pitted against a powerful female who is, if not divine, certainly of mythic proportions. What had formerly been an issue of religion was now a political matter, and one couched in sexual terms, as we see in the famous conclusion of this chapter, where political success and sexual prowess are explicitly linked:

> I conclude then (with Fortune varying and men remaining stubborn in their ways) that men are successful while they are in close harmony with Fortune, and when they are out of

> harmony, they are unsuccessful. As for me, I believe this: it is better to be impetuous than cautious, because Fortune is a woman and it is necessary, in order to keep her under, to cuff and maul her. She more often lets herself be overcome by men using such methods than by those who proceed coldly; therefore always, like a woman, she is the friend of young men, because they are less cautious, more spirited, and with more boldness master her.[59]

This is a rather bald statement about sex and power, about the importance of predation and conquest to sexual attraction. Fortune and the men she favors form political alliances, which Machiavelli describes in terms of sexual politics. Fortune is not just a "mistress," but a "match" for her lovers: she is always a rival, whose powers must never be underestimated. Because Fortune is ruthless, irreligious, and brutal, these are the qualities that attract her and that characterize the only treatment she desires and understands. Like Boethius, Machiavelli emphasizes the necessity of manly strength in controlling Fortune's powers; here, however, it has nothing to do with stoicism, but with boldness and with being in harmony with the times. For Machiavelli, what is good is what works, so that virtue is no longer defined by godliness but by manliness. Machiavelli does not recommend that statesmen turn away from Fortune; instead, they should attempt to subdue her and keep her favor by displaying their virility.

The *Tercets* are generally consistent with *The Prince* in their representation of Fortune as a woman to be both wooed and feared, but the *Tercets* describe Fortune's nature and powers more elaborately, using highly figurative language, so that new details appear that become features of the later iconographic tradition. For example, Machiavelli's description of Fortune's palace, with its many wheels, becomes a major literary and iconographic motif that surfaces ubiquitously—notably in Hogarth's engravings, if not finally in the Crystal Palace itself. And his description of Fortune as a "witch" with "two faces" has important implications not only for his own fiction, in which she is figured forth as a cronelike mother and sexy daughter, but for Dickens's as well: we see the avatars of Machiavelli's Fortune most plainly in Mrs. Skewton and Edith and their doubles Mrs. Brown and Alice, Miss Havisham and Estella. The *Tercets* begin by personifying Fortune as a "cruel goddess" who "rules with fury," but the poet hopes that she may favor a man who has "courage to sing of her dominion." Nevertheless, she must not be trusted, for she never keeps promises, and she delights in perversity: "She turns states and kingdoms upside down as she pleases." The very arbitrariness of her actions increases her power: "She times events as suits her; she raises us up, she puts us down without pity, without law or right." Indeed, she is predictable only in her variability: "Always her choice is not to favor one man in every season; she does not always keep afflicting a man at the very bottom of her wheel."[60]

This general account of Fortune's qualities is followed by a long description of the palace, where the world gathers to seek her favors and where Machiavelli, improvising on the tradition, depicts the goddess as having not one but "as many wheels . . . as there are varied ways of climbing to those things which every living man strives to attain." These many wheels, which "are ever turning, day and night," suggest the constant workings of political machinery, and the risks inherent in vying for success and power. The luckiest man is therefore the one who chooses a wheel "befitting [Fortune's] wish, since the inclinations that make you act, so far as they conform with her doings, are the causes of your good and ill." This procedure is no guarantee of continued success, however, "because while you are whirled about by the rim of a wheel that for the moment is lucky and good, she is wont to reverse its course in midcircle." In her palace, Fortune is fully in control, even if Machiavelli does entertain the momentary fantasy of unlimited success for a man "who could leap from wheel to wheel," thereby indicating the gymnastic virility needed to stay always on top: "a man who could leap from wheel to wheel would always be happy and fortunate, / but because to attain this is denied by the occult force that rules us, our condition changes with her course."[61] Once again we are reminded that the only constant is mutability, and as its goddess, Fortune has supreme power.

Moreover, by characterizing Fortune's power as "occult," Machiavelli suggests the nature of this power and its source. Unlike Dante's "blessed" Fortune, who assists in working out God's providential plan, Machiavelli's Fortune wields the powers of darkness, for she is a witch and her palace a prison: "And this aged witch has two faces, one of them fierce and the other mild; and as she turns, now she does not see you, now she beseeches, now she menaces you. / Whoever tries to enter, she receives benignly, but at him who later tries to go out she rages, and often his road for departing is taken from him."[62] This horrific image of Fortune as an all-powerful, two-faced goddess communicates a shocking contempt for a female formerly described as a "mistress"; but Machiavelli's insistence on the combative—even abusive—treatment of Fortune needed to keep her in line suggests the complexity of his feeling for the goddess, if not for women in general. Indeed, as Hanna Pitkin argues in *Fortune Is a Woman,* her excellent book on gender and politics in Machiavellian thought, such imagery hints at a fear and ambivalence about a "hidden feminine power" that lurks behind the masculine world of politics as a destructive force. This power manifests itself as of "two distinct kinds" in his fiction: the first is the passive seductiveness of young women, and the second, the vengeful and duplicitous power of older women. In keeping with this numbers game, Pitkin tells us that the two types of women appear frequently in "linked pairs: daughter and mother, servant and queen, or beautiful virgin who is transformed into shrewish wife." The pairing is a reminder and a visible analogue of the inherent duplicity of every woman, of the double nature of the feminine. Moreover, the vengeful, usually older women who themselves double-deal serve as local personifications of the goddess, "with superhuman power over the outcome of events in the world of men." For example, in the play *Mandragola,* the mother Sostrata plays the pivotal role in convincing her daughter Lucretia to commit adultery. In the unfinished poem *The [Golden] Ass,* the witch Circe serves as the threatening power behind the gorgeous damsel who seduces the narrator. And even in the *Tercets,* as Pitkin notes, Fortune is a matriarch, with Occasion appearing as one of her young daughters: "She is 'a tousel-haired and simple maiden,' the only person who 'finds sport' in fortune's terrible palace, 'frisking about among the wheels.'"[63] Like Fortune herself, the older woman in each case functions as a memento mori: the man enamored of her youthful, attractive counterpart should heed the warning inherent in the other female presence so that he does not *fall* in love. In other words, every woman is a femme fatale who will effect a reversal in fortune for the man who gives himself over to her power.

Machiavelli's characterization of Fortune therefore reveals that he interprets all politics, in one way or another, as sexual politics. As Pitkin argues,

Machiavelli's great theme is maleness (*virtù*) pitted against "the other," which is consistently understood to be feminine. Moreover, "As a counterpart to his concept of *virtù,* no epithet is more frequent or more powerful in Machiavelli's vocabulary of abuse than 'effeminate.' What men and states must avoid at all costs is resembling women."[64] Nevertheless, the effeminate man, one who is foolish and weak, is someone quite different from the female Fortune in her own right, who shows no signs of such feminine weakness. Besides indicating that the issue of gender in Machiavellian thought is more complicated than it first appears, this reasoning suggests that what is really "occult" about Fortune's power is its (sometimes hidden) location: it exists *within* men (as Boethius knew) as well as without them. Machiavelli's waffling about how much control Fortune leaves to men ("she leaves the other half, or almost, under our control") can be explained by this internal and external operation. When the witchlike Fortune casts her "spell" on a man, thus taking him in her power, she has effected a momentary stay that is like a gender reversal: a man's vulnerability becomes a female opening. Just as love and poison both work from the inside (as the term "intoxication"—applicable to both—suggests), so when Fortune wins her man, she does so by canceling or killing (even if only temporarily) the quality essential to his manhood. He becomes like a woman because he is Fortune's minion, completely at the mercy of her power. Thus Machiavellian man must be adaptable in every way, except in his unilateral resistance to Fortune's sexual attraction. He may court Fortune's favor, but he must never sacrifice his manliness in the process. Almost paradoxically, the strength of his gender is the only power he has.

Machiavelli's ideas about Fortune seem to have been assimilated almost immediately in English culture. For example, Francis Bacon's pragmatic advice and many images in the essay "Of Fortune" reflect Machiavelli's view that success requires strategic versatility and discernment of the plural and often hidden nature of causality. According to Bacon, a man succeeds when "the wheels of his mind keep way with the wheels of fortune"; and "the way of fortune is like the milken way in the sky, which is a meeting or knot of a number of small stars, not seen asunder but giving light together."[65] Bacon's linking fortune and the stars is also a reminder of Fortune's association with astrology and divination, which seems to have intensified, perhaps thanks to Machiavelli's influence: the OED's earliest recorded usages of the term "fortune-telling" occur in the second half of the sixteenth century. In any case, Fortune achieved her highest visibility as a multimedia personality in the sixteenth and seventeenth centuries following Machiavelli's instructions on how to master the goddess—how to harness her powers to one's own ends. These instructions were not lost on the urbane world of London and the Elizabethan theater. The goddess's majesty over the dramatic world was proclaimed with the erection in 1600 of the Fortune Theater, where her image as either a statue or painting was probably displayed.[66] Moreover, as Frederick Kiefer documents, the dramatic imagery of the major Elizabethan playwrights mirrors a conflation of Fortune with Occasion that occurred throughout Elizabethan culture—one that could have been inspired in part by Machiavelli's imagery in the *Tercets.*[67]

Shakespeare's interest in Fortune is well documented in the numerous references that appear throughout his career, references suggesting a familiarity with her image derived from a broad range of sources, visual as well as strictly literary. In *As You Like It,* Rosalind and Celia's debate about the rival powers of Fortune and Nature echoes Chaucer, whose view that these two goddesses are "the twin agents of Providence" derives from Boethius.[68] Rosalind's comment that "Fortune reigns in the gifts of the world, not in the lineaments of Nature," locates and limits Fortune's power within the larger—and essentially more powerful—natural order.[69] That this order is providential can be deduced from *Hamlet.* If "there is special providence in the fall of a sparrow," then indeed, "There's a divinity that shapes our ends, Rough-hew them how we will": in both speeches Hamlet asserts a faith in a God-directed design of nature.[70] Frederick Kiefer argues that Hamlet's worldview becomes providential during the course of the drama, and with this new emphasis, he "re-enacts the shift from Fortune to Occasion that was taking place in so much Renaissance thought and iconography. That is, he moves from a world dominated by an antagonistic Fortune, to one inhabited by a more responsive Occasion."[71] Nevertheless, Hamlet's many references to Fortune during the early part of the tragedy indicate that she is still a formidable personage with whom both playwright and hero must come to terms. Moreover, in Hamlet's exchange with Rosencrantz and

Guildenstern, Fortune can be identified as Machiavelli's completely secular and highly sexualized goddess:

> GUIL. . . . On Fortune's cap we are not the very button.
> HAM. Nor the soles of her shoe?
> ROS. Neither, my lord.
> HAM. Then you live about her waist, or in the middle of her favors?
> GUIL. Faith, her privates we.
> HAM. In the secret parts of Fortune? O, most true! she is a strumpet.[72]

The play of sexual puns ends with a reminder of Fortune's Latin epithet "meretrix," but the bawdy humor is surely Machiavellian.

Emblematic Fortune

The sixteenth century marks the beginning of a print culture, when illustrations proliferated as woodcuts in books produced for a greatly expanding audience. It is not surprising, then, that Fortune—in her own person or in the form of one of her avatars—figures prominently in the emblem books that came into vogue during this period and that continued to exercise an enormous influence on pictorial and literary art into the Victorian period, well after their popularity had passed. Indeed, it was in the nineteenth century that Henry Green first noted the many "similarities of thought and expression" between Shakespeare's imagery and the iconographic tradition as recorded in emblematic literature.[73] And Dickens's indebtedness to this same tradition is apparent in much of his imagery, which, as we shall see, employs a distinctively emblematic approach to representation throughout his career. Inspired by a Continental fashion that began with Andrea Alciati's *Emblemata Liber,* published in Italy in 1531, Renaissance emblem books—to use Rosemary Freeman's definition—were really "picture books" that combined emblematic (i.e., allegorical) illustrations with a verbal explanation or commentary.[74] In its strictest formulation, the Renaissance emblem comprises three parts: the *pictura,* or symbolic picture; the *inscriptio,* a motto or title; and the *subscriptio,* a prose or verse passage that explains the picture.[75] The parts interrelate thematically, so that the emblem in its entirety serves as allegorical show-and-tell: its approach to representation—for the purposes of instruction and/or entertainment—works by *equation,* by offering a series of one-to-one correspondences between the details of a visualizable image and their significations.[76] An example of the emblematic influence on Shakespeare's drama—and evidence of the frequency of Fortune's appearance in both genres—can be found in Fluellen's speech in *Henry the Fifth:* "Fortune is painted blind, with a muffler afore her eyes, to signify to you that Fortune is blind; and she is painted also with a wheel, to signify to you, which is the moral of it, that she is turning and inconstant, and mutability, and variation; and her foot, look you, is fixed upon a spherical stone, which rolls, and rolls, and rolls. In good truth, the poet makes a most excellent description of it. Fortune is an excellent moral."[77] Fluellen's speech describes the artist as a "poet" and the art as something "painted," a curious shift from one medium to another that makes sense if the referent is an emblem. In its adaptation of the emblematic method, the speech reveals what Freeman calls the "deep-rooted . . . Elizabethan and Jacobean taste for allegory." According to Freeman, this taste, carried over from the Middle Ages, would after the Restoration become "the property of a lower social class and an inferior type of intellect."[78] Nevertheless, as the generic precursor of Bunyan's *Pilgrim's Progress,* Blake's illuminations, Hogarth's engravings, and the moral tracts of the eighteenth and early nineteenth centuries, the emblem book is an important ancestor of the Victorian illustrated novel, and certainly a major influence not just on Dickens's narrative imagery, but on his successful collaboration with his illustrators, especially Browne.[79]

Essentially, the emblem books catalogued (to some extent rather haphazardly or arbitrarily) a cultural history of symbolic images; and even though these books may have endeavored (in the words of Panofsky) "to complicate the simple and to obscure the obvious," they nevertheless were intended to be sources not only of delight but of moral instruction. From the beginning (as Fluellen's speech intimates), they seem to have served for the semiliterate as training books in cultural literacy.[80] Charles Moseley explains that the emblematic method of combining the visual and verbal operates as a form of programmed learning: "the symbolical design and its verbal accompaniments, of equal importance, aim to teach a moral truth so that the memory will grasp it not as a mere formula but—this is important—as an experience, which will be a guide to understanding and conduct."[81] In other words, the complexity of the image required that the viewer/reader become involved in "figuring out"—quite literally—its significance, a process that presumably caused the image and its lesson to become fixed in the mind. The efficacy of this process must have been considerable, for the appeal of emblematic literature was widespread, and emblem books imported from the Continent inspired numerous English productions, beginning with Geffrey Whitney's *A Choice of Emblems,* first published in 1586.

Whitney's emblem of Occasion dramatizes the method of "figuring out" characteristic of the genre and also reveals what a simple matter conflating Occasion with Fortune could be. In the pictorial part of this emblem, the nude Occasion, with winged feet poised on a wheel that lies horizontally and floats in the sea, holds a razor in her right hand and what appears to be a scarf in the other (plate 4). Her long hair blows forward, in front of her face. The accompanying poem explains the imagery in question-and-answer form as follows:

> What creature thou? *Occasion I doe showe.*
> On whirling wheele declare why doste thou stande?
> *Bicause, I still am tossed too, and froe.*
> Why doest thou houlde a rasor in thy hande?
> *That men maie knowe I cut on euerie side,*
> *And when I come, I armies can deuide.*
>
> But wherefore hast thou winges uppon thy feete?
> *To showe, how lighte I flie with little winde.*
> What meanes longe lockes before? *That suche as meete,*
> *Maye houlde at firste, when they occasion finde.*
> Thy head behinde all balde, what telles it more?
> *That none shoulde houlde, that let me slippe before.*
>
> Why doest thou stande within an open place?
> *That I maye warne all people not to staye,*

But at the firste, occasion to imbrace,
And when shee comes, to meete her by the waye.
Lysippus so did thinke it best to bee,
Who did deuise mine image, as you see.[82]

As the verses indicate, the emblem attempts to render graphically the aphorism "Seize the occasion" by explaining significant details of the picture, most of which emphasize Occasion's elusive nature, the speed and ease with which she can slip from her pursuer's grasp. The winged feet, the forward-blowing locks, and the whirling wheel attest to the necessity of grasping the right moment quickly if one is to take advantage of the time(s) to obtain good fortune. The emblem therefore fuses Occasion not only with Fortune, but also with Time; and we can see how one of Dickens's most colorful expressions, "to take time by the forelock," evolved in part from this emblem.[83] Left out of the verbal description, however, is any mention of the two ships in the background of the picture, one of which seems to be sinking. The ships, and the sea itself, are reminders of the duality and duplicity of Fortune, who is often associated with the risks of travel on the high seas and who appears in many illustrations with a sail draped about her as the scarf is here. And the wheel, of course, is Fortune's own. Various details in Whitney's emblem reveal his debt to Alciati for the image and idea, but the addition of the ships and the wheel urge the comparison of Occasion to Fortune more insistently in this English version.[84] Nevertheless, despite the fact that the danger of Fortune is shadowed forth in the pictorial part of the emblem, Occasion appears as something positive and desirable, in many respects strikingly like the "mild" version of Machiavelli's secularized and sexualized Fortune.[85]

The most influential emblem book throughout Europe was another Italian production, first published in 1593 (without illustrations) and translated into English in 1709, when it became the official sourcebook for artists working to supply an expanding fine-art market that by then included increasing numbers of the newly affluent middle class. According to Ronald Paulson, Cesare Ripa's *Iconologia* was adapted as a virtual "lexicon," providing a "primitive linguistic system" that was employed by every eighteenth-century artist, and most imaginatively by the great William Hogarth, whose importance to Fielding and Dickens cannot be overrated.[86] Ripa's *Iconologia* offered copious directions for visually personifying almost every conceivable abstraction, including instructions concerning the allegorical figure's gender, degree of physical beauty, age, dress, accoutrements, gestures, and the addition of thematically appropriate secondary personages. These choices were not arbitrary, but informed by (mostly) classical writers, whom Ripa frequently acknowledges in his descriptions. Edward Maser (compiler of the first twentieth-century English version of the *Iconologia,* in 1971) explains that Ripa also made use of other pictorial compendiums, like medieval encyclopedias, bestiaries, and herbals, as well as Alciati's *Emblemata Liber,* Boccaccio's *Genealogy of the Gods,* and a couple of popular volumes on Egyptian hieroglyphics (which were the most exotic pictorial productions influencing emblem literature—emblems themselves were also known as "hieroglyphics").[87] Since these were the common sources for all the works in the emblematic tradition, Ripa's work contains a wealth of standard or generic iconographical information, and so serves as a reliable guide to the tradition of allegorical conventions. His Fortune, therefore, is a composite figure typical of representations of the goddess during the Renaissance, but Ripa makes explicit a connection between Fortune and Time that was only implied in other emblems. In Maser's edited version of Ripa's 1603 edition of the *Iconologia,* the goddess is described as follows:

> The personification of Fortune is a beautiful, nude, winged female, blindfolded, who stands balancing one foot on a large ball. She holds a cornucopia under each arm. From the one on the left spill money, crowns, medals, scepters, and marshal's batons; from the one on the right, pens, brushes, and scrolls. Above her on the left floats the winged figure of Father Time, holding his scythe and admonishing Fortune. Above her head a sphere covered with stars is suspended, and in her left hand she holds a staff topped with a wheel. The pedestal on which she stands is inscribed "Quisque suae Fortunae Faber" (Each man forges his own fortune).[88]

Up to the inscription or "motto," this Fortune sounds most like the goddess described by Shakespeare's Fluellen, who is "painted blind, with a muffler afore her eyes"; "painted also with a wheel"; with "her foot . . . fixed upon a spherical stone, which rolls, and rolls, and rolls." The inscription itself is reminiscent of Boethius's resigned and stoical "You can make of your fortune what you will; for any fortune which seems difficult either tests virtue or corrects and punishes vice." But the entire description suggests the more positive, secularized Renaissance conflation of Fortune with Occasion.

The explanation for Fortune's appearance, her accoutrements, and especially for the interesting addition of Father Time reinforces the connection with Occasion:

> Fortune is lovely, for she is desired by all. She is blind, for she does not favor one over the other, and this without any apparent rhyme or reason. She balances on a ball, for she is unstable and always shifting and changing. She dispenses all riches and honors of this world, hence the two cornucopias. Time is present, for he has the only influence on Fortune: with time, fortune changes. The celestial sphere above her head refers to the stars, which are in continual motion and in some unfathomable way influence the fortunes of men. The wheel atop the staff she holds (itself a symbol of authority) refers to the age-old symbol of Fortune, the turning wheel, with those on top soon to be those on the bottom.[89]

Like Occasion, this Fortune is unquestionably worth seizing: "she is desired by all." And just as Occasion is by definition inseparable from Time, so Fortune must also be considered in her inextricable relation to Time. The two are cast as rivals in Ripa's emblematic scheme because they share authority over the same territory—that is, reiterating Chew's formulation, "the World of Time, governed . . . by Fortune." Indeed, as the god and goddess who direct human affairs, they can in many respects be viewed as male and female aspects of the same thing. Although Time is old, male, and patriarchal, he is both preserver and destroyer, both good and bad, but relentlessly changing—all qualities he shares with Fortune, even though she appears, in her age, gender, and character of elusive mistress, to be almost his opposite. Moreover, Time's most familiar attribute, his scythe, carries many of the same connotations as Fortune's wheel. Both devices can signify fate and/or fatality: the scythe cuts down just as the wheel crushes. But both are also connected with the idea of cyclicality, fulfillment, and eternal return. As an instrument of the harvest, the scythe metonymically represents farming—taking the life of plants to give life to animals, devouring for the sake of preserving.[90] And this sense of exchange or reversal is of course at the heart of "the age-old symbol of Fortune, the turning wheel, with those on top soon to be those on the bottom." Ripa's emblem therefore preserves a positive, worldly view of Fortune, one that accepts the idea that Fortune governs in the affairs of the world, but the plethora of detail also has the effect of calling attention to her status as a metaphor or artistic device.

The positive view of Fortune implied in more conventional emblematic representations is not found, however, in the crowning achievement of the English emblem books, that produced by the poet Francis Quarles in 1635, shortly before the civil wars, which is when the English Renaissance officially comes to a close. Quarles's *Emblems* differed from his English predecessors' productions in several respects, beginning with his devoutly religious—not just professedly moral—purpose: to portray the human soul's quest for divine love. But even if Quarles's religious asceticism seems at odds with an increasingly secular culture, his *Emblems,* as Barry V. Qualls demonstrates in *The Secular Pilgrims of Victorian Fiction,* were a crucial part of the emblematic/allegorical heritage of the Victorian novel in general, and those of Dickens in particular. Qualls discusses Dickens's debt to *Emblems* at length in his chapter "Transmutations of Dickens' Emblematic Art."[91] Quarles's contribution to the emblematic tradition was to make his work a more unified narrative as well as an aid to Christian meditation, so that the figuring-out process of the earlier emblem books becomes in Quarles part of a sequence of spiritual exercises. The result is a work that more closely resembles a medieval book of hours than a picture-puzzle compendium like Whitney's. Moreover, instead of a series of discrete personifications of abstract qualities, Quarles offers scenes or episodes in which the emblematic "characters" take part in an action that relates to the larger allegory of the soul's quest.[92] The overall "plot" (most apparent in the last three of the *Emblems*' five books) is a pilgrimage of life, couched in terms of romance.[93] Following a Continental fashion in Catholic devotional books that turned originally erotic emblems into religious ones, Quarles represents his central protagonist, the Soul (Anima), as a young girl who is courted, counseled, admonished, and guided by Divine Love (Amor) as the Infant Jesus in the guise of a holy Cupid.[94] This curious fusion of sacred love with erotic passion has the effect of domesticating the latter and sentimentalizing both; and it is not difficult to see how Anima, the female child-pilgrim searching for rest and union with Christ, becomes the prototype for Little Nell and thus for all Dickens's good little women thereafter. Even though Quarles debunks the positive Renaissance view of Fortune, he nevertheless continues the tradition of linking Fortune with wheel imagery through his particular version of the Renaissance pilgrimage-of-life topos.

In Quarles's emblematic return to Christian asceticism, Fortune is once again cast in a negative light as a false temptress, the "smiling" and "fawning" mistress of the world's vanities, as she is characterized in the imagery of emblem 1.6. Fortune appears in the illustrations only twice—both times in book 1; but her presence as a personification of material desire is implied throughout, so that the "feeble, faithless, fickle world" from which Quarles's Anima needs to escape is the world of time governed by Fortune. Emblem 1.9, which provides the first illustration featuring Fortune, makes this connection clear (plate 5). While Father Time on the left holds up an hourglass, Fortune grasps a cross attached to a globe, as if to turn the latter. The globe (with or without a cross atop), which figures prominently in Quarles's *Emblems,* represents the world; but in this illustration it also functions as a wheel of Fortune, since the goddess is controlling its operation, causing Cupid (distinguished from Divine Love by the former's lack of an aureole) and Plutus (the personification of riches) to fall from it. The rather cryptic epigram to this emblem serves partly to gloss the picture:

> If fortune fail, or envious time but spurn,
> The world turns round, and with the world we turn:
> When fortune sees, and lynx-ey'd time is blind,
> I'll trust thy joys, O world: till then, the wind.[95]

As in Chew's formulation of the pilgrimage-of-life topos, the world is the province of both Time and Fortune because temporality defines all three:

when considered *sub specie aeternitatis,* as in this emblem, the world, like Time and Fortune, is identified with mutability and thus characterized—like a wheel—by its turning.

Quarles's interest in Fortune, and his desire to denigrate the goddess explicitly, is indicated by a comparison of this emblem with its source in the Jesuit emblem book, *Typus Mundi.* Both emblems use the Latin motto *Frustra quis stabilem figat in orbe gradum* ("In vain does one fix a stable place on a ball"), and both picture the globe, Cupid, and Plutus; but Father Time and Fortune are Quarles's additions.[96] A similar addition occurs in Quarles's next emblem (1.10), in which Fortune appears holding a fool's cap as a prize for the winner in a worldly game of bowls, played between Mammon and Cupid and sponsored by Satan (plate 6).[97] Although the goddess is wearing a gown in this emblem and the fool's cap is an attribute specific to the context, Fortune can nevertheless be identified with Whitney's Occasion by the billowing sail-like scarf behind her head and by the horizontal wheel on which she stands. But unlike Whitney's Occasion, Quarles's Fortune is clearly in league with the World, the Flesh, and the Devil as enemies of Christianity and thus of humanity. The reward proffered by Quarles's goddess must be very tempting indeed, but it is not worth seizing, for it partakes merely of the world of time, and is of no value to the Christian who aspires to things eternal. Quarles explains in the poem the terms of the allegory as follows:

> Come reader, come; I'll light thine eye the way
> To view the prize, the while the gamesters play:
> Close by the jack, behold, jill fortune stands
> To wave the game; see in her partial hands
> The glorious garland's held in open show,
> To cheer the lads, and crown the conqu'ror's brow,
> The world's the jack; the gamesters that contend,
> Are Cupid, Mammon: that judicious fiend
> That gives the ground, is Satan: and the bowls
> Are sinful thoughts; the prize, a crown for fools.[98]

This verse epitomizes the aspect of Quarles's wit that Mario Praz characterizes as "all on the surface, gaudy and provincial," but that nevertheless served a large and unsophisticated audience as a "cheap substitute" for the more cultivated metaphysical wit of a poet like John Donne.[99] To be sure, the implied connection between "jack world" and "jill fortune" is not one of Quarles's most felicitous poetic effects, but it once again establishes the partnership of the two in Quarles's emblematic design (although usually when Quarles assigns the world a gender it is female, as in "base adult'ress" and "crafty strumpet"—epithets that apply equally well to Fortune herself).[100] Yet despite the "gaudiness" of the wit, the tone of the poem suits the cartoonish illustration and the emblem's theme: life in this world is a trifling game that fools alone take seriously.

An interesting variation on the theme of the world's temporality and mutability occurs in the following emblem (I.II), whose illustration of the world on wheels suggests the inextricable connection of both to Fortune (plate 7). Using an image reminiscent of Pluto's rape of Proserpine, the illustration shows Satan driving a chariot drawn by a goat and sheep, while the world rides in the car behind him. In the upper left of the picture, Divine Love stands on a hill overlooking the chariot and tugs on a rope attached to the cross at the world's top. The questions that open the poem recall the traditional emblematic form, but they prove to be largely rhetorical:

> O whither will this mad-brain world at last
> Be driven? Where will her restless wheels arrive?
> Why hurries on her ill-match'd pair so fast?
> O whither means her furious groom to drive?
> What, will her rambling fits be never past?
> For ever ranging? Never once retrieve?
> Will earth's perpetual progress ne'er expire?
> Her team continuing in their fresh career:
> And yet they never rest, and yet they never tire.[101]

The destination of the world—and the apparent answer to three of the stanza's first four questions—is "hell": the world's present course on "her restless wheels" is a headlong, breakneck dash toward disaster, not a "progress" in the later, positive, Victorian, and historical sense of the term. Here, as elsewhere in Quarles's ascetic, meditative scheme, all movement is evil and dangerous; and just as Divine Love's effort in the picture is to stay the world's forward progress, so Quarles's repeated wish is to find "rest," to achieve stasis and therefore peace. Both the Latin motto *Mundus in exilium ruit* ("The world rushes on in captivity") and the poem's reference to the "Poor captive world" indicate that Quarles has some sympathy for the world's plight here; but it is the poet's world-weariness, expressed as a kind of motion sickness, that best explains the terms of the image. Considering that the source for the first two books' illustrations was the *Typus Mundi,* it is understandable that the "Image of the World" is the subject of many of Quarles's emblematic equations. Nevertheless, Quarles persistently reiterates metaphors that on the one hand emphasize the world's roundness, hollowness, and emptiness, and on the other, its perpetual, but purposeless, motion. Like a "bubble" or a "ball," the world is "vain" and "void"; like "a rolling stone without a tenter," the world moves erratically and aimlessly.[102] This image of the rolling, restless world stripped to its essentials easily becomes a wheel, since its function is motion and nothing else—it is a means to an end, but not an end in itself.

A final example of this world-wheel connection, established by function and asserted thematically as discussed above, occurs in emblem 2.12 (plate 8), entitled with a reference to Galatians 6:14, "God forbid that I should glory, save in the Cross." Here Divine Love stands on the cross, attached at its base to the hub of a horizontal wheel that is, in turn, balanced on a globe. The four winds are depicted blowing the wheel to suggest its erratic movement. The explanation for this curious picture is suggested by the refrain "My trust is in the Cross," which begins the final two stanzas of the accompanying poem, and by the emblem's motto, *In cruce stat securus amor,* translatable either as "Love stands safe on the Cross," or "An abiding love bases itself on the Cross."[103] In other words, the cross is (using T. S. Eliot's terms) "At the still point of the turning world," and the wheel placed between cross and world helps to suggest, once again, the dynamics of movement in an otherwise static picture. Although the accompanying poem mentions neither the wheel nor Fortune specifically, it implies the connection between the two. Quarles refers to many of Fortune's traditional gifts, such as "wealth," "fame," and "honour," as well as "mirth," "joy," and "beauty," only to lament their transiency and ultimate worthlessness. This emblem shows that for Quarles the world and the wheel have figuratively joined forces against the cross and Divine Love; in their turning, they symbolize treachery and the vanity of misdirected desire. Just as Divine Love must find a safe post on a cross to rise above worldly concerns, so it must seek the center of the wheel of Fortune (the place formerly reserved for the goddess herself) to avoid being lashed about on the rim.

Rosemary Freeman asserts that the vogue for emblem books during the Renaissance can be accounted for by a love of allegory; when allegory ceased to be fashionable among a more sophisticated readership, "the emblem book became what it had always been in danger of becoming, a trivial and rather childish mode of expression instead of a serious literary form."[104] Nevertheless, the popularity of Ripa's *Iconologia* among eighteenth-century artists reveals that the emblematic tradition survived in painting and the visual iconographic tradition. Moreover, the emblematic method of narration employed by Quarles continued into the nineteenth century, influencing the novel in many ways and more directly than works with presumably better aesthetic reputations. For example, this method found its way into popular middle- and lower-class spiritual literature via the best-known (if not the most appreciated) allegory in the English language, John Bunyan's *Pilgrim's Progress,* first published in 1678 and reprinted in many editions thereafter through the next three centuries.[105] In narrating the celebrated pilgrimage of Christian (and later Christiana) from the City of Destruction to the Celestial City, Bunyan capitalized on his original readers' "emblematic habits of thought," habits evidently formed by their regular perusal of religious and/or "moral" emblem literature.[106] As Qualls has most comprehensively demonstrated, Bunyan's emblematic method prominently resurfaces in the Victorian era as a major motif and structuring device of the novel. Thackeray's title and motif *Vanity Fair* is only the most obvious example of many novels that lifted—either in small bits or wholesale chunks—symbols, icons, emblems, narrative patterns, and/or central visions and themes from Bunyan's humble masterpiece. Dickens's many references to *Pilgrim's Progress* in his novels attest to Bunyan's place as a major influence; and Qualls establishes Dickens's debt to the emblematic tradition by demonstrating Dickens's thematic dependence on such memorable emblems as the shipwreck, the labyrinth, the birdcage or prison, and the dunghill.[107] These emblems have sources not only in Bunyan, but in Quarles, who alone of the two continues the emblematic tradition of Fortune. The enduring appeal of the emblematic method and allegorical narrative among a less literate audience was also evident in the republication of Quarles's *Emblems* in the Victorian Age, when, according to a contemporary commentator in *Chambers's Book of Days,* it continued to be "delighted in by the common people, but despised by the learned and refined."[108]

Ironic Fortune

The appropriation of Ripa's *Iconologia* by visual artists in the early eighteenth century accelerated the standardization of iconographic meaning, but it also led to the tradition's lapse into cliché. Thus it was up to the most imaginative and innovative artist working in (perhaps "out of" would be more accurate) this tradition to bring the iconographic Fortune to her apogee as the "speculator's goddess." An engraver by trade, William Hogarth mastered the conventions of iconography in order to perform such typical engraver's tasks as producing shop cards and signboards for merchants and coats of arms for the newly affluent middle class. But Hogarth considered himself a serious, enterprising artist rather than an artisan; and just as he refused to limit himself to the usual business and methods of his trade, so he rejected other artistic limitations as well, especially those formal iconographical and generic constraints that, for his purposes, had become obsolete. For illustrating "modern moral subjects" as he called them, slavish imitation and fidelity to convention were serious impediments.[109] To use Ronald Paulson's terms, Hogarth chose to disregard the rules of decorum so as to re-open the closed system of signs that eighteenth-century English graphic art had become, turning it into something capable of expressing new ideas rather than simply alluding to old ones.[110] Hogarth's purpose was in fact twofold: to offer a commentary on the times through the depiction of scenes from urban life in highly realistic—we would say photographic—detail; and to make these works accessible—both in price and in message—to as wide an audience as possible. This latter Hogarth accomplished by capitalizing on the essence of his trade, its power of reproduction; and by selling many inexpensive prints of his own paintings to a general public, Hogarth carved out a hugely successful—and lucrative—career for himself. As Paulson notes in his commentary to *Hogarth's Graphic Works,* his prints could be found everywhere: not only were they displayed in shops for passersby and potential customers to see; Paulson tells us, "they were framed and hung on the walls of middle-class houses, inns, taverns, and mounted on screens or kept in cabinets in the houses of the nobility."[111]

Thus by midcentury Hogarth had created what must be considered a new genre of art, custom designed for a growing middle class. Taking up the term that Fielding coined in *Joseph Andrews* (1742), Hogarth named this genre "comic history painting"—a term intended to establish its relationship to history painting, the most prestigious art of the day.[112] Whereas history painting dealt with noble themes and heroic characters, comic history painting dealt with the ignoble and the unheroic, the reduction of the sublime to the ridiculous. In other words (as Fielding suggests), comic history painting was to history painting what the new genre of the novel was to the epic: an admittedly mongrel species in comparison to its aristocratic precursor, but one that substituted the vigor of the hybrid for the outmoded and clichéd decorum of the pure type.[113] Hogarth's progresses, works of the 1830s and 1840s, exemplify his comic history painting at its finest; but even his earliest works—the ones that will primarily concern us here—break new generic ground. These works are more conventionally emblematic than the progresses, but even so, they relinquish the humorlessness and conventionality of Ripa for the comedy and originality of social satire. And since Hogarth's abiding subject is the world of fortune in its contemporary incarnation as eighteenth-century London, the goddess Fortune necessarily figures prominently in these early works. In the later, more realistic, works she—like the god of the Deists—exists only by implication; but even there her presence is felt by way of the obsessions that drive the characters, whose existence is defined and limited by a world under her governance, and by the accoutrements that have come to be associated with her ascendancy in an acquisitive, urban culture.

Fortune first appears atop her wheel on a benefit ticket for an impoverished actor named Spiller that was probably printed in March 1720 (plate 9). Like Whitney's Occasion in many respects, she is shapely and nude, with forward-blowing hair and with a banner behind her that recalls Occasion's scarf. But what is most notable about this Fortune is her obvious status as an emblem or icon: diminutive and spritelike, she is a different order of being from the other, presumably mortal, and solidly eighteenth-century Londoners on the street below her. What is unconventional here is Hogarth's shrewd juxtaposition of iconographic and realistic detail. Thus the pole that supports Fortune and cuts through the center of the wheel is also the fulcrum of a scale (for weighing contributions of coins on one side against Spiller's heavier bills on the other), and a stake at which, apparently, Spiller is soon to be burned, the pyre being fueled by the unsold benefit tickets that cover his feet.[114] Once all the details of the print are apprehended, the viewer grasps the fact that, while Fortune herself is presented straightforwardly and emblematically, the context for her presentation is wholly ironic, thereby rendering her presence ironic. Already we see the Ripan tradition transformed through Hogarth's subtle adaptation of its methods.

Hogarth's trick in the *Benefit Ticket for Spiller*—employing straightforward emblematic details that are ultimately subsumed in a larger ironic context—foreshadows his fullest appropriation of the emblematic tradition in *The South Sea Scheme* and *The Lottery,* two engravings probably issued together and certainly satirizing the widespread fever of speculation that infected England and the Continent during the first quarter of the eighteenth century.[115] Products of 1721, these two works represent Hogarth's first foray into political satire. They attack national money-raising schemes that exploited the gambling impulse and gullibility of the English people. Both critique the world of Fortune that London has become, a world for whose evils the sellers and buyers are equally responsible. The first engraving refers to the recent failure of the South Sea Company, the joint-stock corporation that, according to the latest European vogue in government debt-management tactics, had taken over the national debt in the hopes of making huge profits on English trading concessions received in exchange. The company sold shares on time to an enthusiastic public, who were convinced by the directors and the government itself that this was a surefire get-rich-quick enterprise. When the profits did not materialize, investors began to suspect that the venture was merely a government-supported boondoggle—which it ultimately proved to be—and withdrew their funds, causing the company to collapse and ruining many shareholders in the process. The bursting of this bubble soon after a similar disaster in France did, however, prove immensely profitable in one respect: it was a gold mine for political cartoonists, led by the Dutch masters in the genre, whose influence on Hogarth is apparent in these two satirical engravings. Both designs draw heavily on the emblematic tradition in their use of allegory and inscription; and, despite their visual complexity, they both employ symbolic wheels of fortune as organizing principles, a strategy that links them with their Continental models.[116]

The South Sea Scheme once again combines the realism of a contemporary London street scene with the fanciful props of parody and allegory, all of which serves to demonstrate that the recent wild enthusiasm for speculation has turned the world of Fortune into a devil's carnival, one in which such values as "Honour" and "honesty" have been subverted by "Monys magick power," as the accompanying inscription tells us (plate 10). The central focal point in this carnivalesque scene is a giant merry-go-round representing a wheel of Fortune and thronged by a sea of people, all presumably eager to take a ride. To ensure that the sinister nature of the goings-on is not lost on the viewer, this playful version of Fortune's wheel is offset by a wheel of torture lying in the scene's foreground, on which the allegorical and nude figure of "Honesty" is stretched, while being broken by "Self-Interest," who is dressed in contemporary costume—no doubt as a sign that the latter abstraction (like "Vilany" [*sic*], who punishes "Honour") is a personage peculiar to these bedeviled times. On the left, the nude and blindfolded figure of Fortune herself appears as a surreal parody of Ripa's goddess: instead of balancing on her ball with her forelock blowing forward, she hangs by her hair from the balcony of the Guildhall while a devil who looks uncannily like Father Time dismembers her with a scythe, tossing pieces of her body to the frenzied mob. The first lines of the inscription gloss this bizarre image as follows:

See here ye Causes why in London,
So many Men are made, & undone,

That Arts, & honest Trading drop,
To Swarm about ye Devils Shop, (A)
Who Cuts out (B) *Fortunes Golden Haunches,*
Trapping their Souls with Lotts & Chances.[117]

The implication of the illustration and the inscription is that the times have caught up with Fortune: even though this is clearly still her world, the goddess, like the figures of Honor and Honesty, has herself become a martyr to the cause of speculation. But unlike these other martyrs, she is the object of the crowd's worship, and her sacrifice is a grim parody of the Christian doctrine of death and resurrection: Fortune must die so that others can have fortune. As in Ripa's emblem, Fortune's value and desirability are insisted on by the image, but it also ironically communicates an old truth about the economics of Fortune: there is never enough to go around.

The Lottery satirizes another national fund-raising strategy that exploited the public's willingness to put faith in Fortune by buying "Lotts and Chances." Hogarth (as well as Addison and Fielding) considered the government's sponsorship of lotteries unethical because the promotion of gambling effectively devalued effort and labor—which is the moral of this emblematic extravaganza (plate 11). The scene is the interior of the Guildhall where the lottery drawings took place, set up like a *tableau vivant* from pantomime (which was much in vogue and was satirized for its tastelessness in a subsequent engraving by Hogarth). This set comprises three major sections: an upper stage level illustrating the action of the drawing, a lower level illustrating its consequences, and in the center, rising from the lower to the upper level, a large pedestal on which are arranged the four figures who oversee the action: National Credit, Apollo, Justice, and Britannia. The device of using a stage set allows Hogarth to exploit the emblematic tradition to its limits while also moving his art in the direction of more realistic representation. The characters—who are identified in the explanation that accompanies the engraving and that serves as the inscription—pose and dress like the conventional figures of emblem literature, whether allegorical, like National Credit, Justice, and Britannia, or mythic, like Apollo; but they are also, in a sense, real (if we assume that they represent costumed actors). Although National Credit, personified as a regal woman, sits at the top of the pedestal and presides over the activities like an Olympian deity, the whole scene has to do with the characters' relationship to fortune, in all its permutations of meaning: luck, chance, fate, and status with regard to wealth. Appropriately, then, the goddess Fortune and her various avatars are among the principal characters in the emblem's narrative; and the wheel of Fortune is the primary recurring motif. On the upper level of the stage and flanking the pedestal are two large wheels of fortune used for the lottery drawings, the one on the left filled with numbered slips corresponding to the tickets; and the one on the right, with slips that designate the amount of the prize (from a "blank" to ten thousand pounds), to be matched with the slips drawn from the first wheel. One of Fortune's avatars, Wantonness, dressed as half man and half woman, draws the numbers from the first wheel, while a nude, blindfolded, and forelocked Fortune executes the decisive step, the win-or-lose drawing from the second wheel.

On the lower level of the stage the consequences of the drawing are enacted by groups of allegorical characters clustered around two male figures representing good and ill fortune, respectively. On the right, directly below Fortune, Good Luck, holding a purse, is being "seized by Pleasure and Folly," while "Fame [is] persuading him to raise sinking Virtue, Arts &c." Fame's efforts, however, appear to be hopeless, since the floor has already given way under the personification of "Virtue, Arts &c," a woman sitting beside a globe and leaning on a stack of books, who holds her head as she wearily draws circles with a compass. The visual pun encourages the viewer to compare the drawings executed by Wantonness and Fortune with Virtue's equally random, if more artistic, "drawing," and to conclude that the fascination with Fortune increases at the expense of Virtue: as in Machiavelli (the gender differences notwithstanding), Fortune and Virtue are thus pitted against each other, becoming mutually exclusive terms. This allegorical vignette about the effect of Good Luck is balanced by its alternative on the left side of the lower stage. Under the wheel of Wantonness we have Misfortune holding a blank and being "opprest by Grief, [as] Minerva supporting him, points to the Sweets of Industry."[118] This last personification, who shares the foreground with "sinking Virtue" to her right, is flanked by appropriate accoutrements symbolizing work: on one side Industry's traditional emblematic attribute, a beehive, and on the other a pickax and a spinning wheel.[119] As Minerva (Wisdom) points to her, Industry leans back in a pose of supplication, holding out a honeycomb, the sweets to which the caption refers.

Just as the goddess Fortune and the characters allegorizing fortune are placed at focal points throughout the engraving, so there are wheels of various kinds used as graphic accents throughout to reinforce the theme. On the upper level, both lottery wheels stand inside their opened, wheel-shaped cases, so that the upper stage virtually reverberates with wheels, making it look like the inner workings of a curious machine or clock. Fortune stands on her signature wheel and Wantonness holds a small windmill, an icon associated with the London pantomime and a metaphorical Fortune's wheel in its association with inversion or reversal.[120] On the lower level, Industry's spinning wheel also repeats the wheel motif, serving as a humble reminder that the wheel was invented as an aid to labor rather than as an instrument to use in games of chance. Hogarth's association of female Industry with spinning, which finds its source in the linguistic and social rather than the Ripan tradition, recurs in *The Industrious 'Prentice,* in which women spinners can be seen tending their wheels in the weavers' workroom (plate 12). (This later work also transforms the beehive as a symbol of industry, for the working-class denizens of the weaving shop, the church, and the streets—in association with their looms, pews, coffins, garrets, and gallows—most closely resemble the drones and workers in a hive and at their honeycomb, unable to escape their destiny as creatures subordinated to a society both dependent on and resentful of its industry.) Finally, the placement of all the characters in *The Lottery* suggests a human wheel of Fortune around a central hub represented by a turnstile, located at the base of the pedestal, on which Suspence sits, being "turn'd to and fro by Hope and Fear." This arrangement reinforces the Boethian idea that those who put themselves in Fortune's power are subject to her reversals, and that in her world—as in this design—Industry and Virtue frequently find themselves at the bottom rather than at the top.

As suggested above, *The South Sea Scheme* and *The Lottery* serve as emblematic previews for the much subtler, more realistically expressive symbology of the progresses, all four of which narrate man's and/or woman's pilgrimage of life through the world of fortune that is contemporary London. But unlike Quarles's and Bunyan's, Hogarth's progresses are wholly concerned with this-worldly rather than otherworldly rewards. The harlot, the rake, the young couple who marry to promote their parents' fortunes in *Marriage à la Mode,* and the idle apprentice in *Industry and Idleness* have obviously given themselves over to Fortune's power; but even the fourth progress's industrious apprentice is depicted via Hogarth's symbolism as the embodiment of Occasion—one of Fortune's emblematic avatars—who takes Time by the forelock to secure worldly success (plate 12). In the plate whose full title is *The Industrious 'Prentice a Favourite, and entrusted by his Master,* the apprentice Francis Goodchild stands behind a desk on which hangs the "London Almanack," featuring an illustration of a winged and nude youth grasping Father Time's forelock. The latter figure is recognizable by his scythe and hourglass.[121] Using the terms of *The South Sea Scheme,* all the protagonists of the progresses have opted for a metaphorical ride on the wheel of Fortune: the first three progresses narrate a devil's bargain that effects for Moll Hackabout, Tom Rakewell, and the newlyweds, respectively, a brief rise and peak and then a precipitate fall, while the fourth juxtaposes the steady rise of one apprentice, Goodchild, with the equally steady fall of the other, Tom Idle. Because the characters seem to get what they deserve, Hogarth's vision appears to be providential; but his fascination with the progress as a fall suggests another possibility: that the erring protagonist may simply be a victim in a culture whose emphasis on fortune overrides every other consideration. Indeed, the double narrative of *Industry and Idleness* calls the simple morality of the other three progresses into question by hinting that Goodchild and Idle are both hostages to Fortune, since a world in which it appears to be a matter of utter indifference whether one is hanged or made lord mayor of London must be a world that turns by her command. But since Hogarth's irony is visual, it is subtle, apparent primarily in the extreme detachment with which the artist seems to treat his subjects. Consequently, even though the progress's roots are in moral allegory, Hogarth has transformed it for his successors into an ironic genre, a form eminently adaptable to a broad spectrum of forms ranging from the political cartoon to the novel.

Providential Fortune

Hogarth's brilliant success in depicting the world of Fortune in pictures was matched by Henry Fielding's equally extraordinary depiction in words, and perhaps the apparent difference in worldview in the works of these two friends has more to do with the medium than with the artist. In any case, if Hogarth's irony calls into question the providential plot of his progresses, no such questioning occurs in Fielding's masterpiece, *Tom Jones,* in which Fortune makes her most celebrated literary appearance in the eighteenth century. Like the Hogarthian progress, Tom's progress requires a precipitate fall, but in his case it appears to be the fortunate fall of the Christian tradition, and thus the necessary precondition for his eventual rise to prosperity and happiness. Just as Fielding's allusion to *Paradise Lost* in Tom's ouster from Paradise-Hall places the novel in the postlapsarian world, so Tom's triumphal return to Somersetshire as the recognized Allworthy heir is the novel's appropriate providential conclusion.[122] But, as in Hogarth's progresses, the bulk of the novel is given over to a consideration of Fortune's world, so that "fortune" in all its permutations as a personage or concept is one of Fielding's chief themes and topics, the discussion of which becomes a running learned joke through the novel. Hogarth's influence is apparent in Fortune's appearance in her own right as an iconographic "character," but Fielding also draws from a literary tradition in which such mixing of ontological states, forms, and genres is more familiar, as we have seen in Boethius, Dante, Machiavelli, and Shakespeare. Nevertheless, Fielding saw himself as an innovator like Hogarth, and as the self-proclaimed "Founder of a new Province of Writing," he delights in the "novel" exploitation and juxtaposition of conventions and genres that made this new form revolutionary (59).

Thus Fielding's Fortune is as rich, varied, and lively as the surface of his comedy; so that if her real existence is treated with only mock seriousness, that is, after all, the general tone of the novel. In any case, the goddess is ubiquitous: Christine van Boheemen notes that the word "fortune" appears more than 150 times in *Tom Jones,* and besides numerous references to the goddess herself, it has at least two other meanings: "money" and "luck." Van Boheemen argues that the novel "falls totally under [Fortune's] sway"; moreover, that Mrs. Waters has a special role as Tom's alleged mother and "a woman of fortune whose erratic appearance and behavior in the fiction suggests that she embodies the goddess herself."[123] While van Boheemen's argument concerning Mrs. Waters seems correct, the same argument can be made concerning at least five other female characters in *Tom Jones*, all of whom significantly alter Tom's fortune through the course of the novel: Bridget Allworthy, Molly Seagrim, Mrs. Western, Harriet Fitzpatrick, and, most importantly, Lady Bellaston, who appears preeminently as the incarnation of duplicitous Fortune. All of these fleshed-out versions of the goddess derive most directly from the two-faced sexy goddess of Machiavelli (and Shakespeare), while their primary foil, as her emblematical name, "Sophia Western," indicates, is Boethius's Philosophy, the embodiment of the wisdom of the Western philosophical tradition.[124] Moreover, Fielding's many learned references or allusions serve, themselves, as a kind of comic supertext, offering a rather comprehensive history of the goddess's own fortune in literature and iconography, for they include everything from the classical debate about her status as a divinity to a continual rumination about her actual fleshly or figurative existence. Hogarth and Fielding alone, therefore, could have provided Dickens with the rich soil needed for his own iconographic development of Fortune.

For example, when, toward the end of the novel, Squire Allworthy reveals that he always thought of Tom "as a Child sent by Fortune to my Care," Fielding suggests not only that Tom's real mother, Bridget Allworthy, is an avatar of the goddess in her Machiavellian matriarchal mode, but that her two sons—like Francis Goodchild and Tom Idle—have inherited her duality of "good" and "bad" fortune (715). Consequently, the siblings are in continual rivalry for Fortune's favors throughout the novel, and the plot is a record of their reversals: as in the case of Hogarth's two apprentices, the rise of one inevitably synchronizes with the fall of the other. Moreover, the fact that both Tom and Blifil are conceived out of wedlock indicates that all Fortune's whorish epithets apply to Bridget. Thus when, at the beginning of the novel, she refers to the (then) "unknown Mother" of Tom as "an impudent Slut, a wanton Hussy, an audacious Harlot, a wicked Jade, a vile

Strumpet," she leaves both the record of her own duplicity, as well as Fielding's clever personification of her as Fortune (33).

Molly Seagrim plays the role of the young fair-faced goddess, one as whorish as Bridget but more sexually attractive. Nevertheless, Fielding reveals the danger inherent in her sexiness by emphasizing the virile quality of Molly's beauty, which has "very little of Feminine in it, and would have become a Man at least as well as a Woman." We are reminded of Hogarth's bisexual figure of Wantonness here, especially when Fielding tells us about Molly, "So little had she of Modesty, that *Jones* had more regard for her Virtue than she herself" (131–32). This is not to say that Molly is not duplicitous, however, as we see when she convinces Tom that he has gotten her pregnant, and, most dramatically, when he finds Square hiding in her bedroom behind a curtain "in a Posture (for the Place would not near admit his standing upright) as ridiculous as can possibly be conceived." When Fielding compares Square's "Posture" to "that of a soldier who is tyed Neck and Heels," we realize that the scene is an emblematic visualization of Hamlet's exchange on Fortune with Rosencrantz and Guildenstern, for Tom has discovered Square in Molly's "secret parts," as the philosopher's soldierly but shameful posture signifies (173). By bedding Molly, both Square and Tom have been pressed into service as Fortune's "privates."

The most extravagant parody of Fortune in *Tom Jones* is Sophia's aunt, Mrs. Western, who, having "lived about the Court and seen the World," considers herself an authority on sexual politics and wages a Machiavellian battle of the sexes, not with a lover, but with her brother, the brutish Squire Western (207). The violence of this gender war is one of the delights of the novel, and that Fielding's reading of Machiavelli informs it quickly becomes obvious through many references, among them Mrs. Western's chiding the Squire for his ignorance of women, specifically, his daughter Sophia: "The Judgment which can penetrate into the Cabinets of Princes, and discover the secret Springs which move the great State Wheels in all the political Machines in Europe, must surely, with very little Difficulty, find out what passes in the rude uninformed Mind of a Girl" (209). Ironically, Mrs. Western is perfectly matched with her brother, not just in their mutual obtuseness about Sophia, but even in her physical and mental attributes: "her masculine Person, which was near six Foot high, added to her Manner and Learning, possibly prevented the other Sex from regarding her, notwithstanding her Petticoats, in the Light of a Woman" (208). If the youthful Molly's "very little of Feminine" fairness nevertheless has the capacity to charm, Mrs. Western's "masculine Person" has no such effect, and she is clearly a comic Machiavellian goddess, a Fortune manqué. This lack of attractiveness, however, has not stopped Mrs. Western from entertaining the possibility of an amour, as we learn from her niece Harriet Fitzpatrick, who plays both her rival in this affair and Fortune's other, fair, if duplicitous, face. When Harriet describes her aunt's blindness to Fitzpatrick's real intentions with regard to the two women, we are thus reminded of another conventional attribute of Fortune: "my Aunt never saw, nor in the least seemed to suspect that which was visible enough, I believe, from both our Behaviours. One would indeed think, that Love quite puts out the eyes of an old Woman." Fitzpatrick, described by Harriet as typical of "Men, who in all other Instances want common Sense, are very *Machiavels* in the Art of Loving," is therefore more correct than he knows in thinking that both aunt and niece are "Fortunes" (445).

The larger design of *Tom Jones* undergoes its major reversal in the unlucky book 13, which is dedicated, both literally and figuratively, to the goddess Fortune.[125] Fielding—like his friend Hogarth before him—signifies that London is Fortune's realm; but Fielding goes further by suggesting, like Machiavelli, that, as women create and preside over the intrigues of the fashionable world, so they are also its would-be destroyers. Appropriately, the plotting, world-weary, sophisticated, licentious Lady Bellaston is sovereign as *Tom Jones*'s most treacherous incarnation of the goddess: "the aged witch," as Machiavelli says, "with two faces, one of them fierce and the other mild" who "does not see you," "beseeches," and then "menaces." Indeed, she plays Circe to Tom's golden ass by turning him into a kept man. Tom falls into her trap because he thinks he needs Fortune before he can have Sophia—and to some extent he is right. In any case, book 13 equates Tom's arrival in London with entering Fortune's domain and demonstrates the dangers in becoming intimate with the goddess. Tom's first encounters duplicitous Fortune in the person of Harriet Fitzpatrick, who tricks Tom about Sophia's whereabouts, introduces him to Lady Bellaston, and later plots against him; but her primary role in book 13—as the harbinger of

Lady Bellaston—suggests that she is a garden-variety embodiment of the dangerous goddess, and thus merely an Occasion, as it were, to set the scene for Fielding's major dramatization of Fortune and her realm.

This dramatization occurs in chapter 7, which depicts Tom's attendance at a London masquerade as the guest of "the Queen of the Fairies," an alias, he discovers later that night, for Lady Bellaston, who beds Tom at the chapter's end. The masquerade brings us, therefore, to the deceitful core of fashionable London and into the "secrets" of Fortune. In other words, we enter with Tom the phantasmagoric circle of two-faced women and manifold deception that is Fortune's realm. Fielding's brilliant narrative adaptation of the emblematic technique makes it clear that the masquerade represents the pagan goddess's palace/prison, a surreal and suffocating underworld where the wheels of female plotting create a vicious circle of duplicity and sexual intrigue. Just as the hunt metaphorically serves as the organizing principle for Tom's adventures on the road, thereby advancing the plot in a (more or less) linear and presumably manly fashion despite Fortune's many reversals, so chapter 7 employs strongly allegorical devices to emphasize that Tom has entered an alien, feminine "demimonde" and is now in the clutches of the pagan goddess. Fielding, for example, describes the building as a "Temple," and the master of ceremonies as a "High Priest of Pleasure," who "imposes on his Votaries by the pretended Presence of the Deity, when in Reality no such Deity is there" (545). Like the pantomime, the masquerade was, despite its great popularity, noteworthy primarily for its artificiality and tastelessness, according to both Hogarth and Fielding; and the arch tone serves as preparation for the atmosphere of deceit and intrigue borne out in the rest of the chapter, in which everything moves by disguise. This is true for the reader as well as for Tom, through whose limited vision we observe the masquerade.

Wearing the domino and mask sent him by "the Queen of the Fairies," Tom blunders from disguised woman to disguised woman hoping to find Sophia, but finds instead Lady Bellaston, whom he mistakes for Harriet Fitzpatrick. Tom's inability to see, except as "masks," the women who are present suggests his loss of masculine control. Fielding emphasizes the moribund, hallucinatory quality of this female space by giving us a peevish fortune-teller, disguised as an old woman, who entertains herself "by telling

People rude Truths," so "to spoil as much Sport" as possible and thus to "satisfy her Spleen" (547–48). This description resonates with the chapter title, "Containing the Whole Humours of the Masquerade" and recalls Pope's "Cave of Spleen" in *The Rape of the Lock,* another emblematic female hell that is also a revelation of feminine "secrets." But Lady Bellaston plays the pivotal role in this chapter as the confidential Fortune who bewitches Tom, and Fielding's repeated references to her simply as "The Mask" indicate her occult and sovereign power. She explains to Tom that he is the only person present who is fooled by the disguises; what is strange to him is familiar and boring to all the others, who come "'to kill Time in this Place'" (548). This lassitude and the "killing" of Time indicate the fate of men under the spell of Fortune: where she holds sway, her masculine counterpart and rival becomes the victim. There may be movement, but not forward; repetition, but no progress.

The masquerade, therefore, marks the beginning of Tom's most serious loss not only of virtue, but *virtù.* By submitting to Lady Bellaston's amorous advances, he loses his manly independence and his honor, however impoverished both have become. And when, thanks to Lady Bellaston's "violent Fondness," Tom is "raised to a State of Affluence, beyond what he had ever known," the reader can be assured that a disastrous reversal will follow (554). Indeed, before Tom can escape the clutches of Fortune in the guise of Lady Bellaston to be rewarded in the novel's happy conclusion, it appears that, in accordance with "the universal Opinion of all Mr *Allworthy's* family"—and like Hogarth's Tom Idle and, later, Dickens's Oliver Twist—"he was certainly born to be hanged" (89). Nevertheless, despite his faults and the Hogarthian prophecy of ill fortune carried by his given name, Tom, rather than Blifil, proves to be the Good-child of this history. His marriage to Sophia and the inheritance of two estates are presumably the providential rewards he earns through his in most respects manly behavior.

Tom Jones's pilgrimage through the "World of Time, governed . . . by Fortune" requires many spins on the goddess's wheel, but these reversals, we come to realize early on, are all "under God's ordinance." Indeed, the novel's happy ending is ultimately a matter of generic necessity. Despite the huge generic latitude that Fielding gives himself—the ability to range freely among forms and appropriate them at will—*Tom Jones* is throughout a comic history, like *Joseph Andrews,* and therefore must end with the hero at the height of his fortunes—after, of course, proving himself "Allworthy." Thus as the "founder" of this new genre and author of the tale, Fielding wills the providential conclusion: like certain "Brokers" for the "Lottery" held "at *Guild-hall,*" Fielding is himself privy to the "Secrets of Fortune" and so can decree how she dispenses her favors (59). But as the novel evolved over the next century, it began taking its commitment to moral instruction more seriously. When the taste for earnest reportage superseded the picaresque pleasure in leading the reader on "a wanton kind of chase," Fortune as the multiform goddess of riches and sex began to fade from the novelistic scene.[126] In several respects, therefore, it was Fortune's offense against new standards of generic decorum that caused her to vanish from bourgeois literature in the next century.

Chapbook Fortune

But if Fortune was fired from service in the literature of the strictly conscienced bourgeoisie, she maintained her status as a beloved, popular goddess in the literature of the street. After the English Civil Wars, cheap publications of all kinds began to enter the homes of the poor; and because telling, seeking, and finding fortunes were favorite themes of these works, the goddess Fortune makes frequent appearances as a personage in the narratives, and occasionally appears in the accompanying illustrations as well. Much (in some cases most) of the appeal of these works lay in the accompanying illustrations, cheaply produced as woodcuts; consequently, chapbooks, penny merriments, almanacs, and fortune-tellers helped to keep alive the allegorical and iconographical imagination of the unskilled reader, who could participate in the narrative more immediately—or, in some cases, perhaps exclusively—by virtue of its visualizable elements.

The most familiar chapbook representations of Fortune occur in the popular tale "The History of Fortunatus," an old romance recounting the adventures of the eponymous hero, who, as the son of a formerly wealthy but improvident father, must seek his own fortune and who is noteworthy primarily because of his exceptional good luck—a sign that he (as his name suggests) is the favorite of Fortune. Although it is difficult to fix publication dates precisely, there are at least two distinct variants of this tale published during the eighteenth and nineteenth centuries as chapbooks, both of which illustrate the central moment of the plot and the scene with the most emblematic potential: the moment when Fortunatus, on meeting Fortune in a wood, receives from the goddess a magical, refillable purse. The first variant I will discuss is probably the later one, because it clearly emphasizes the tale's moral elements, presenting a thoroughly Christianized Fortune who instructs Fortunatus in a most Boethian fashion. When Fortunatus explains himself to the goddess by telling her, "poverty constrains me to wander till Providence giveth me a competent living," Fortune answers as if she were, in fact, that very Providence. The goddess lays out the celestial chain of command for Fortunatus, indicating that she has been "sent" by "the will of the Divine Power," for whom she acts as no more than an emissary. In her words: "Fear not, . . . I am Fortune, and by the influence of the stars and planets, are given to me these six powers, Wisdom, Riches, Strength, Health, Beauty, and Long Life, now I am sent to bestow one of these on thee, such is the will of the Divine Power, and which soever of these thou shalt choose thou shalt enjoy to thy utmost with, so choose freely." When Fortunatus chooses riches, his expression of gratitude prompts another instructive speech that reveals the moralizing and allegorizing tendency of this variant, as well as its use of the emblematic method: "had you chose Wisdom you would have known better than to have thanked me, perceivest thou not that I cannot see whom I favour, render thanks only where they are due, that is to the giver of all good, to whom you can yield no better recompense, than of thy riches to bestow freely on the poor and needy; in short be charitable. Charity is always represented as a widow with three children, therefore never neglect the widow and fatherless."[127] Here the emblematic tradition continues with its twin purpose of moral instruction and pictorial exegesis. As a complement to the emblematic description in the text, one of the accompanying woodcuts features Charity with her three children—even though Charity really has nothing to do with the story. The utterly gratuitous introduction of Charity may well have occurred because the chapbook's author/printer happened to have the woodcut already on hand—a common practice in the publication of chapbooks that accounts for much of their interest.

The two woodcuts of Fortune (which are mirror images of each other) depict her as the text describes her: "a beautiful woman . . . with a bandage over her eyes and a wheel by her side." She is voluptuous and gorgeous, but respectably clothed in classical garb, clearly portrayed as a dignified lady who is worthy to play the noble patroness as she hands a kneeling Fortunatus the magical purse. And when she exits from the text, the goddess's counsel and curious warning to Fortunatus are reminiscent of Lady Philosophy: "Fortune then pointed to him a path, telling him to keep in it, and not to trust her anymore. Fortunatus soon got out of the wood."[128] This beatific Fortune, one who not only provides riches but also offers excellent moral instruction about keeping to the straight and narrow path, has been tamed by Christian principles and made into a providential deity (with the visible sign of Fortune's upright Christian character being her modest, classical dress). She is the ladylike and domesticated—or, using Gombrich's more graphic terms, the "bloodless" and "etiolated"—Fortune of the Victorian middle class, the handmaid of Providence and closely allied to the latter, as indicated by Fortune's answer to Fortunatus's initial supplication.[129] There is none of the treachery or witchery of Machiavelli's Fortune in this goddess: she is only "good" Fortune, reduced by religion to a shadowy abstraction, a pale imitation of her formerly fascinating self.

This Christianized, or providential, version of the Fortunatus story manifests its sensitivity to the moral, emblematic tradition with its addition of the next woodcut (one not included in the second variant I will discuss), which illustrates Fortunatus stretched on a rack, his fortune having taken a sudden, unexpected turn for the worse. The crisis develops when Fortunatus tries to buy some horses and is suspected by a nobleman of having stolen the purchase money, since Fortunatus's "mean appearance" is evidence of poverty. As punishment, Fortunatus is strapped to the rack, which is described in the text and illustrated as a "wheel."[130] Because Fortune has just in the previous chapter warned Fortunatus not to put faith in her, the text and the illustration force a comparison, suggesting that Fortune's wheel and the rack are one and the same. Thus, Fortune's two accoutrements in the illustrations, the purse and the wheel, momentarily come to represent the traditional doubleness of the goddess, another sign that the author is attempting to turn this history into an emblematic "divine and moral" tale. But Fortunatus is soon released, with what seems like very little effort on his part; and considering that even this moral, but still self-professedly "delightful," story of Fortunatus is most memorable for its hero's great good fortune, the emblematic episodes and illustrations described above set a more moralistic, admonitory tone about the liabilities of fortune than the narrative seems to warrant.

The second variant, and what appears to be the more typical version of "The History of Fortunatus," is—like the accompanying illustration of the goddess—stripped to its bare essentials as a romantic comedy, one written primarily to celebrate the delights of worldly riches and the pleasure of great good fortune. After all, Fortune's gift of the purse that always contains "ten pieces of gold" (in variant A) or "ten pounds" (in variant B) of the coin of the realm is no small treasure; and for the most part, it serves Fortunatus well, in all versions of the story, through what in almost every respect is a prosperous and happy life. Thus in variant B all the righteous dignity and noble decorum of the providential Fortune have vanished with her clothing; and although she is described in the text as "a fair Lady with her eyes muffled" and addressed by Fortunatus as a "sweet virgin," the illustration recalls the pagan goddess, as well as Machiavelli's highly sexualized Fortune (plate 13).[131] In the cover scene, a blindfolded, bare-breasted Fortune extends the magical purse to Fortunatus with one hand and holds her belly with the other, a gesture presumably intended to remind the viewer of Fortune's intrinsic connection to the pleasures of the flesh—the appetite for food, sex, or both. Like an amalgamation of Whitney's Occasion and Quarles's Fortune, both of whom stand on wheels that lie horizontally, variant B's Fortune is seminude (more like Occasion), but rendered in the cartoonlike style of Quarles's emblems, which here (as it does not with Quarles) seems generically appropriate. Placing the wheel underneath Fortune has the effect of rendering her image unmistakably iconic, but the result is to give the image even more totemic power: there is no possibility of confusing this woman with a mortal female (however saintly) like St. Catherine, nor of mistaking her for another goddess born of personification like Justice, or even Providence. And this Fortune is literally fleshier and figuratively more colorful than her counterpart in variant A. Although caricatured and comic, she has more visual "presence" than variant A's goddess, obviously representing, in her own person, both temptation and opportunity. In this respect she is rather like Eve, who, also "in a wood," held out an offering to Adam—an offering of fruit, which carries the same symbolic values of temptation and opportunity as Fortune's purse.

And what the picture suggests, the text delivers: a celebration of Fortune as ripe Opportunity or Occasion, a reveling in the delights of this-worldly success. Although Fortune tells Fortunatus that she has "the power of Six gifts" granted "by permission of heaven," the choice of recipient is apparently hers alone; and the goddess's autonomy is underscored by the fact that the Divine Power mentioned in variant A is really of no consequence here—Fortune's power is all that the story requires. Moreover, there is no mention of Providence in variant B. Unlike the first Fortunatus, with his smugly confident "[p]overty constrains me to wander till Providence giveth me a competent living," variant B's Fortunatus explains to the goddess, "I am constrained by poverty to seek my fortune." His comment indicates a realistic, no-nonsense assessment of his situation—one that does not confuse chance—surprising good luck—with providential expectation and reward. When Fortunatus asks for and receives the gift of riches in the form of the purse, Fortune does not reprove him for not choosing wisdom, nor does she caution him about the risks inherent in putting faith in fortune. Instead, "she bid him follow her out of the wood, and so vanished." Later, when Fortunatus is put on the rack, we are told, "Then did Fortunatus wish he had chose Wisdom before Riches," but his regret is even more transitory than in variant A; and there is no attempt to connect the briefly mentioned rack with Fortune's wheel by way of illustration or narrative imagery.[132] In variant B the world of Fortune is a materialistic world—a worldly world, as Dickens might say—where good fortune comes and goes as if by magic, which is a fair metaphor for the essentially unpredictable laws of chance. Fortunatus is a plucky guy; not at all a bad man, but on the other hand, not an overly moral one. He is an entrepreneur who seizes the opportunity to make himself rich, never revises his materialistic, opportunistic philosophy, and lives to the end of his days (as his name implies) a remarkably fortunate man. Both versions narrate what is virtually a secular pilgrim's progress. Variant B, however, is fantasy unadorned by all but the most basic allegiances to family and society, whereas variant A, with its moralizing and providential trappings, professes the values of the middle class.

Despite their differences in class allegiance and/or class identification, both chapbook versions of "The History of Fortunatus" show how the iconographical tradition of Fortune was kept alive in street literature by an audience comprised of a cross-section of social classes and interests. At its heart were the middle-class producers of these works, the printers: small-time (at least originally) capitalists who were in business not so much to instruct "the street" and its occupants, but to make a living from them. Most of the publishing houses were in London (Seven Dials, commemorated by Dickens in *Sketches by Boz,* became famous for its chapbook trade), but other cities became centers as well. Probably the most famous publishers during the late eighteenth and early nineteenth centuries were William and Cluer Dicey, John Pitts, and James Catnach—the last the most notorious, for his sensationalist publications, his gin-swilling hacks, and his general association with printed trash during the first quarter of the nineteenth century.[133]

But the clientele for these works was as open and various as the term "street" implies. The primary audience was no doubt the newly literate who had leisure enough for reading, which usually meant the lower classes and children; but it also included anyone, regardless of class or education, who was interested. Since these works were cheap and available on the street in bookstalls, they were ubiquitous; they helped define what we mean by an appeal to a "mass audience," and they might be said to be the first documents produced by and for a thoroughly heterogeneous British popular culture. In short, everyone in England during the late seventeenth, eighteenth, and nineteenth centuries must have been familiar with these chapbooks, and it was not unusual for the more aesthetically elite throughout this period to regard street literature with amusement and touching (if sometimes patronizing) affection. In the late seventeenth century the Cambridge-educated Samuel Pepys could be counted as one of the most devoted fans and collectors of street literature; and the next two centuries abound with testimonials to its far-reaching influence, as Leslie Shepard says, not only "in propagating and supporting literacy," but "in stimulating creativity" as well. Street literature was, in fact, most instrumental in its educative function: "in helping a poor man to rise in the world of culture."[134] These were works one grew out of or left behind, but evidently did not forget. They were an abiding, pervasive influence on Dickens's art, as has been carefully documented by Harry Stone in *Dickens and the Invisible World*.[135] Dickens's writings are littered with references to chapbook characters and imagery, not the least of which is the wonderful purse given Fortunatus by Lady Fortune herself.

The history of Fortune and her wheel after the English Civil Wars brings us to the nineteenth century literally and figuratively by way of the street, for the most distinctive feature of this segment of Fortune's own journey is her disappearance from more serious art only to turn up as the goddess of the street's most representative inhabitants, the working class and the poor. When the widespread assimilation of the Puritan ethic endowed members of the middle class with the ability to distinguish the blessings of God by empirical evidence, and thus to consider their own newly acquired prosperity as providential reward, the "lower orders," as the Victorians called them, necessarily became the greatest sinners in this formulation, for, by the same logic, their impoverished condition proved that they had been disavowed by God. Consequently, for the less ascetic, less spiritual portion of this socially condemned populace—not the devotees of Bunyan and Quarles—there was no other deity but Fortune left to worship.

The literature of the street—its dreambooks, fortune-tellers, its stories of adventure and miraculous success—preserves the record of Fortune's continued popularity among the poor. The chapbook "History of Fortunatus" most notably articulates the fantasy of all those who, in the language of the tale, were "constrained by poverty to seek [their] fortune," to hope that it would materialize—if not actually in the shape of a beneficent goddess—in a life delivered from penury. The magically refillable purse is the perfect metaphor for this fantasy: like the guaranteed "living"—whether earned or inherited—of the upper orders, Fortunatus's purse provides the necessary cash at the necessary moment, thereby avoiding all the usual economic liabilities of wealth, such as concerns with budgeting, saving, investing, and otherwise guarding against shortages or protecting surpluses. A purse providing an inexhaustible supply of the coin of the realm was the one thing needful to get off the street and into comfortable circumstances; and, in the tradition of street literature, the purse becomes more emblematically meaningful than the cornucopia as an accoutrement symbolizing Fortune.

The goddess's other, more famous accoutrement—her wheel—remains unambiguously symbolic of Fortune in popular, primarily middle-class culture only in its association with gambling. By the end of the eighteenth century this wheel appears as the E. O. Table—the roulette wheel—in the political cartoons of James Gillray, who, like Hogarth, condemns governmentally sanctioned gambling in its various forms.[136] Hogarth's giant merry-go-round in *The South Sea Scheme* and his representation of the great Lottery wheels emphasize the dangerous aspect of risk rather than the wonderful possibilities of striking it rich. The imagery of both *The Lottery* and *Industry and Idleness* proclaims female Industry with her humble spinning wheel as the only wholly reliable woman/wheel combination. The other wheels so conspicuous in eighteenth-century popular art—those attached to the carts, wheelbarrows, wagons, coaches, and carriages that bring harlots to London, move aimlessly about the city, speed across England, deliver the mail, turn over, catch fire, transport the lord mayor to the Guildhall or the condemned to Tyburn Tree—are as surely associated with fate as the medieval wheel of Fortune; but the eighteenth-century popular artist leaves this connection to be inferred by the viewer or reader. Nevertheless, in the world of metaphor that is art, wheels so frequently serve as the salient features of vehicles that their tenor must have to do with fortune. After all, along with the brawling mobs, these wheels characterize the street, which has become Fortune's domain and completely under her sway.

Fortune's banishment to the street can be traced rather accurately through the works of Hogarth and Fielding because they, more than any other eighteenth-century artists, were successful in bridging the aesthetic gap between so-called serious and popular art. As perhaps the first truly great artists of the middle class, together they provide the expert visual and verbal testimony that allows us to fix the period of the goddess's apogee and the beginning of her descent as the first half of the eighteenth century. Hogarth's wholly ironic treatment of Fortune in his early engravings demonstrates that, even though the world of contemporary London is obsessed with the idea of fortune, the goddess herself has lost the iconographical dignity that she claimed during the Renaissance and in the emblematic tradition. By the 1740s Fortune has been sacrificed to Providence and tossed to the street like a losing lottery ticket. As in *Tom Jones* or with Tom Idle, the goddess oversees only hazard or ill fortune as it manifests itself in whoring and gaming, losing and hanging; she is a figure more like *The Lottery*'s Wantonness, associated only with illicit behavior. Winning, on the other hand, is no longer really "Good Fortune," but the providential gift of God to his "Goodchild": the entrepreneur whose industry and ambition are the outward signs of Christian virtue. The beauty of this formulation is that in one stroke it sanctifies the opportunistic materialism of the middle class as the only morality, at once condemning the members of the orders above and below as asocial hedonists who, in the form of luxury on the one hand and pleasure on the other, have recklessly abandoned themselves to a pagan deity.

SPRING 1840–1849

The Patriarch and the Goddess

2

The leuedi Fortune is both friend and fo,
Of pore che makit riche, of riche pore also,
Che turneth wo al into wele, and wele al into wo,
Ne triste no man to this wele, the whel it turnet so.

"Lady Fortune and Her Wheel"

He that hath wife and children hath given hostages to fortune, for they are impediments to great enterprises, either of virtue or mischief.

—FRANCIS BACON, *"Of Marriage and Single Life"*

Waxing: The Rochester Wheel of Fortune

Toward the end of April 1840, a renovation project in Rochester Cathedral led to a surprising discovery that, in several respects, must have seemed like an uncanny stroke of good fortune. While dismantling the old pulpit at the north wall of the choir, workers uncovered the remains of a large mural, which was immediately identifiable as a fine specimen of medieval religious art, presumably dating from the thirteenth century. The graphic description, accompanied by an artist's rendering (plate 14), of this fresco in the *Gentleman's Magazine* just a few months later demonstrates a Victorian enthusiasm for the Gothic as well as the reporter's knowledge of medieval iconography:

> It is very evident that the subject of the design is the Wheel of Fortune. The personification of Fortune is habited as a Queen, (not blindfolded as in more classical compositions,) and she holds her wheel in her right hand, the left being obliterated in the lost half of the picture. At her feet is seen a man struggling to attain a position upon the wheel; above is another who has mounted half the ladder; and at top is the present favourite of the Queen, seated in ease and dignity, but looking with a mixture of complacency and dread at those who were no doubt represented falling and fallen on the contrary side of the wheel. . . . The defaced part of the subject had been covered, at some distant time, with a strong coating of oil paint. We are happy to add that the remaining portion is likely to be preserved.[1]

This discovery of the Rochester wheel of Fortune testifies to the fact that, despite the aspersions cast on her character, Fortune had found a respectable place in Christian iconography by the Middle Ages, as discussed in chapter 1. Medieval representations of Fortune's wheel like this one were rather common in ecclesiastical manuscripts and murals;[2] and Fortune's being "habited as a Queen" reveals not only the dignity she had achieved, but a certain reverence for her powers. As the *Gentleman's* reporter notes, Henry III had ordered Wheels of Fortune to be painted in several English churches, and the Rochester fresco probably dates from that feckless monarch's long but turbulent reign. In Henry's expense records for Clarendon Palace, there is mention of a "Wheel of Fortune and Jesse" to be painted in the King's own chamber—the latter referring to the genealogical tree of Christianity tracing Christ's ancestry to the "stem" of Jesse, perhaps intended as a symbol of the ultimately divine source of Henry's monarchical and patriarchal power. The reporter speculates about Henry's choice of iconographic images thusly: "The connection between the Wheel of Fortune and Jesse is not very obvious; but if Dame Fortune introduced the patriarch into the palace, it is not impossible that the patriarch brought her ladyship into the Church."[3] Henry's actual motives for selecting this combination of images for Clarendon are unclear, but the record documents a fascination with Fortune's image that suggests—like the "mixture of complacency and dread" apparent in the face of the king at the top of the wheel—not just a healthy respect for the goddess and a desire for her favor, but a fear of the threat she poses to patriarchal—and kingly—authority.[4]

In short, the icon is primarily a warning, for Fortune's wheel illustrates the mutability of humanity's sublunary world, however providential humanity's place may be in a larger cosmic order. It refers to the originally pagan philosophy concerning fortune articulated by Boethius, which—stripped of explanations that attempt to accommodate it within a larger ethical system such as Christianity—offers a tragic vision of human fate as controlled utterly by chance, personified as the goddess Fortune. The wheel itself, then, becomes primarily a symbol for punishment and an instrument for its execution—meanings it would continue to convey less ambiguously in later depictions of St. Catherine (or Katherine) of Alexandria.[5] One hundred or so years after this fresco was painted, such a view becomes the text and theme of Chaucer's monk, who offers his seventeen examples of tragedy just as the Canterbury pilgrims reach Rochester—a coincidence suggesting that Chaucer himself was thinking of the Rochester wheel when he composed the monk's tale. Moreover, manuscript records of fourteenth- and fifteenth-century vernacular sermons show that medieval preachers frequently took Fortune's wheel as their text, probably pointing to pictorial representations like the one in Rochester Cathedral for visual reinforcement of their message. G. R. Owst, in *Literature and Pulpit in Medieval England,* tells us: "Of all . . . graphic caricatures of the medieval artist none made greater appeal to the pulpit than that well-known pictorial device known as the Wheel of Fortune. It illustrated with a peculiar vividness the preachers' own favourite view of life, fundamentally harsh and pagan as it had remained, the inevitable round of existence for every mortal human being, the successive stages of man's tragic journey upon earth from cradle to grave, the varying temporal fortunes of a world that offered him no abiding security." It can be inferred from Owst's comment that the "fundamentally harsh and pagan" aspect of Fortune's wheel is its representation of a vicious cyclicality unrelieved by any linear, providential, masculine, or fatherly protection. And since the men featured in the illustration are literally at the mercy of the woman who turns the wheel, the icon is apprehensible as a symbol not just of mutability, but of female hostility. Indeed, one preacher compared the goddess to a "contrary wife" who "shifts the wheel contrary to the wishes of him who is propelled on it or sits upon the top."[6] In other words, the Rochester fresco attempts to warn against the eminently attractive but terrible power of the Romans' favorite goddess by pitting men against a femme fatale, thereby illustrating "man's tragic journey from cradle to grave" as directed by female power. And even the most culturally purblind thirteenth-century observers would have noticed that the image depicts a gender struggle, with a gigantic woman controlling the fate of male subjects who are half her size. As in the words of the anonymous medieval lyric "Lady Fortune and Her Wheel," the goddess is "both friend and foe," and therefore not to be trusted: "she turns woe into weal, and weal into woe, / Trust no man to this weal, the wheel it turneth so."

What is most curious, therefore, about the fresco is its highly suggestive half-obliterated form—no doubt intended to mitigate the icon's cautionary message by preserving the image only of waxing fortune. Uncannily, this drastic alteration, perhaps the work of iconoclasts during the Reformation or civil wars, seems to speak directly to the historical moment of the fresco's recovery; for it calls attention to the prevailing mood of the times even while the opposing mood can be inferred from the figure. As Jerome Buckley explained in *The Triumph of Time,* "The great polar ideas of the Victorian period were . . . the idea of progress and the idea of decadence, the twin aspects of an all-encompassing history. Poised at their high moment in time, the Victorians . . . surveyed their world, its past and its future, with alternate hope and fear."[7] Appropriately, therefore, the fresco conveys "the idea of progress," and although its twin, or opposite, "the idea of decadence," can be projected onto the figure, the deliberate erasure of Fortune's waning or "contrary side" certainly correlates with the sense of youthful hopefulness and destiny that characterized England at that point in the nineteenth century.

In that spring of 1840, England's monarch was not a king, but a young and popular Queen who had come to the throne just three years before, who had just married that winter, and whose reign was now anticipated to be long, fruitful, and prosperous. Indeed, Victoria seemed to be good Fortune herself, with her attention directed toward increasing England's prosperity and preserving the glory of the common *wele,* to use the medieval term from the lyric. Although we know through historical hindsight that this decade would come to be known as the Hungry Forties, it was also the decade of the railway, and thus of the greatest fortune-producing wheels the world had ever seen. J. M. W. Turner's 1844 painting *Rain, Steam, Speed: The Great Western Railway* captures the new, dizzying sense of technological acceleration that would come to define the collective imagination of the age. And Tennyson, then in his thirties, provided what might be called the official script for the new Victorian vision of progress in 1842 with "Locksley Hall," whose self-congratulatory speaker identifies himself as "heir of all the ages," and who sees a bright future accessible by rail: "Not in vain the distance beacons. Forward, forward, let us range, / Let the great world spin forever down the ringing grooves of change." The speaker's faith in linear progress is made explicit in the lines that follow: "Thro' the shadow of the globe we sweep into the younger day: / Better fifty years of Europe than a cycle of Cathay" (lines 181–84).[8] Tennyson's speaker thus rings in the new in romantic (if chauvinistic) terms, which reflect a season of youth. According to John Dodds, "In 1841 those who were to be remembered by later generations as bearded patriarchs were, for the most part, young men. . . . These people had already begun to shape the ideas and feelings of the Victorian age. Their energy was that of young men and women coming into the prime of life. And on the throne there was a young woman of twenty-two, with a husband the same age."[9] Those young people who were later to be known as the first "Victorians" gave the decade of the Romantic Forties its vision and voice, and no one among them was more influential or romantic than Charles Dickens, for whom the image of waxing prosperity seemed like a special prophecy. Of all those British subjects who looked to the stately gray walls of Rochester Cathedral for inspiration, no one could have so easily found an augury there as Dickens, who would prove to be Rochester's favorite and most fortunate son.[10] Did we not know otherwise, we could imagine Dickens himself, his illustrator Phiz, or perhaps one of Dickens's characters furiously brushing "the strong coating of oil paint" over the waning side of the fresco's wheel, in an effort to stay the hand of Fortune forever; then triumphantly proclaiming, like the *Gentleman's* reporter, "[W]e are happy to add that the remaining portion is likely to be preserved."

For this half-told story about waxing Fortune graphically represents the confident vision of life already realized in Dickens's popular novels and apparently coming to be realized in the career of the young author as well. Just four springs earlier, Dickens's own fortune had taken an amazing upswing with the appearance of the first number of *Pickwick Papers,* featuring a soon-to-be famous picaresque, if aging, hero who has himself been preserved in the British imagination as an icon of providential good fortune. Dickens's first popular character, Pickwick undergoes many reversals of fortune, but ultimately lands on his feet. He remains in cultural memory as a comic Boethius who, when imprisoned and forsaken by Fortune (in the abstract sense), learns to be philosophical about the fickle goddess and eventually gets the best of her. Pickwick's story contains what might be called the deep structure of Dickens's early comic narratives: it is the picaresque pilgrimage of life, the story of a "harmless" Tom Jones passing through "the World of Time, governed under God's ordinance by Fortune."[11] In Dickens's version of the picaresque narrative, however, only the "chase" is "wanton": there is no place left for Fielding's latitudinarian idea that a hero can be both virtuous and incontinent. *Oliver Twist* and *Nicholas Nickleby* similarly adopt a providential pattern. The former novel's subtitle, "The Parish Boy's Progress," and the assertion by Oliver's adoptive father Mr. Brownlow that Oliver was "cast in [his] way by a stronger hand than chance" indicate that Dickens's early vision is informed by the Christian optimism (and respectability) so characteristic of the Victorian gentility (*OT,* 377). Nicholas Nickleby's story is in effect also a "progress," since Nicholas rises from financial disaster brought on by his late father's unfortunate speculations to financial prosperity and happiness in the employ of the fatherly Cheeryble Brothers. In all these novels, fortune figures prominently as a theme, but the characters' rewards are unquestionably providential. It is not until Dickens's fourth novel, begun in the spring of 1840, that a darker vision with regard to the fate of his central character emerges. Little Nell in *The Old Curiosity Shop* not only represents Dickens's first heroine; she is also his first tragic protagonist.

The Old Curiosity Shop*: Allegorical Nell*

Dickens married Catherine Hogarth in April 1836, the same spring that

Pickwick began serialization, and by 1840 Kate's labors seem to have synchronized with Dickens's own, for he had fathered as he had noveled: now there were three children—a boy and two girls. With this new pattern in the life and household of the young writer, Dickens could now be said to have entered "women's time." That is, he had become keenly aware of felt time as a series of the maternal cycles of gestation, birth, and child-rearing that had been established (and would continue) in his own home, just as he had painfully experienced the larger cyclicality of life; for the domestic increases had been interrupted by one decrease, the traumatic (especially for Dickens) death of his seventeen-year-old sister-in-law, Mary Hogarth, on May 7, 1837. That Dickens was chafing under the yoke of this new temporal dispensation is apparent from a February 1840 letter to his friend John Forster, in which he describes his response to his domestic situation with mock-hysteria: "I saw the Responsibilities this morning, and burst into tears. The presence of my wife aggravates me. I loathe my parents. I detest my house." Writing two days after Victoria's wedding and continuing a running joke about his unrequited passion for the queen, Dickens pretends that his despair is the consequence of a broken heart, but the fantasy romance itself reflects Dickens's growing concern about "Fortune" and his fear that his wife and children were her "hostages"—impediments to the queen's favor and the other great enterprises envisioned by this ambitious young man. In the same letter Dickens threatens to get the queen's attention by "murdering [his publishers] Chapman and Hall and becoming great in story (SHE must hear something of me then—perhaps sign the death warrant: or is that a fable?)."[12] Dickens would indeed soon become "great in story" once again, and the metaphorical appropriateness of this phrase as a description of pregnancy as well as legend perhaps reflects Dickens's new temporal awareness. In any case, given the increasing demands placed on Dickens in his role as head of a household with numerous dependents, especially of the female gender, it is not surprising that by 1840 his fiction should reflect a more serious consideration of the female psyche and of women's time than ever before. Up until this point, Dickens's women characters had been absolutely two-dimensional: females seen from rather a distance and falling into a few caricaturish types. The most memorable of these—as Michael Slater has well documented in

Dickens and Women, his exhaustive assessment of these types—are the prostitute Nancy from *Oliver Twist* and Mrs. Nickleby; but both of these women must nevertheless be regarded as peripheral figures in the novels they inhabit.[13] In the spring of 1840 Dickens's interest in what it is like to be female, to experience life as the other gender, becomes a focal point of his fiction. This new narrative emphasis must have been owing in part to his recent domestic experiences; but whatever the cause, Dickens channeled all his capacity for imaginative sentiment—which was vast—into Little Nell, his first female character to complete the archetypal Christian pilgrimage of life. Consequently, *The Old Curiosity Shop* is Dickens's first rather faltering step in his artistic journey into women's time.

The focus on female temporality is most appropriate when we consider the novel's evolution. Originally serialized in Dickens's new weekly, *Master Humphrey's Clock,* and beginning in the fourth number, published on April 25, 1840, *The Old Curiosity Shop* was at first intended to be only one of many stories told within the frame of the periodical. But with the seventh number, the novel began running weekly as the *Clock*'s sole content, until the conclusion of the story in the forty-fifth number, published February 6, 1841.[14] *The Old Curiosity Shop* thus ran a forty-week course, eerily paralleling the normal cycle of human gestation, until *Barnaby Rudge* took over the *Clock*'s narrative burden. Moreover, the eponymous *Clock* itself represents a kind of womb, as we learn from the reclusive Master Humphrey, who narrates the frame story of the periodical and begins the narration of the novel. Introducing himself in the *Clock*'s first number as "a misshapen, deformed, old man," Humphrey explains that he and three aged friends entertain themselves one night each week by reading stories kept in the base of Humphrey's old grandfather clock (*MHC,* 7, 11). Thus, despite the fact that the clock has been assigned by its type to the masculine gender, it gives birth to the narrative and most particularly to the girl child who so captures Humphrey's (and Dickens's) imagination. And considering the other gender reversals apparent in the generation of the novel, as well as its allegorical quality, it is not unreasonable to conclude that the clock prefigures Nell's grandfather as a personification of Father Time, whose patriarchal worries about "fortune" in some ways reflect Dickens's own.

Dickens's willingness to edit—and write—a periodical in the voice of such a torpid character is in itself rather telling. Thus far in his career the young author's literary exertions had been Herculean; and the sense of felt time communicated by the *Clock* project is exhaustion, a need to slow the pace and (as it were) unwind, while still maintaining the necessary income from writing. By assuming the quietly reflective character and voice of Master Humphrey, Dickens himself must have hoped, like Humphrey and his comrades, to "beguile time from the heart of time": to work in such a way as to ensure his own physical, emotional, and spiritual renewal (*MHC,* 11). Dickens at twenty-eight had already gone through a lifetime of experiences, and in this spring of 1840, his own need to regenerate—to restore his youth and life—expresses itself in his initial identification with opposite qualities: with age and death. In the course of the novel, this identification with "otherness" manifests itself in the characterization of Nell herself, who does double duty as both heroine and allegorical personage. J. Hillis Miller has described *The Old Curiosity Shop* as Dickens's "most dreamlike novel," and this quality is surely tied to the sense of otherness that is suggested by the title, is so pervasive in the narrative, and even defines its protagonist.[15]

Although the actual plot of *The Old Curiosity Shop* begins when Master Humphrey removes himself at the end of chapter 3 "for the convenience of the narrative" (he tells us), his introduction of Nell helps to establish her allegorical character (*OCS,* 28). When on one of his habitual nocturnal walks he meets "a pretty little girl" who asks his help in finding her way home, Humphrey is immediately struck by the inappropriateness of one so young being out alone (*OCS,* 2); and his interest is further piqued when he discovers that the child lives with her grandfather in the shop that gives the story its name. After Humphrey leaves the child, her youthful presence, which is so incongruous with her circumstances, takes possession of him to such an extent that he imagines her sleeping in her bed, surrounded by "the images of fantastic things . . . huddled together in the curiosity-dealer's warehouse." Nell captures Humphrey's imagination because she is the antithesis of all around her; thus the task of the narrative is to accommodate this antithesis by determining "the kind of allegory" in which the little girl exists, to understand Nell's profound otherness in a way that provides thematic synthesis (*OCS,* 13). From the outset she is clearly one of Alexander Welsh's "spirits of love and truth," but the nature and essence of the truth that Nell symbolizes is as yet left to be discovered.[16]

The illustration by Samuel Williams of Nell lying in bed ("The Child in her Gentle Slumber," plate 15) that appeared with the novel's original publication in *Master Humphrey's Clock* not only attests to Nell's association with allegory; it also points rather directly to what she allegorizes, even though Dickens himself had not yet decided on Nell's specific role in the novel. In his instructions for illustrating the scene, Dickens had directed Williams to place the sleeping "child in the midst of a crowd of uncongenial and ancient things," "grim, ugly articles . . . giving a notion of great gloom."[17] Dickens, in effect, is establishing a gothic setting, and his intuitive understanding of genre must have informed his directive, for the gothic trappings indicate that Nell's story is in some way metaphysical, and is therefore defined by her intrinsically problematic relationship to narrative or pictorial context. In other words, Nell is always out of place, for her existence is generically delimited by her allegorical status, her role as an abstraction rather than as a living, flesh-and-blood child. Thus what Dickens may first have thought of as ethereal in her nature turns out to be "ghostly" or deathly, a quality emphasized not just by the "ancient things" that surround her, but by her sleep. Interestingly, as John Harvey notes, it was an early review—by Thomas Hood in the *Athenaeum*—that called attention to the way the illustration made explicit Nell's allegorical status, which the accompanying *Clock* text originally had merely implied. Writing in November 1840, before the novel was completed, Hood instructed readers, "Look at the Artist's picture of the Child, asleep in her little bed, surrounded, or rather mobbed, by ancient armour and arms, antique furniture, and relics sacred and profane, hideous or grotesque:—it is like an Allegory of the peace and innocence of Childhood in the midst of Violence, Superstition, and all the hateful or hurtful Passions of the world. How sweet and fresh the youthful figure! how much sweeter and fresher for the rusty, musty, fusty atmosphere of such accessories and their associations!"[18] Evidently it was Hood's way of describing the illustration that caused Dickens to add—in the first complete volume edition of *The Old Curiosity Shop,* published in 1841—the following passage: "I had her image, without any effort of imagination, surrounded and beset by everything that was foreign to its nature, and furthest removed from the sympathies of her sex and age. . . . she seemed to exist in a kind of allegory" (*OCS,* 13). Thus, although Nell's allegorical character is implicit in Dickens's original conception of her, Hood's review undoubtedly helped Dickens to articulate his reasons for emphasizing her otherness.

The gothic quality of Williams's illustration is accentuated by the medieval effects like the armor and the ornate chairs, but the "relics sacred and profane" that Hood mentions have a special function of calling attention to Nell's spiritual role, even though, in the general disorder of the room, everything is so out of context that these "relics" seem at first to signify nothing more than a heap of broken images. Nevertheless, the clutter of objects in the lower-right corner of the picture may assert greater signifying power than objects elsewhere in the design. Because Nell's face is turned in that direction and because of the rather unsettling representation of the crucifix leaning against the trunk below her, this corner seems to invite careful scrutiny. Propped between a helmet and sword on one side and grotesque masks on the other, the crucifix appears as an emblem of discarded religion, diminished in size and importance when compared to the demonic, bestial carving—perhaps intended to be the top of a scabbard—that also leans against the trunk. Together, the crucifix and the carving draw attention to the third item against the trunk, a circular object that may be—as a continuation of the armor motif—a shield. But it could also suggest (and this interpretation makes more sense thematically) a roulette wheel, placed in the design to signify the passion for gambling, the love of games of fortune, that is Nell's grandfather's downfall. Furthermore, because these three objects—the crucifix, the carving, and the wheel—rest against a trunk that in size and general appearance is reminiscent of a small casket, this corner of the picture seems unusually meaningful as an adumbration of Nell's fate.

But it is in George Cattermole's less interesting drawing of Nell dead ("At Rest," plate 16), which appeared in *The Old Curiosity Shop*'s penultimate *Clock* installment, that we find the confusion of "Passions" and disorder of "relics sacred and profane" rearranged and intelligibly ordered to create a thoroughly Christian context. The "profane" idols of "The Child in her Gentle Slumber" are gone; Christianity is no longer represented by a discarded crucifix, but by the image of the mother and child behind Nell's bed, the book in her hand (presumably a Bible or prayer book), and more generally by the Gothic architecture that represents a church ruin (thus clarifying the purpose of the first illustration's gothic treatment). The sprigs of holly on Nell's bed, the open window, and the bird on the sill also reflect the Christian context, as (using Jane Cohen's terms) "hackneyed symbols of immortality."[19] By including the holly as well as the hourglass, Cattermole was following Dickens's instructions; however, Dickens had actually specified that "an hour-glass running out" be used in the illustration that follows this one in the text, to indicate the fate of Nell's grandfather rather than of Nell herself.[20] Because Cattermole obviously referred to Williams's illustration when he created "At Rest," his design serves as a counterpoint to the earlier illustration. The hourglass and bird in Cattermole's design hold positions in the window comparable to those of the bottle, the mirror, and the snuffed candle of Williams's design. Standing in front of the closed window, these three items seem intended to symbolize the imprisonment of self and spirit—especially when they are compared to Cattermole's open window, with its bird on the sill symbolizing the liberation of spirit. Cattermole's hourglass, then, in its association with Nell, seems not so much intended to suggest time "running out" (in Dickens's sense) as to signify escape—by the completion of a life cycle. But the hourglass also serves as a symbol and a memento mori for Nell's grandfather, who has proven to be sorely in need of such a reminder and who finally dies from grief at the end of the number. Thus the hourglass conveys an idea of completion, but also serves, perhaps, as a symbol of tragic reversal, and therefore as a traditional reminder of time's cyclicality.[21]

The importance of illustrations in general and of these two in particular in determining the public's response to *The Old Curiosity Shop* cannot be overestimated. In his early plans for the periodical, Dickens had wisely directed that woodcuts be "dropped into the text" of the *Clock* as a way of enhancing its visual appeal and adding interest to its stories.[22] Thomas Hood's response to "The Child in her Gentle Slumber" is an early indication of the illustrations' crucial role. Forster, too, first in an unsigned review in *The Examiner* and later in his biography of Dickens, acknowledges the importance of the illustrations in his recording of how *The Old Curiosity Shop* developed into a novel:

> It began with a plan for but a short half-dozen chapters; it grew into a full-proportioned story under the warmth of the feeling it had inspired its writer with; its very incidents created a necessity at first not seen; and it was carried to a close only contemplated after a full half of it had been written. Yet, from the opening of the tale to that undesigned ending; from the image of little Nell asleep amid the quaint grotesque figures of the old curiosity warehouse, to that other final sleep she takes among the grim forms and carvings of the old church aisle; the main purpose seems to be always present. The characters and incidents that at first appear most foreign to it, are found to have had with it a close relation. . . . In the first still picture of Nell's innocence in the midst of strange and alien forms, we have the forecast of her after wanderings, her patient miseries, her sad maturity of experience before its time.[23]

Forster's comment makes clear how influential were the illustrations both in helping readers to picture Nell and in helping Dickens to generate and complete her story. The "necessity at first not seen" and the "undesigned ending" of course refer to Nell's death as a narrative imperative; and her fate is clearly "forecast" in Samuel Williams's drawing. The fact that these two illustrations could so exactly complement and mirror each other is visual proof that Dickens was more than usually tempted into thinking in iconographic and allegorical terms as he wrote this most improvised (excluding *Pickwick*) of all his novels.

Thus, from the outset of *The Old Curiosity Shop,* Dickens seems to have intuited Nell's allegorical nature, if not her precise role in the allegory. Dickens tells us that Nell "had often pored whole evenings" over "an old copy of the Pilgrim's Progress"; and when she and her grandfather set out from home, Nell comments, "I feel as if we were both like Christian"—thereby explicitly acknowledging that their journey is the archetypal pilgrimage of life (*OCS,* 116, 117). As Alexander Welsh notes and as Nell's remark suggests, *The Old Curiosity Shop* is "visibly modelled on Bunyan's allegory." In their escape from London and their hopes of finding peace in the country, the two characters participate in "Bunyan's repudiation of the earthly city," although neither seems to consider that death must inevitably mark the end of their journey.[24] But Nell's allegorical role is further complicated by the fact that she is not only a pilgrim through "the World of Time, governed under God's ordinance by Fortune"; when she assumes the role of Grandfather's "guide and leader," she becomes the embodiment of his spirit, his only reason for living (*OCS,* 96).[25] Once out of London Grandfather tells Nell: "I can do nothing for myself, my darling. . . . I don't know how it is, I could once, but the time's gone. Don't leave me, Nell; say that thou'lt not leave me. I loved thee all the while, indeed I did. If I lose thee too, my dear, I must die!" (*OCS,* 11). In other words, Nell's inextricable connection to her grandfather indicates that she has become his anima: because all his love is projected onto her, she is both real and ideal, a physical presence and the image of all that is holy in his eyes. In Jungian terms, Nell is the feminine principle who exists to a great extent as a projection of Grandfather's imagination; as such, she personifies Dickens's own anima, the archetypal female originating as a "spontaneous product" of the author's unconscious.[26] As in Francis Quarles's *Emblems, Divine and Moral,* she is the author's (female) soul, whose task it is to manage the spiritual affairs of the (male) author and help him proceed safely to his long home. Thus Nell bears a striking resemblance to Quarles's images of the bedridden soul who "would fain have rest" and of the pilgrim soul who leaves the city to find "country sweets" and "lesser trouble."[27] Moreover, like Quarles's soul, Nell combines childlike innocence with feminine desirability, as her pubescent age of "nearly fourteen" seems intended to suggest. Thus Nell does duty as quintessential female, the child, the mother, and the lover, "both old and young, Demeter and Persephone," while Grandfather plays "spouse and sleeping suckling rolled into one."[28] The symbolic burden that Nell is forced to bear in the novel causes her destruction; for, as she is the embodiment of Grandfather's spirit or soul, her death must be inextricably connected to his own.

Nell's tragedy, then, occurs not because the other characters fail to perceive her spiritual, symbolic nature, but because they do not fully grasp the extent of its otherworldliness. Instead, they interpret Nell's angelic qualities as a promise of worldly good fortune. For example, Grandfather tells Nell: "there must be good fortune in store for thee. . . . Such miseries must fall on thy innocent head without it, that I cannot believe but that, being tempted, it will come at last!" (*OCS,* 26). Indeed, Grandfather believes that the "triumph" that must be preordained for Nell will come by way of his "tempting fortune" through gambling (*OCS,* 76). Grandfather's need to seek fortune against time results from the fact that his biological clock is sounding loudly in his own ears. He begins "to think how little [he] had saved, how long a time it took to save at all, how short a time he might have at his age to live" (*OCS,* 74). And even after he has lost everything through this ill-advised method of trying to provide for Nell, he never doubts that "[t]he means of happiness are on the cards and in the dice," nor does he lose faith in his ability to predict fortune's behavior. As he tells Nell, "Fortune will not bear chiding. We must not reproach her, or she shuns us; I have found that out" (*OCS,* 223). Because Grandfather never doubts that Fortune is a fair lady who ultimately metes out reward or punishment according to the deserts of the recipient, he has no compunction even about stealing Nell's gold for gambling. But Grandfather's certainty comes from confusing faith with desire, and he can beat the odds only in his continual ability to lose, as Quilp implies: "'I thought,' sneered the dwarf, 'that if a man played long enough he was sure to win at last, or at the worst, not to come off a loser'" (*OCS,* 75). Grandfather's reply of "And so he is" simply states his absolute, never-wavering belief that he is the favorite of the goddess who will satisfy his lust for riches (*OCS,* 75).

Dick Swiveller, with the encouragement of both Nell's brother Fred and Quilp, also associates Nell with Fortune—in the usual contemporary sense that conflates the goddess with a rich, marriageable woman. Like Bassanio, Dick proposes to "ring fancy's knell"—to fulfill his destiny and make his fortune through marriage by wooing Nell for her grandfather's money (*OCS,* 161). Dick imagines himself (as Quilp so eloquently interprets this fancy) a "lucky dog" and a "made man": "'I see in you nothing now but Nelly's husband, rolling in gold and silver'" (*OCS,* 164). But because Dick's fate rests firmly in the comic portion of the novel, which does not partake of religious allegory, the "young lady saving up for him" is not Nell, as Dick had fancied, but Nell's comic double, the Marchioness, who is as thoroughly an inhabitant of this world as Nell is of the next (*OCS,* 551). Thus Nell is a character whose very name defines her association and literal identification with death. As the pun of her name suggests, she is a death knell for her grandfather, and ultimately for herself. In being mistaken for Fortune, Nell becomes at once Fortune's victim and the first of her avatars in Dickens's novels, the young and innocent manifestation of the third Fate, Atropos, "the destroyer," Freud's and Dickens's "silent goddess of Death."[29]

From the Magic Reel to Ixion's Wheel: "The Cry of the Children"

Dickens begins the final chapter of *The Old Curiosity Shop* with an image that presumably refers to the thread of his narrative unwinding as if from a spool: "The magic reel, which, rolling on before, has led the chronicler thus far, now slackens in its pace, and stops. It lies before its goal; the pursuit is at an end" (*OCS,* 547). The image, which describes linear progress through circular movement, suggests the successful progress, the happy conclusion to the romantic quest. The hopeful, forward progress of this reel reflects Dickens's fundamentally optimistic vision during the waxing portion of the Victorian era and of his own career. This view is still operative in 1846, when Dickens concludes *Pictures from Italy* using a comparable image. Reflecting on his Italian journey, Dickens posits that we can learn from Italy's ruins "the lesson that the wheel of Time is rolling for an end, and that the world is, in all great essentials, better, gentler, more forbearing, and more hopeful, as it rolls!" (*PI,* 433). Although at least two of the positive changes accruing with the advance of "the wheel of Time"—i.e., the world's becoming "gentler" and "more forbearing"—might be considered as feminine, the image itself, like *The Old Curiosity Shop*'s magic reel, communicates a progressively linear historical view that can be equated with masculine temporality. It was for a woman, Elizabeth Barrett Browning, to introduce the wheel as a symbol for an unambiguously tragic fate into Victorian artistic discourse by associating the wheels of industry with a critique of British patriarchy. Later, Barrett would use the wheel as a symbol for women's time.

In August 1843, when *Blackwood's Magazine* published "The Cry of the

Children," Barrett (not yet Browning) became one of the first of many artists to protest the exploitation of child labor, by graphically rendering in her poetry images of suffering taken from the governmental bluebooks—the Parliamentary Commission Reports, which eventually shocked the nation into passing its first labor laws. Before the year's end, like-minded artists Thomas Hood and Dickens would publish, respectively, the "Song of the Shirt" and *A Christmas Carol,* thus mobilizing a major literary assault on labor practices in England's mines and mills that both appropriated and extended the bluebooks' influence on industrial reform.[30] Barrett, an invalid who knew nothing about the workaday world beyond her Wimpole Street bedroom, was particularly indebted to R. H. Horne's report, which included the following horrifying description of a typical factory he visited: "It is a frightful place, turn which way you will. There is a constant hammering roar of wheels, so that you could not possibly hear any warning voice. . . . Little boys and girls are here seen at work at the tip-punching machines (all acting by steam power) with their fingers in constant danger of being punched off once in every second, while at the same time they have their heads between two whirling wheels a few inches distant from each ear."[31] The "whirling wheels" that figure so ominously in this description become the central image of "The Cry of the Children."

Barrett begins the poem by appealing to her "brothers" in the "happy Fatherland" of England to hear the cry of these suffering child laborers (lines 1, 24).[32] The phrase "happy Fatherland" ironically points to the poem's theme: that in its treatment of these children, English industry not only ignores but violates its patriarchal and parental responsibilities. In the pivotal seventh stanza, which most dramatically employs the wheel image, Barrett makes the case for the children by letting them speak for themselves:

> For all day the wheels are droning, turning;
>   Their wind comes in our faces,
> Till our hearts turn, our heads with pulses burning,
>   And the walls turn in their places:
> Turns the sky in the high window, blank and reeling,
>   Turns the long light that drops adown the wall,
> Turn the black flies that crawl along the ceiling:

All are turning, all the day, and we with all.
And all day the iron wheels are droning,
And sometimes we could pray,
"O ye wheels" (breaking out in a mad moaning),
"Stop! be silent for to-day!" (lines 77–88)

This stanza captures the dizzying effect of the roar and relentless speed of the steam-powered "whirling wheels" described in the commission report. Metaphorically, the children are presented as Ixionic prisoners and victims of wheels that bring fortune only to the captains of industry. The breakneck speed of the wheels sets an inhuman pace not only for the children's work, but for their lives as well, causing them to grow old and "die before our time," as they tell us in stanza 4 (line 52). The centrifugal force of these factory wheels therefore destroys the lives of these children just as it accelerates the cyclical rhythms of nature. In her use of wheel imagery, Barrett suggests that the laboring children are sacrifices to an inevitable clash between notions of technological advance and biological "felt" time. These children, still part of nature in their innocence and powerlessness, are tortured on the iron wheels of industry, turned by masters who choose to ignore the dangers of their power.

In a poem probably written the following year, but first printed in *Blackwood's* in 1846, Barrett again uses the wheel as a symbol, this time to indicate quite specifically women's work and women's time. "A Year's Spinning" tells the story of a cottage spinster forsaken by her lover and cursed by her mother for allowing herself to be seduced. In the course of the year recounted in the poem, the spinster first meets her lover, bears his child, buries both her mother and the child, and anticipates her own death, presumably because of her moral and physical suffering. This spinster's year has no seasons, only biological cycles and the diurnal round of work: the laboring woman is distanced from the natural world moving through spring, summer, fall, and winter by and through her enforced physical labor—in both its senses as childbirth and daily toil. The final line of each stanza is a refrain offering some variation of the phrase "And now my spinning is all done," suggesting the cyclicality of the woman's traditional occupation and of the female's biological destiny. The woman's spinning in the poem therefore becomes an emblem of fate, and we are reminded of those most famous spinners, the Greek Fates—Clotho, Lachesis, and Atropos, the three goddesses of destiny—who (respectively) spun, measured, and cut the thread of each person's life. In the myth of Er, recorded several centuries before the Christian era, Plato envisioned the Fates as Necessity's daughters and handmaids, who assisted in turning a huge cosmic spindle, further suggesting, for the later tradition, their connection with the spinning wheel (and, ultimately, with Fortune).[33] Here, the spinster is assuredly Necessity's daughter: she has no choice but to attend to the natural cycles of conception, gestation, and birth because they take place in her own body. In the year that passes in the poem, these three cycles, as well as three deaths, are brought to completion. In the final stanza, only the now-emblematic wheel remains as the reminder of the spinster's work and life. It is thus an appropriate symbol of her death as well, and one she hopes will eventually register on the lover who deserted her:

> And let the door ajar remain,
> In case he should pass by anon;
> And leave the wheel out very plain,—
> That HE, when passing in the sun,
> May see the spinning is all done. (lines 31–35)[34]

Barrett's poem is reminiscent of Walter Savage Landor's "I Cannot Mind My Wheel" (1806), which was printed as a Manchester broadside ballad and which tells a similar story of a young woman spinning and mourning a lost lover.[35] The spinning/mourning story is archetypal, but it also is grounded in reality. As the term "spinster" in law and common usage indicates, such narratives serve as an etymological elaboration of a long history that metaphorically equates woman's longing for a man to help her complete her biological vocation with the most traditional of British female domestic industries—spinning. As the Wife of Bath said, God gives women "wit" for three things: "deceite, wepyng, and spynnyng."[36]

Barrett's wheel imagery in "A Year's Spinning," as in "The Cry of the Children," thus works to register a critique of patriarchy. Despite their obvious differences, both poems record suffering and victimization at the hands of men who are indifferent about the power they exercise over the children's and spinsters' lives and work. In both poems those who must "mind the wheel" as an industrial and/or biological necessity are punished capitally for being bound to it: a bond enforced by youth, innocence, and poverty in the first case, and by gender in the second. Barrett's wheel imagery negates the idea of progress communicated by Dickens's "magic reel" and later by his "wheel of Time"; she transforms the industrial wheel into a symbol for tragedy, for the relentless cyclicality of existence going nowhere but to the grave. In *Dombey and Son,* Dickens would follow Barrett's lead, adapting his wheel imagery to a comparable critique of patriarchy that adumbrates a similarly tragic view.

Dombey Time

When Dickens began writing *Dombey and Son* from Lausanne on June 27, 1846, he was well on his way to becoming the undisputed international master of the genre that was rising with him to the foremost place in popular literature. Kathleen Tillotson points out in *Novels of the Eighteen-Forties* that by the end of this decade the novel had begun its long season of flowering as "the form of expression most suited to the age."[37] The period of *Dombey*'s serialization—from October 1846 to April 1848—would see the publication of *Jane Eyre, Wuthering Heights, Vanity Fair,* and *Mary Barton* as well, fixing the reputation of their respective authors, the Brontës, Thackeray, and Gaskell, as Victorian giants of the novel. As Raymond Williams explains, the "unprecedented" burst of creativity in the genre that took place in a twenty-month period during 1847 and 1848 can be understood as an articulation of a "new consciousness" of this "critical and defining stage" in British history. England's place as "The first industrial civilisation in the history of the world" brought with it the need for a massive reassessment of society—especially of this new, predominantly urban society—and the protean suppleness of the novel made it the most felicitous form for carrying out such an assessment. Dickens's "radically innovating *Dombey and Son*" led the way.[38]

Like *Pickwick, Nickleby,* and, most recently, *Martin Chuzzlewit, Dombey and Son* was a production in twenty numbers and nineteen monthly installments, the last presented as a double issue. Popularized by

Dickens and adapted by other writers as one model for serialization, this period of almost elephantine gestation (or more precisely, a doubling of human gestation) was frequently described in terms of pregnancy and parturition, perhaps most notably by the complaining *Fraser's* reviewer who characterized the model as "the monstrous anomaly of a twenty-month's labour and a piecemeal accouchement."[39] Such metaphors suggest a process perceived as a birth, however anomalous, and therefore connected to a temporality that, if gendered, would be considered female. Certainly, the cycle of regular monthly publication sustained for over a year and a half not only swelled the size of these novels, but also affected the patterns of writerly production and readerly expectation and consumption in ways that integrated congenially with the rhythm of at least middle-class, literate women's lives. D. A. Miller has argued that such novels virtually enforced the reader's "leisured withdrawal to the private, domestic sphere" not once but many times, thereby establishing a regular round of work and leisurely reading, as well as creating and justifying the form's celebration of domesticity.[40] The novel, especially in its expansive multivolumed or twenty-numbered form, became the ideal medium for presenting a wide range of temporalities; but as an extension of Miller's argument suggests, it was especially adaptable to the sympathetic treatment of women's time in its various manifestations. By making female worth and a sympathetic appreciation of women's time his explicit themes, Dickens in *Dombey and Son* offered his first novel to take full advantage of the form's implicit and explicit ratification of domestic values.[41]

Indeed, *Dombey and Son* is Dickens's first "domestic novel," the subgenre defined by Steven Marcus (with reference to *Dombey*) as "a novel which regards society and individual existence through representing the life of a single and rather small family as it persists through time."[42] The emphasis in Marcus's definition is on diachronic presentation: *Nickleby* and *Chuzzlewit,* while also certainly revealing an interest in family ties, used the synchronic activities of a wider range of kin as a backdrop for picaresque narratives more concerned with following the adventures of individual heroes and villains. By contrast, *Dombey* is an inside story of family life and relationships as they change over time: the narrative covers something over twelve years in the life of the Dombey family, a period marked at noticeably regular intervals by some domestic crisis, including three births, three deaths, two weddings, and two flights from home.[43] These significant domestic events are explicitly calibrated with the heroine's life: as both the text and the working notes for *Dombey* reveal, Dickens keeps time in the novel via Florence Dombey's biological clock, as she grows from a child of six through adolescence and puberty to marriage and young motherhood.[44] But if the waxing half of a female's life cycle sets one large, unifying rhythm of the novel, the actual plot moves in a complementary fashion, by a downward turning of Fortune's wheel in the life of Florence's father. For *Dombey and Son* is also Dickens's most sustained effort in the Victorian novel's version of the *de casibus* tragedy: the fall of a hero from fortune to ruin that serves as the theme of Chaucer's monk's tale and the deep structure of the great Elizabethan tragedies.

The *de casibus* plot concerns the wealthy and proud head of the house and firm named in the title who fails—personally and financially—because of his inability to define his relationships—patriarchal, domestic, economic, or otherwise—in anything but the most self-interested, commercial terms. Thus Dickens tells us about "Dombey and Son": "Those three words conveyed the one idea of Mr. Dombey's life. The earth was made for Dombey and Son to trade in, and the sun and moon were made to give them light. Rivers and seas were formed to float their ships; rainbows gave them promise of fair weather; winds blew for or against their enterprises; stars and planets circled in their orbits, to preserve inviolate a system of which they were the centre. Common abbreviations took new meanings in his eyes, and had sole reference to them: A.D. had no concern with anno Domini, but stood for anno Dombei—and Son" (*DS,* 2). Although Dombey becomes a more complex character as the novel proceeds, at the outset this magnificently hyperbolic description of Dombey's sense of place and time tells us almost everything we need to know about his character. Dombey sees himself not just as the head of the house, the "Colossus of commerce," as Major Bagstock aptly describes him; Dombey believes himself to be lord of the universe, with power over time, life, death, and fortune (*DS,* 363). Nevertheless, his very Dombey-centrism satirically identifies him as a type rather than an original. As one of the first number's reviewers remarked, "The world of London is filled with cold, pompous, stiff, purse-proud men like this."[45] Dombey and his kind were all those commercial magnates, traders, champions of laissez-faire, and captains of industry who accepted Carlyle's doctrine that "Work is Worship," so long as everyone was clear about what was sacred here: a habit of life and guiding principle best summarized by that other great Protestant tenet, "Time is money."[46] Since Dombey controls the wealth in his dominions and domicile, he controls time there as well; and wielding this sort of temporal power, as Dombey's name and Dickens's joke about it suggest, is tantamount to playing God.[47] In the words of the villainous Carker, "Dombey and Son know neither time, nor place, nor season, but bear them all down" (*DS*, 526).

Dombey time can therefore be defined as that temporality arising from a sense of patriarchal power and privilege that recognizes no other standard and that requires full obedience to its reckoning. Appropriately, Florence's early impression of her father can be summed up in a few deft strokes, which include his association with time: "The child glanced keenly at the blue coat and stiff white cravat, which, with a pair of creaking boots and a very loud ticking watch, embodied her idea of a father" (*DS*, 3). The synecdochic details presented here give us the essential Dombey: his sense of class superiority and rigidity, the "firmness" he shares with his "tensely masculine world," his insistence on control, and his aggressively masculine temporality.[48] Thus Dickens punctuates Dombey's dying wife's silence with the "loud ticking" of the husband's and the attending doctor's watches, "which seemed in the silence to be running a race" (*DS*, 9). The competition between the two timepieces indicates a similar temporal imperialism on the part of both men, thereby hinting that the doctor (a court physician) operates by his own version of Dombey time, which by definition must overbear against any rival temporal standard.

As the foregoing discussion suggests, Dickens intends Dombey time to be at once a parody and a perversion of what can be called patriarchal time, the temporality sanctioned by both Victorian capitalism and nineteenth-century British Christianity, which advocated obedience to the Victorian paterfamilias as the earthly, temporal representative of a heavenly father. Like patriarchal time (at least in its Evangelical and Calvinist formulations), Dombey time is teleological: it has a beginning and an end shaped by an all-powerful, all-knowing father and significantly notched by the birth of a son, whose sole reason for existence is to execute his father's will. As Dombey himself puts it, "This young gentleman has to accomplish a destiny. A destiny, little fellow!" (*DS,* 4). That Dickens intends to parody patriarchal time is suggested everywhere in the novel, but this theme is most apparent in the conclusion of Paul Junior's story.[49] Since patriarchal time requires the sacrifice of the son for and by the father, Paul is the "Boy born, to die" described in the first of Dickens's working notes for the novel.[50] For as in the Christian, so in the Dombey story: the death gives meaning to the birth and provides the motive for its presentation. Paul's death, which occurs about a quarter of the way through the novel, is fated from the beginning as the crucial incident necessary to advance the *de casibus* plot.

Following a characteristic pattern, Dickens highlights his temporal theme by offering numerous variations on it throughout the novel, thus corroborating Lindley Murray's explanation regarding time's gender in his *Grammar:* "Time is always masculine, on account of its mighty efficacy."[51] *Dombey and Son* is saturated with imagery associated with clocks, watches, and timepieces of all kinds and littered with references to Time personified as a powerful masculine force: Time is "another Major"; he is "remorseless," "all-potent," "sure of foot and strong of will" (*DS,* 89, 1, 473, 542). In only one instance is Time personified in its moderating capacity as healer, and this significantly occurs with regard to Dombey and Edith's relations after their marriage: "Time, consoler of affliction and softener of anger, could do nothing to help them" (*DS,* 646). This exception to the general rule nevertheless serves to underscore Time's role in the novel as a masculine, dominating force, since one implication here is that, in a marriage with Dombey, Time's gentler qualities would have to originate with the wife. Instead, Dombey and Edith's marriage gives new meaning to the term "wedlock": they are "jined together in the house of bondage," to use Captain Cuttle's colorful designation for the state of matrimony (*DS,* 702, 783).

The most obvious parallel to Dombey and his watch is Dr. Blimber's relationship to his great hall clock, whose loud ticking seems to repeat its owner's first question to Paul, "how, is, my, lit, tle, friend?" (*DS,* 145, 150). Like Dombey's watch, this clock's assertive animism functions as a form of masculine display, in this case to represent Blimber's more patronizing, but equally insistent, version of patriarchal time. The image Dickens uses to describe Blimber's "forcing system" of education suggests both an Ixionic wheel and its association with the great clock in the hall: "The studies went round like a mighty wheel, and the young gentlemen were always stretched upon it" (*DS*, 163). This image recalls Barrett's suffering young factory workers in "The Cry of the Children," who, like Paul, "die before [their] time" because their work demands that they operate at an accelerated pace.[52] Ultimately, the clock proves to be as unreliable as the pedagogical timing inherent in Blimber's "forcing system" of education (*DS*, 141, 143). Nevertheless, during its repair the clock maintains its power over Paul, who thinks that its face is still "ogling him," even though it has been temporarily removed and propped against a wall (*DS*, 192). These references to Blimber's clock show that, like Dombey time, Blimber time is highly suspect in point of accuracy, but its authority concerning household and institutional matters goes without question.

Dickens parodies patriarchal time as a function of religion through his brief but memorable characterization of the Reverend Melchisedech Howler "of the Ranting persuasion," whose apocalyptic pronouncements include a prediction of "the destruction of the world for that day two years, at ten in the morning" (*DS*, 207). Like Tony Weller's nemesis, Mr. Stiggins, in *Pickwick;* the Shoemaker Divine of Little Bethel in *The Old Curiosity Shop;* and, later, Mr. Chadband of *Bleak House,* Howler is a type of spiritual father who serves as a stock figure of Dickensian satire. These dissenting ministers respond to the divine call by lording it over or preying on gullible women (in this case, Mrs. MacStinger) in various ways, thereby abusing their patriarchal power. But the eschatological twist added in this instance serves as a reprise for *Dombey*'s attack on patriarchal time. No doubt part of Dickens's fun in creating the Reverend Melchisedech derived from the circumstance that, if his prediction were accurate, the end of the world would come close on the heels of the end of the novel. Thus on the reverend's next—and last—appearance in the final number, we learn that he "had consented, on very urgent solicitation, to give the world another two years of existence, but had informed his followers that, then, it must positively go" (*DS*, 856). Blimber and Howler time can be considered ridiculous versions of Dombey time's sublime because each exhibits its two essentials: (1) each wields patriarchal power by controlling time in other people's lives; and (2) each is a willful, arbitrary reckoning in which accuracy always gives way to egoistic desire. Taken together, these three temporalities suggest a pervasive abuse of patriarchal power in the four most important areas of Victorian society: in the home, commerce, education, and religion. The only masculine time that escapes Dickens's attack is that of Walter's uncle Solomon Gills, who keeps an eminently reliable chronometer, but who thinks the world has passed him by—until the end of the novel (*DS,* 34, 38). When Dickens finally tells us "that instead of being behind the time . . . as he supposed, he was a little before it, and had to wait the fulness of time and the design," we realize that Sol's temporality, like the solar system suggested by his name, is not linear, but cyclical (*DS,* 874).

Dickens's portrayal of Dombey time therefore registers a complaint against "patriarchy" by criticizing it in its most insidious form of "paternalistic dominance," as feminist historian Gerda Lerner defines these terms in *The Creation of Patriarchy.* Lerner explains that, even though the latter concept evolved historically "from family relations as they developed under patriarchy, in which the father held absolute power over all the members of his household," it implies a more ossified sense of social inequality and a refusal to admit differences in ability except along class lines: "paternalistic dominance describes the relationship of a dominant group, considered superior, to a subordinate group, considered inferior, in which the dominance is mitigated by mutual obligations and reciprocal rights. The dominated exchange submission for protection, unpaid labor for maintenance." In other words, a system of paternalistic dominance requires that all parties be complicit in a hierarchical social arrangement based on a pervasive attitude of gender (or racial) superiority—which is its most contemptible feature. Consequently, females, categorized by gender as subordinates in this system, have no possibility of achieving autonomy. Lerner tells us: "As applied to familial relations, it should be noted that responsibilities and obligations are not equally distributed among those to be protected: the male children's subordination to the father's dominance is temporary; it lasts until they themselves become heads of households. The subordination of female children and of wives is lifelong. Daughters can escape it only if they place themselves as wives under the dominance/protection of another man."[53]

Within the terms of this definition—noting of course that Dombey pays for labor—lie the major concerns of Victorian domestic fiction and the entire plot and theme of *Dombey and Son.* When Dorothy Van Ghent noted some time ago that Dickens's two great interrelated and "formally analogous" themes are "the crime of the parent against the child, and the calculated social crime," she was describing the crime inherent in a system of paternalistic dominance. The "form" of both crimes, "the treatment of persons as things," is another way of describing the exploitation of human beings by making them objects of exchange.[54] Via the characterization of Dombey as the arch-patriarch, *Dombey and Son* is the first of Dickens's novels to unify these two themes successfully. Whether as head of the house near Portland Place or the one in the City, Dombey reinstitutionalizes the traditional patriarchal prerogative of "absolute power over all the members of his household" in exchange for "maintenance"—for food, clothing, shelter, and/or financial support. His relationship with everyone who falls within his sphere of control becomes primarily economic: Dombey literally buys time from his subordinates, presumably gaining more of it for himself. It is therefore Dombey's fortune—not just his maleness—that is the key to his omnipotence and his ability to "choose [his] own times," as he tells Edith (*DS,* 562–63). That this is the case can be demonstrated by looking at the makeup of Dombey's "subordinate group, considered inferior," which actually comprises two groups that include both sexes but divide along gender lines. There is the predominantly female group at home, which includes his wife (either of the two), his two children, his relatives, and his domestic servants; and an exclusively male group at the office, which includes all his employees from the top manager to the lowliest messenger. Moreover, because he is the wealthiest member of his merchant class, Dombey considers himself to be in a class by himself; membership in his "dominant group, considered superior" can be shared with only one other person, the son who is heir to these domestic/female and corporate/male dominions. Such immense wealth creates a kind of staying power that seems to make its possessor immune to time's movement. As Carker, with his usual slimy sycophancy, tells his chief in a passage restored for the Penguin edition of the novel: "One who sits on such an elevation as yours, and can sit there, unmoved, in all seasons—hasn't much reason to know anything about the flight of time. It's men like myself, who are low down and are not superior in circumstances, and who inherit new masters in the course of Time, that have cause to look about us. I shall have a rising sun to worship, soon."[55] Carker's remark is of course double-edged, but it accurately comments on one of the curious effects of position and power on anyone's consciousness of temporality, regardless of gender—an effect illustrated by Dombey's exalted place at top center of the novel's cover wrapper. While the powerful seem to have a place above time, the weak and dependent are battered about as if caught in a temporal maelstrom. Major Bagstock's "Native"; Mrs. Skewton's manservant, Withers; Rob the Grinder; and the boys at Blimber's Academy all have "cause to look about": like prisoners or beasts of burden, their consciousness of time alternates by a pendulum swing between the pain or drudgery of labor and fear for their lives. In simple economic terms the value of their time—like the value of their lives—is measured by the Dombey standard of paternalistic dominance. In fact, the crimes of Carker, Dombey, Blimber, Howler, Bagstock, and even Skewton and Pipchin differ in degree, but not in essential kind: they are all crimes that derive from and are sanctioned by the widespread institutionalization of paternalistic dominance in Victorian society. Time in this society is unquestionably a father.

Lerner's definition of "paternalistic dominance" also explains Susan Nipper's gnomic assessment of Florence's and Paul's relative positions in Dombey time: "Miss Floy being a permanency, Master Paul a temporary" (*DS,* 25). Susan's comment most obviously serves as a prophecy of both children's larger temporal fate, but she is actually attempting to contrast the Dombey children's places, by virtue of gender, in reference to their tenure as subordinates in the domestic organization. Ultimately Florence's escape from Dombey time comes, as Lerner's definition predicts, when she places herself, as a wife, "under the dominance/protection of another man." Florence's subordinate position in the patriarchal institution continues to be "a permanency," although in its final configuration—her role as Walter Gay's wife and Dombey's adored daughter, nurse, and savior—it is indeed more thoroughly "mitigated by mutual obligations and reciprocal rights."

The Bosom of the Family

Because Dombey time is expanded into such an absurdity at the beginning of the novel, the reader understands immediately that Dickens's sympathies lie elsewhere. Initially they reside with Dombey's dying wife, whose consciousness of time at that critical moment, we can be sure, is rather different from her husband's, but whose death leaves her opinion about all things temporal largely a matter of speculation. As Juliet McMaster says in her fine essay on women's biological clocks, Fanny Dombey's story—that of a mother's "courage unto death"—"receives an indirect spotlight as a tale pathetically untold."[56] By leaving Fanny's story at the shadowy edge of the narrative, Dickens employs what we might call a technique of refraction to bring the domestic economy of the Dombey household into sharper focus and to suggest that the indomitable will of the husband is just as responsible for Fanny's death as the difficult birth of the child. Fanny's death serves as the first indication that an unhappy fate is likely to await any female who must live within striking distance of Dombey time. But Fanny's death is more than just a foreshadowing device. By pairing the event of the son's birth with the mother's death, Dickens quickly establishes what the rest of the novel sets about to realize: that *Dombey and Son*'s complaint against patriarchy is inextricably tied to—is in fact designed primarily to be—a celebration of women and a virtual sanctification of women's time in its maternal mode. Through Dickens's representation of Fanny, maternal time is immediately connected not just with the biological, with matters of life and death, but with the spiritual—in a way that does not parody religious belief. As Fanny breathes her last, the profound silence that meets the loud ticking of Dombey's watch throws Dombey time into unflattering relief as an artificial and mechanical temporality that willfully disregards the quieter but truer rhythms of nature and the cosmos, which are first associated with Fanny. Throughout the novel Dickens suggests these larger cosmic rhythms by way of ocean imagery, so that Fanny's death (like Paul's later) is characterized as a going out with the tide: "the mother drifted out upon the dark and unknown sea that rolls round all the world" (*DS*, 10).[57]

If Dombey is the embodiment of masculine time, then the first representative of the novel's preferred temporal values is not Dombey, but his wife. Consequently, Fanny's role does not end with her death; instead, she continues as a spiritual presence throughout the novel. Fanny and Christ appear to Paul as he is dying (*DS,* 226). And the frontispiece (first included with the final double number) recalls this moment by depicting Fanny as if she were the Virgin Mary after her Assumption (plate 17). Dressed in a robe, with her hair about her shoulders and her arms held out to receive her infant, Fanny takes her symbolic place in the clouds and among the angels at the top of the design like *Maria Regina,* the Queen of Heaven.[58] Fanny's exalted position in this frontispiece parallels Dombey's position at top center on the novel's monthly wrappers (plate 18), thus offering an iconographic revision of the parents' respective places that accords with Dickens's theme. Fanny, not Dombey, is the parent whose place at the top—the place of Fortune, above and outside time—is permanent and eternal. Though her death is treated like an Assumption in the iconography of the novel and the frontispiece, in which she represents transcendent, idealized maternal love, Fanny has nevertheless been removed from the temporal flow, which is, after all, the location of the novel's events and concerns.[59]

In the sublunary world of the narrative, Dombey immediately sees that Fanny's absence creates a maternal void in the household that he must somehow fill, and so her death carries far greater significance to Dombey than her life ever did. In fact, the rest of the narrative is generated by Dombey's botched attempts to supply this domestic need in one way or another. In Deirdre David's words, imperial Dombey is himself "Governed by his desire to control the female body on which he is dependent for his own patriarchal reproduction, and hence for his projected importance in the world of business and empire."[60] We might say that Fanny's is a pregnant absence; thus she continues to haunt the novel not just through the religious iconography described above, but also through more grotesquely comic representations intended to call attention to the position she has vacated. Dickens and later Phiz (presumably taking his cue from the passage quoted below) continue Fanny's story through imagery that suggests a house in mourning for its mistress. When Dombey orders the furniture to be covered up after the funeral, the place takes on a grief-stricken, ghoulish appearance: "mysterious shapes were made of tables and chairs, heaped together in the middle of rooms, and covered with great winding-sheets. Bell-handles, window-blinds, and looking-glasses, being papered up in journals, daily and weekly, obtruded fragmentary accounts of deaths and dreadful murders. Every chandelier or lustre, muffled in holland, looked like a monstrous tear depending from the ceiling's eye. Odours, as from vaults and damp places, came out of chimneys. The dead and buried lady was awful in a picture-frame of ghastly bandage" (*DS,* 22). This imagery affirms, however ludicrously, that Fanny's "broken spirit" nevertheless remains in the house as some kind of watchful presence (*DS,* 2); and several of Phiz's illustrations work to continue her memory by recalling this passage. Muffled chandeliers appear in the first two plates in the novel, "Miss Tox introduces 'the Party'" (plate 19) and "The Dombey Family" (plate 20). In each case, the chandelier hangs rather ominously above the woman temporarily trying to discharge the duties of the house's mistress—Louisa Chick and Polly Toodle, respectively. In three later illustrations, "Mr. Dombey introduces his Daughter Florence," "Mr. Dombey and the World," and "'Let him remember it in that Room, Years to come,'" Fanny herself, rather like the Duke of Ferrara's Last Duchess, peeps out of a partially obscured picture frame. Fanny's numinous presence in these three illustrations is appropriate, since her appearance in each case coincides with a moment when the house loses or gains one of its two subsequent mistresses, Edith and finally Florence, who has been "the spirit of [Dombey's] home" all along (*DS,* 504). In this final plate, as Michael Steig points out, Florence—like her mother before her—appears to be a "ghostly image": as she stands in the doorway with sunlight streaming down upon her, Florence is the genius of the place returned to save her father, close up the house for good, and put her mother's spirit to rest at last.[61]

As the female closest to Dombey after Fanny, Florence is heir to her mother's difficulties; but Florence's suffering at the hands of Dombey is more unjust because she has entered the Dombey household through no desire or fault of her own. Moreover, Florence's particular place there makes her more objectionable than anyone else in the eyes of her father. A little girl is property that has no value in the Dombey corporate or domestic economy: "In the capital of the House's name and dignity, such a child was merely a piece of base coin that couldn't be invested—a bad Boy—nothing more" (*DS,* 3). Like many Dickens children before and after, Florence is guilty only of being born; but in this single instance in all of Dickens's novels, the problem is primarily gender rather than simply ill-fated germination. Florence's crime against patriarchy (besides inspiring the love of her brother, which is denied the father), is to have been born female—a crime that must be paid for through the temporal sentence outlined by Van Ghent. That is, Florence is the principal child "who must necessarily take upon [her]self responsibility for not only what is to be done in the present and the future, but what has been done in the past, inasmuch as the past is part and parcel of the present and future."[62] In the patriarchal system, the temporal "responsibility" described here usually devolves on the patriarch himself: if he is reaping the rewards of having everyone's time at his disposal, then he ought, according to the operating principle of exchange, to bear the burden of time in some way or other for them all. But this is the temporal burden that seems to weigh on Dombey's son and heir, Paul Junior, from birth—a burden that shortly proves too heavy for his delicate frame.[63] In his "old fashion," Paul is marked from the beginning by "Time and his brother Care" (*DS,* 1); he is femininely sensitive and delicate, more like his mother and sister than his father—which partly accounts for his natural attachment to any woman, even to the unmaternal Pipchin. Nevertheless, in his symbolic role as the novel's Christ, Paul—though surely a sacrifice to patriarchal time—is not intentionally punished by his father for being born, but rewarded with his father's blessing and affection. It is Florence who, because she is a girl, is perceived to be the criminal, the enemy of Dombey and the system of paternalistic dominance that he represents. Florence is Dickens's only character whose victimization by a parent (and, by extension, society) takes the form of sexism. For this reason *Dombey and Son* is Dickens's most far-reaching complaint against patriarchy.[64]

Dombey's mistreatment of Florence escalates as the narrative proceeds; but during Paul's infancy, she suffers mostly from her father's neglect. In the meantime, the actual pressure of Dombey time bears more heavily on the entourage of women—Polly Toodle, Susan Nipper, Lucretia Tox, and Dombey's sister Louisa Chick—who attempt to fill the domestic vacancy left by the dead mother.[65] Although Dombey deeply resents having to admit it, Fanny's death forces him to recognize that the wife's value and the value of her time significantly increase when all domestic life centers on an infant. In such circumstances the clock that takes charge in the daily, practical operation of the domestic sphere is again a biological one, the infant's; and to keep Paul's ticking—as the title of the second chapter tells us—"Timely Provision" must be made in the form of a wet nurse. Consequently, Polly Toodle, the working-class woman brought in to supply the child's animal needs, finds herself in the most uncomfortable position in the Dombey household. Polly becomes an object of Dombey's closest scrutiny because she shares the domestic spotlight with young Paul. She has none of the rights or privileges that would ordinarily go with this position if she were the mistress of the house; but she nevertheless performs admirably in her awkward, temporary role as the literal and figurative bosom of the Dombey family—its maternal center and source of nourishment of both the physical and the psychic kind.

Dombey's abuse of patriarchal privilege in its wider social operation is at its worst in his shameful dealings with all the Toodle family, but especially with Polly. As conditions of employment, Polly must move into the Dombey establishment and virtually cut off ties with her own family, leaving the Toodle infant, presumably, to be "brought up by hand" by her sister Jemima.[66] Polly must also assume the businesslike alias "Richards" and wear mourning for the woman whose position she is attempting to fill. But while depriving Polly of her maternal position in her own family and insisting that she be made over in a businesslike but genteel image appropriate for her new situation, Dombey at the same time tries to strip Polly's relationship with Paul of all its affective, maternal quality. Polly is to be simply the hired bosom, responsible for supplying milk but no other form of maternal nourishment. Dombey tells her: "It is not at all in this bargain that you need become attached to this child, or that my child need become attached to you. I don't expect or desire anything of the kind. Quite the reverse. When you go away from here, you will have concluded what is a mere matter of bargain and sale, hiring and letting; and will stay away. The child will cease to remember you; and you will cease, if you please, to remember the child" (*DS,* 16). Dickens is brilliant in his depiction of

Dombey through such speeches, and the use of the term "attached" in this passage is quite telling. Suckling a child is an attachment in the most literal terms; moreover, it is one of those acts—like giving birth, having sexual intercourse, or dying—in which the literal, the physical attachment, cannot be separated from the symbolic, the emotional involvement. And certainly in Dickens's world—as in Christian iconography—a woman with an infant in her arms or nursing at her breast calls up associations regarding the mother-child bond thus represented that go far beyond the biomechanics of milk production and consumption.[67] For symbolic purposes, the nursing woman *is* the mother, because she performs the task which, next to bearing the child, is essential to its existence (this seems to be the point of Phiz's illustration "The Dombey Family," which features, per Dickens's instructions, Polly in *loco materis* [plate 20]).[68] In short, Dombey is asking Polly to do the impossible, for this plump, "apple-faced" woman is maternal to the very core of her being: it is her nature to treat Paul as if he were her own child. Polly therefore plays flesh to Fanny's spirit. Like Fanny, Polly is an avatar of the Holy Mother, as her name, which is the diminutive of "Mary" (not to mention the feminine for "Paul," the novel's Holy Son), suggests. But Polly is more thoroughly secularized and humanized: if Fanny represents *Maria Regina,* the Queen of Heaven, Polly represents *Maria Lactans,* the nursing Madonna.[69] Her first appearance as "a plump rosy-cheeked wholesome apple-faced young woman"; her five children; and her dark, hairy, "strong, loose, round-shouldered, shuffling, shaggy" engine-stoking husband call greater attention to Polly's humble origins and her earthbound humanity than to her divinity (*DS,* 13–14, 16; see plate 19). Indeed, her husband seems more like the deity, if of the chthonic sort: as he tells Dombey, he worked "mostly underground" until he married Polly, when he "come to the level" (*DS,* 18). And Polly is assuredly no Virgin: her fertility, her apple face, and even her home in Staggs's Gardens call up associations instead with Eve and earth motherhood—fecundity rather than chastity. But these details concerning Polly's humble background only serve to highlight Dickens's point that nursing is a class-leveling as well as a sacred activity. Polly represents idealized maternity not despite, but because of, her common humanity, her ability to bring food for the spirit and the flesh into the Dombey household—and of course to the novel.

There seems to be no limit to Polly's maternal resources, her wellsprings of affection and milk of human kindness. Like the Holy Mother, Polly is all tenderness and sympathetic feeling—all "wetness," to use Julian Moynahan's term for the female, maternal principle operating in the novel.[70] Polly is easily moved to tears for the misfortunes of others, and constitutionally unable, it seems, to see a child suffer without trying to relieve its pain. She takes Florence to her bosom as well as Paul and tries to console the little girl for the loss of her mother, a circumstance that seems to affect Polly, "who naturally substituted for this child one of her own," almost as much as it does Florence herself (*DS*, 23–24). It is solely through Polly's influence that Florence gets to spend time with her baby brother, and both children take pleasure in this arrangement, as Dickens tells us and as Phiz's "The Christening Party" illustrates. In fact, the first four illustrations of the novel—those for the first two numbers—feature, as their only constant, Polly's bond with children. In three of these she is holding a baby at her bosom as a sign of her role, and in the fourth she is acting as intercessor to defend her son Rob from being attacked by a mob of boys. Dickens's instruction to Phiz that "the Toodle family should not be too much caricatured, because of Polly" further suggests the seriousness—and sacredness—of her function in the novel.[71] This visual focus on Polly helps to establish her thematic importance—despite her relatively minor role—as a working-class version of Dickens's "Womanly Ideal," to use Michael Slater's term.[72] Indeed, Dickens uses his characterization of Polly to praise the female as the more virtuous gender regardless of class. He tells the reader, "she was a good plain sample of a nature that is ever, in the mass, better, truer, higher, nobler, quicker to feel, and much more constant to retain, all tenderness and pity, self-denial and devotion, than the nature of men" (*DS*, 27). In this novel that, as Merryn Williams says, "almost wholly turns on the differences between the sexes," Polly is the first fully realized indication of Dickens's theme "that men will perish if they reject the 'feminine' values of sympathy and love."[73]

The traditional symbolic locus of these values is of course the heart, but through imagery first noticeably associated with Polly (and later with Edith and Florence), the female bosom serves as the more gender-specific anatomical part for signifying the source and site of all that is noblest and best in a woman. To emphasize the female bosom's power of signification in the novel, Dickens eventually makes comically and textually explicit what is implied via Polly's role as wet nurse for Paul. This occurs in a description of the Toodle family many years after Polly's abrupt dismissal from Dombey's employ and after Paul's death (presumably hastened by his abrupt weaning concomitant with the dismissal [*DS*, 141]). In a "Pleasant family scene" depicting "the Toodles' [*sic*] at home,"[74] Polly's bosom takes on gigantic proportions as the creative and restorative agent for Toodle domestic harmony and especially for Mr. Toodle's equanimity. Dickens sets the scene as Paul's godmother and Dombey groupie Miss Tox arrives at the Toodle residence

> one evening, what time Mr. Toodle, cindery and swart, was refreshing himself with tea, in the bosom of his family. Mr. Toodle had only three stages of existence. He was either taking refreshment in the bosom just mentioned, or he was tearing through the country at from twenty-five to fifty miles an hour, or he was sleeping after his fatigues. He was always in a whirlwind or a calm, and a peaceable, contented, easy-going man Mr. Toodle was in either state, who seemed to have made over all his own inheritance of fuming and fretting to the engines with which he was connected, which panted, and gasped, and chafed, and wore themselves out, in a most unsparing manner, while Mr. Toodle led a mild and equable life. (*DS*, 533)

Although the narrative spotlight here is on Mr. Toodle and his routine of work and rest as an employee of the new London-Birmingham railway line, this passage can be interpreted as Dickens's homage to Polly Toodle. Since Polly's is the bosom that has contributed the most toward creating this warm, comfortable family scene, it must be the signifying bosom, as it were: the one metaphorically represented here. Not only Polly's husband, but a whole brood of Toodles and Paul Dombey have "tak[en] refreshment in the bosom just mentioned"; and all but Paul and one infant out of at least nine Toodle offspring have survived, owing in part to this salutary nourishment. Dickens's play here with the cliché "bosom of the family" therefore signals that "bosom" carries more than its usual signifying power in the novel as the bodily part most suggestive of womanly value.[75] Moreover, in this passage the Toodle bosom is once again (as it was in chapter 2) connected with domestic temporality and with biological and maternal time: presumably, the "timely provision" of tea and sympathy supplied mostly through Polly's efforts helps to create "calm" in the Toodle household and keeps Mr. Toodle "peacable, contented, easy-going" despite the fact that his work forces him to move at breakneck, inhuman speeds. Mr. Toodle is a graphic illustration of a rare phenomenon during this critical period of the Industrial Revolution: a working-class man who has satisfactorily negotiated what E. P. Thompson calls "the violent technological differentiation between work and life."[76] Were it not for the counterbalancing effect of rest and relaxation "in the bosom of his family," Mr. Toodle might be as careworn and harried as Major Bagstock's Native. The Toodles represent a Dickensian ideal as one of those "best-regulated families" ironically used to refer to the Dombey family in the full title of chapter 2 ("In Which Timely Provision is made for an Emergency that will sometimes arise in the best-regulated Families"). According to Dickens's imagery, the feeling fostered by Polly's bosom seems to be the primary factor in helping to establish this sense of domestic equilibrium.

Hell on Wheels

Reference to Mr. Toodle's occupation as stoker and then engineer for the London-Birmingham line is but a small indication of the prominent role the railway plays in *Dombey and Son.* As a symbol for speed, force, and linear progress, the railway had already been celebrated by Tennyson and Turner during the first half of the decade; now it was for Dickens to reinforce the railway's status as the Victorian icon for the new accelerated pace of existence and change that emerged with widespread industrialization. The novel covers the period of upheaval caused by railway construction in Staggs's Gardens. It chronicles the new order that emerges there concomitant with the opening and operation of the first London station and its attendant railway buildings and services; moreover, Dickens's depiction of these changes serves as a way of demonstrating the brisk tempo of technological advance and improvement that characterize the period (*DS*, 62–64, 217–19).[77] But Dickens's imagery does not express unequivocal approval for the railway, even though Mr. Toodle's connection to it allows Dickens to present as generally positive a working man's view of the onset of the Railway Age. On the one hand, the railway makes Mr. Toodle's fortune, such as it is, by first bringing him to "the level" as a stoker and then promoting him to "ingein-driver," so that he rises to become, in his own estimation, "well to do in the world" (*DS,* 836). On the other hand, the railway sets a frenetic pace for Mr. Toodle's working life, and its overbearing temporality is described in the same terms as Dombey time: it has become the official time "observed in clocks, as if the sun itself had given in" (*DS,* 218). Thus railway time is presumably another masculine temporality. Yet the train is never assigned a gender, even though its ferocious nature seems to be as much animal as mechanical. These "conquering engines" are "tame dragons" or "monsters," each one a "giant" or a "fiery devil" with "two red eyes" that can be seen "tearing on, spurning everything with its dark breath," "sometimes lapping water greedily," but most of all, "shrieking, roaring, rattling" through the English countryside (*DS,* 219, 280–82, 776–79). Indeed, the train seems to have taken over a considerable share of the era's animal spirits, while casting on the Victorians an equivalent portion of its mechanical rigidity in return.

But it is not primarily as a representation of time, gender, or linearity that the railway becomes symbolic in *Dombey and Son.* Rather, the train serves as an agent of retribution through the operation of its iron wheels, which are its most salient feature in the novel's spectacular presentation of Carker's death; and there is no question that however deserved the punishment in this case, these wheels symbolize Ixionic instruments of torture. The day before the accident, Carker, newly arrived at an out-of-the-way English railway station and discomposed by his flight from France to escape Dombey, is drawn to the tracks to get a closer look at any stopping train: "He loitered about the station, waiting until one should stay to call there; and when one did, and was detached for water, he stood parallel with it, watching its heavy wheels and brazen front, and thinking what a cruel power and might it had. Ugh! To see the great wheels slowly turning, and to think of being run down and crushed!" (*DS,* 777). Carker's thoughts reveal that, despite the train's animalistic appearance, his fears locate the danger it poses in its wheels, which represent unrelenting force, indifferent and mechanical. From the beginning of his flight, Carker has been haunted by the sound of wheels he mistakenly hears approaching. During the early part of the journey—by phaeton—he is repeatedly plagued by "the monotony of bells and wheels, and horses' feet, and no rest," so that the carriage wheels become symbolic of his own psychic disorder: "the monotonous wheel of fear, regret, and passion, he kept turning round and round" (*DS*, 772–74).

When the train at last fatally realizes Carker's fears, the mechanical imagery predominates over the animal for the actual kill: the wheels are the agents of destruction. Stepping backward onto the railway track, Carker "felt the earth tremble—knew in a moment that the rush was come—uttered a shriek—looked round—saw the red eyes, bleared and dim, in the daylight, close upon him—was beaten down, caught up, and whirled away upon a jagged mill, that spun him round and round, and struck him limb from limb, and licked his stream of life up with its fiery heat, and cast his mutilated fragments in the air" (*DS*, 779). The horrific "jagged mill" is a more terrifying version of the Ixionic "mighty wheel" of studies used by Dickens to characterize Blimber's "forcing system" of education (*DS*, 163). In both cases, the notion of a linear-progressive movement gives way to relentless cyclicality as the wheel becomes a rack: a symbol for punishment and an instrument for its execution. Both instances recall the controlling metaphor of "The Cry of the Children"; more immediately, they are also reminiscent of an episode in *Pictures From Italy* recounting Dickens's tour of an Inquisition "Chamber of Torture" at Avignon. Guided by an old woman whom he nicknames "Goblin" and characterizes as "a fierce, little, rapid, sparkling, energetic she-devil," Dickens presents this fiery crone's dramatic reenactment of the rack in operation in terms that anticipate *Dombey and Son*'s Ixionic wheel imagery: "Goblin is up, in the middle of the chamber, describing, with her sunburnt arms, a wheel of heavy blows. Thus it ran round! cries Goblin. Mash, mash, mash! An endless routine of heavy hammers! Mash, mash, mash! upon the sufferer's limbs!" (*PI*, 275–76). Goblin's demonstration seems particularly to prefigure Carker's execution, since it emphasizes the consequences of the punishment, the mutilation of "the sufferer's limbs." But this image of "a wheel of heavy blows" operated by a witchlike old woman may also foreshadow Dickens's more ingenious use of wheel imagery in *Dombey and Son* to suggest—in the character of Mrs. Skewton—Fortune depicted as a female hell on wheels.

Dickens's timing in introducing Mrs. Skewton helps to suggest this interpretation. Mrs. Skewton dramatically enters the novel steering a Bath chair the morning after Dombey's ominous train ride from London to Birmingham, a journey that mirrors Carker's later phantasmagoric flight with its fatal conclusion. Throughout the trip Dombey, like Carker, is both oppressed by a sense of the ride's "monotony" and persecuted by anguished thoughts—in this case, thoughts concerning the death of Paul. Consequently, Dombey experiences the ride as a psychic projection of his own grief: "The very speed at which the train whirled along mocked the swift course of the young life that had borne away so steadily and so inexorably to its foredoomed end. The power that forced itself upon its iron way—its own—defiant of all paths and roads, piercing through the heart of every obstacle, and dragging living creatures of all classes, ages, and degrees behind it, was a type of the triumphant monster, Death" (*DS,* 280). At this point in the novel, the train's identification as "a type of the triumphant monster, Death," seems to be sui generis, Dombey's private reflection and a memory of the past rather than an adumbration of the future. Paul's recent death is the occasion for the trip, a sojourn in Leamington with Major Bagstock taken as a recuperative measure. Moreover, Paul's death has just been brought painfully to mind at the station by Dombey's encounter with Mr. Toodle, who happens to be stoker for the trip and who tries to offer Dombey his condolences. When Dombey realizes that Mr. Toodle is wearing mourning for Paul, he feels violated by the stoker's presumptuous display of a "community of feeling with himself," a gentleman so clearly above such vulgar connections (*DS,* 277–80). With Toodle literally and figuratively fueling the fire for the journey, the imagery suggests that Dombey, like the engine, is "tearing on resistless to the goal": "All things looked black, and cold, and deadly upon him, and he on them. He found a likeness of his misfortune everywhere" (*DS,* 281–82). In other words, Dombey's train ride is not just a reflection of the past but a foretelling of the future, for it symbolizes his own headlong movement toward disaster, which will come by way of the Fortune that awaits him the next day in Leamington.

Dickens's careful staging of Mrs. Skewton's introduction therefore seems intended to highlight her symbolic importance as that awaiting Fortune. During Dombey and the Major's first stroll through the resort town, their attention is drawn to the following remarkable sight: "they beheld advancing towards them, a wheeled chair, in which a lady was seated, indolently steering her carriage by a kind of rudder in front, while it was propelled by some unseen power in the rear. Although the lady was not young, she was very blooming in the face—quite rosy—and her dress and attitude were perfectly juvenile" (*DS,* 286). The strange apparition of a lady on wheels that turn as if by locomotive power suggests that this vision is a grotesquely logical extension and the metaphorical outcome of Dombey's train ride. Mrs. Skewton's arrival, "propelled by some unseen power," indicates that she is part of the novel's "machinery" both in the literal and in the dramatic senses of the term: she is a supernatural being—a "cruel Divinity" as she is later described—the *dea ex machina* introduced to effect the major downward turn of the plot (*DS,* 367). In fact, the stagy artifice of this entrance resonates further when we later learn that what appears to be a chance meeting has been orchestrated by the Major, who wants to match Dombey with Mrs. Skewton's daughter Edith, thereby setting in motion the plot against Dombey's fortune. Appropriately, the Major privately alludes to his motive—vengeance against Miss Tox for spurning the Major in hopes of winning Dombey—using wheel imagery ("Mrs. Dombey, eh, Ma'am? I think not, Ma'am. Not while Joe B. can put a spoke in your wheel, Ma'am" [*DS,* 128]). Like the personification of a metaphor, Mrs. Skewton embodies "difference," or contradiction: her "blooming" appearance suggests youth, but does not disguise the reality of its opposite. Nor is the sense of her role as metaphor diminished by the discovery that a "flushed page," who is "tall, and wan, and thin," provides "the motive power" for her wheels "by butting at the carriage with his head to move it forward" (*DS,* 287). As the representative victim broken on the wheel, this servant (whose name is the doubly punning "Withers") helps to complete the emblematic suggestion that Mrs. Skewton personifies ill or decayed Fortune, the goddess in her deathly aspect. And this dramatic entrance marks the first in a series of memorable female characters in Dickens's novels who symbolize Fortune in her most terrifying form, thereby literalizing the notion of a hell on wheels: or, in the terms Dickens used to describe the train, she is "a type of the triumphant monster, Death" (*DS*, 289).

Everything about Dickens's outrageous characterization of Mrs. Skewton indicates that she personifies ill or decayed Fortune, but nothing so much as her association with the wheeled conveyance that does duty as her attribute. Dickens's explanation of her "attitude in the wheeled chair" emphasizes Mrs. Skewton's metaphorical status by revealing her former identity as a desirable Fortune:

> Her attitude in the wheeled chair (which she never varied) was one in which she had been taken in a barouche, some fifty years before, by a then fashionable artist who had appended to his published sketch the name of Cleopatra: in consequence of a discovery made by the critics of the time, that it bore an exact resemblance to that Princess as she reclined on board her galley. Mrs. Skewton was a beauty then, and bucks threw their wine-glasses over their heads by dozens in her honour. The beauty and the barouche had both passed away, but she still preserved the attitude, and for this reason expressly, maintained the wheeled chair and the butting page: there being nothing whatever, except the attitude, to prevent her from walking. (*DS*, 288)

Although Mrs. Skewton has formally assumed the "attitude" of a Cleopatra, who is herself an avatar of Fortune in the goddess's dangerous-but-desirable aspect, it is her ongoing connection with wheels—from aristocratic barouche to invalid chair—that gives away her true identity. Moreover, the emblematic nature of the Bath chair is suggested both by the fact that it is merely an affectation and by the circumstance that just such a chair has made a noteworthy appearance earlier in the novel. When Paul is staying at Mrs. Pipchin's in Brighton, and is wheeled to the ocean in a similar contraption by "a weazen, old, crab-faced man," Dickens's description seems to carry a similarly symbolic message. It is as if Paul is also riding on the wheels of Fortune as he moves helplessly, but resignedly, toward his end, represented by the old man and the sea: "and with Florence sitting by his side at work, or reading to him, or talking to him, and the wind blowing on his face, and the water coming up among the wheels of his bed, he wanted nothing more" (*DS,* 108). Thus when Mrs. Skewton later rolls into the novel in an identical machine, she appears to be the incarnation of that very Fortune who had previously delivered Paul to the waves. This metaphorical connection between the two characters is corroborated later when Mrs. Skewton, near death herself, is taken to Brighton and "often wheeled down to the margins of the sea and stationed there" (*DS,* 584). Appropriately, she dies in Brighton shortly afterwards—no doubt to suffer a sea change before being resurrected by Dickens in her later incarnations as Mrs. Clennam and Miss Havisham.

So many images of reincarnation surround Mrs. Skewton that her existence on the same ontological plane as the other characters in the novel is seriously called into question. For example, her maiden name is "Feenix"; her "ashes" are "collected" each night by her maid for the next day's "revivification"; music reminds her of "undeveloped recollections of a previous existence—and all that"; and before leaving on her final journey to Brighton, she repeatedly promises, "I'm coming back" (*DS,* 290, 296, 396, 571–72). Even her author explicitly questions her state of being: "Few people had less reason to complain of their reality than Cleopatra, who had as much that was false about her as could well go to the composition of anybody with a real individual existence" (*DS,* 384). And finally, Mrs. Skewton's enthusiasm for the past as exhibited on the visit to Warwick Castle no doubt arises in part from her having lived through "those darling byegone times" as the most popular but formidable goddess of the Middle Ages and the Renaissance: "'Those darling byegone times, Mr. Carker,' said Cleopatra, 'with their fortresses, and their dear old dungeons, and their delightful places of torture, and their romantic vengeances, and their picturesque assaults and sieges, and everything that makes life truly charming! How dreadfully we have degenerated!'" (*DS,* 387). Needless to say, the fondness for violence expressed in the foregoing passage is not only reminiscent of the Goblin of Avignon, but perfectly in character for the personification of Fortune in her fatal aspect.

But even though Mrs. Skewton can be identified as the literally ancient Fortune who initiates the machinations leading to Dombey's downfall, she represents only one aspect of the goddess met by Dombey in

Leamington. Her daughter, Edith Granger, plays the role of fair Fortune, the goddess in her desirable aspect, who becomes the actual agent of Dombey's ruin. Dickens's clear understanding of the mother and daughter's shared role as the double face of Fortune is evident in his introduction of Edith, one that immediately follows the narrative apparition of Mrs. Skewton steering her Bath chair in the chapter titled "New Faces": "Walking by the side of the chair, and carrying her gossamer parasol with a proud and haughty air, as if so great an effort must be soon abandoned and the parasol dropped, sauntered a much younger lady, very handsome, very haughty, very wilful, who tossed her head and drooped her eyelids, as though, if there were anything in all the world worth looking into, save a mirror, it certainly was not the earth or sky" (*DS,* 286). This description reveals that, despite their differences in age and attractiveness, Edith nevertheless is like her mother in her ability to preserve an "attitude"—in this case of aristocratic hauteur. Thus Edith looks the part of Fortune even though she does not have one. In his instructions to Phiz regarding this episode's accompanying illustration, entitled "Major Bagstock is delighted to have that opportunity" (plate 21), Dickens makes explicit what is similar about the two women as well as what is deceitful about Edith:

> Quite a lady in appearance, with something of a proud indifference about her, suggestive of a spark of the Devil within. Was married young. Husband dead. Goes about with an old mother who rouges, and who lives by the reputation of a diamond necklace and her family.—Wants a husband. Flies at none but high game, and couldn't marry anybody not rich—Mother affects cordiality and heart, and is the essence of sordid calculation.[78]

Both women, either by chance or design, look like "Fortune," a circumstance that greatly assists them in the pursuit of it; for they are fortune-hunters, predatory females or "man traps," as Captain Cuttle would say (*DS,* 857). Like her mother, and despite her air of "proud indifference," Edith is a high roller at the game of marriage, the most profitable venue for conducting the battle of the sexes, which seems ultimately to be both women's greatest purpose and pastime. Indeed, Edith's widowhood suggests that she has already won a first round in this battle (we learn later that she has a dead son as well).

Phiz's illustration reinforces Edith's and Mrs. Skewton's shared role as the double face of Fortune (plate 21). While it nicely conveys the women's social and psychological resemblance by way of similarities in pose and costume, the composition also suggests that the large wheel of the Bath chair, which is visible between the two women, functions as the joint attribute of both. And Edith's parasol, bent back at a forty-five-degree angle over her shoulder, serves as a visual pun for both of the chair's visible wheels. Dickens's instructions to Phiz included the Bath chair, a brief history of Mrs. Skewton's "attitude," and the parasol; but the resulting illustration seems to reveal how the author and illustrator's unspoken understanding of the two women as representing "Fortune" is at work in their collaboration.[79] This same kind of artistic sympathy may account for Phiz's later creation of the *Copperfield* Fortune, the Victorian bag lady and cyclist who appears on the cover wrapper of Dickens's next novel.

The above-mentioned lower-class or "street" version of Fortune may well find her source not just in Mrs. Skewton, but as a composite of that aristocratic lady and her other double in *Dombey and Son*—her witchlike alter ego, Mrs. Brown, who is also a deathly version of the goddess. First appearing as the hoarder of rags and bones who nabs Florence on the street and steals her clothes, Mrs. Brown is directly connected to Fortune when she reappears (like Fortunatus's goddess) in a wood outside Leamington a few chapters after Mrs. Skewton's and Edith's introduction (*DS*, 70). Her sudden apparition before Edith and her frightful appearance as a "withered and very ugly old woman" identify her with numerous storybook sorceresses, but her insistence on telling Edith's fortune links her not only with the goddess Fortune but with Edith herself (*DS*, 380). Their hostile exchange reveals their double connection with fortune:

> "Let me tell your fortune, my pretty lady," said the old woman, munching with her jaws, as if the Death's Head beneath her yellow skin were impatient to get out.
>
> "I can tell it for myself," was the reply.
>
> "Aye, aye, pretty lady; but not right. You didn't tell it right

> when you were sitting there. I see you! Give me a piece of silver, pretty lady, and I'll tell your fortune true. There's riches, pretty lady, in your face."
>
> "I know," returned the lady, passing her with a dark smile, and a proud step. "I knew it before." (*DS,* 380–81)

Because both women can tell fortunes by seeing "riches in [Edith's] face," this confrontation serves as a kind of recognition scene; and Dickens's proliferation of references to fortune in this episode leaves no question about who the two women recognize themselves to be: they are Fortune's faces of death and desire.

The fourth woman necessary to complete Dickens's doubling of mother-daughter pairs representing the two faces of Fortune is Mrs. Brown's daughter Alice Marwood, who, like Edith, has (had) a ruinous involvement with Carker, and who turns out to be Edith's first cousin (*DS,* 825). The mirror image of Edith, Alice is the street version of desirable Fortune, who, deprived of Edith's aristocratic refinement, appears simply as a sinner and whore (*DS,* 488). But just as Edith has something of "the Devil" in her, Alice (like *Oliver Twist*'s Nancy before her), partakes somewhat of the angelic: "there shone through all her wayworn misery and fatigue, a ray of the departed radiance of the fallen angel" (*DS,* 489). In having been "transported" for her crimes, Alice is yet another Fortune who suffers a sea change, like Mrs. Skewton; and her resemblances to these two women reveal that her role serves primarily to provide symmetry and complementarity, rounding out Dickens's theme concerning fortune. In a metaphorical aside ending the chapter entitled "Another Mother and Daughter," which focuses on Alice's return and the telling of her history, Dickens makes explicit the connection between these four women and Fortune's wheel: "Were this miserable mother, and this miserable daughter, only the reduction to their lowest grade, of certain social vices sometimes prevailing higher up? In this round world of many circles within circles, do we make a weary journey from the high grade to the low, to find at last that they lie close together, that the two extremes touch, and that our journey's end is but our starting-place?" (*DS,* 495–96). In this passage, which echoes Ezekiel and Sam Weller's "veels within veels" (*PP,* 571),

Dickens sounds like one of those medieval preachers who used the wheel of Fortune as their text. That is, Dickens here explicitly acknowledges a cyclical temporality in operation in *Dombey and Son,* one that is ultimately in control. Cyclical temporalities circumscribe the progressively linear one embraced by Dombey and his kind: the pilgrimage of life is here revealed to be a journey on a wheel. So in "the fulness of time and the design," the linear projectile of Dombey time curves into a circle (*DS,* 874). Just as the natural world moves round it in cycles of days and seasons, so even the commercial world, as Engels notes, moves in "a continuous series of cycles of boom and slump."[80] Life in *Dombey and Son*—like "Speculation" in *Nicholas Nickleby*—proves to be "a round game" (*NN,* 120).

As Steven Marcus has brilliantly argued, the "several experiences of time" presented in *Dombey and Son* not only indicate a conflict of temporalities among characters; they also reveal Dickens's own "troubled sense of time" at this point in his life and career.[81] Dickens certainly had the capacity to entertain opposing views, and there is evidence in the novel that he had not given up the faith in history's teleological movement that he had expressed just a year earlier in *Pictures from Italy* with his image of the "wheel of Time . . . rolling for an end" toward a happier future. In the long sermon introducing chapter 47 ("The Thunderbolt"), Dickens looks forward to the day when humanity, no longer blind to the new miseries of urban industrial existence, "would then apply themselves, like creatures of one common origin, owing one duty to the Father of one family, and tending to one common end, to make the world a better place!" (*DS,* 738–39). This statement confirms Dickens's continued loyalty to patriarchal ideals rooted in Christian belief and demonstrates that the critique he offers in *Dombey and Son* is a warning and call for reform—not an abandonment of these ideals. Nevertheless, the loss of assurance in his tone indicates an incipient skepticism about what might be called the official Victorian temporality of linear progress—a skepticism compellingly conveyed by Dickens's first conscious, systemized use of wheel imagery as symbol for tragedy—for the "weary journey" of life through a world of suffering and trouble.

SUMMER 1850–1853

Mother Shipton's Wheel of Fortune

3

CELIA. Let us sit and mock the good housewife Fortune from her wheel, that her gifts may henceforth be bestowed equally.

ROSALIND. I would we could do so, for her benefits are mightily misplaced, and the bountiful blind woman doth most mistake in her gifts to women.

As You Like It, 1.2.29–34.

Domesticating Fortune: From David Copperfield *to* Household Words

In 1850 Dickens found himself at the top of Fortune's wheel just as the century—and the Victorian era—moved into a similarly enviable and exalted position. As Carl Dawson explains in his fine assessment of the midcentury literary scene, *Victorian Noon,* Carlyle had accurately predicted that the new hero of the age would be "the hero as man-of-letters"; and certainly *David Copperfield*'s opening sentence reflects Dickens's confidence that he was this literary man of the hour.[1] The narrating "I" who pretends to wonder "[w]hether I shall turn out to be the hero of my own life" is really foretelling the fortune of the novel-writing protagonist and his author alike, for, as the novel was Dickens's, so David is Fortune's "favourite child" (*DC,* preface, 1). Appropriately, the novel's cover wrapper pays playful homage to Fortune and suggests David's privileged position in relation to the goddess (plate 3). At the design's center a baby David—like a Wordsworthian child or the infant Jesus—floats over a globe, while a comically grotesque Fortune holds the supreme position at the wrapper's top, overseeing not only the baby, but also the ups and downs of fortune, here represented as the cycle of human existence from cradle to grave. The wrapper thus implies that Fortune smiles on David, thereby belying at the outset the prophecy of the nurse and other "sage women of the neighborhood" that the newborn baby "was destined to be unlucky in life" (*DC,* 1). The wrapper goddess's rather frightful appearance as a sort of composite Mrs. Skewton and Mrs. Brown is a reminder of her role in Dickens's previous novel, in which Fortune came in two mother-daughter pairs but was immediately recognizable in all four of her permutations as unmanageable and dangerous. The avatars of Fortune who appear within *David Copperfield,* however, prove to be thoroughly domesticated; in either of her two aspects of death and desire, she is a domesticated version of her formerly untamed self.

The first of these Fortunes is David's great-aunt Betsey Trotwood, whose unexpected visit to Blunderstone Rookery in chapter 1 gives the pregnant Mrs. Copperfield "such a turn" that David credits his birth on that Friday midnight (with its attendant omens) to her arrival (*DC,* 4). Her "portentous appearance," her "presentiment" that the child will be a girl, for whom she intends to be godmother and namesake, and her disappearance "like a discontented fairy" when she learns that the newborn is a boy, all suggest that Betsey is a witch or fortune-teller, a woman intimately connected with the supernatural—even if she is not always mistress of its powers (*DC,* 7, 9, 12). As Harry Stone has argued, Dickens's representation of Betsey and her "magical visitation" identify her as a character from the tradition of fairy tales and folklore.[2] This quirky aunt certainly bears some resemblance to Mrs. Skewton and Mrs. Brown, who represent Fortune in her deathly aspect, but Betsey's actual role as bountiful Fortune becomes fully apparent later, when she renders David the greatest service of his young life: dismissing the Murdstones as his guardians and assuming that office herself. In so doing Betsey becomes a traditional folkloric "donor": a witch or other formidable presence who tests, interrogates, or otherwise requires something of the hero, but from whom the hero "obtains some agent (usually magical) which permits the eventual liquidation of misfortune."[3] The magical agent throughout *David Copperfield* is love, and this is the most important gift that Betsey bestows on David. But whether her offerings are protection from malicious forces, economic support, or undying affection, Betsey remains, as David aptly describes her, "the soul of generosity"—that is, a bountiful bestower of goods and services (*DC,* 346). Thus, despite the intimidating appearance and eccentricity that link her superficially to *Dombey and Son*'s deathly Mrs. Skewton and Mrs. Brown, as well as to the Fortune on the *Copperfield* cover wrapper, Betsey proves over and over again to be, like the goddess who favors Fortunatus, nothing but great good Fortune.

David's child-wife, Dora, is of course the novel's young and desirable Fortune, as I discussed in chapter 1. The docile Dora is as much a creature of domesticity (however impervious to its skills) as David's aunt—or perhaps more accurately as Dora's dog Jip. In fact, it is her character as a domestic dependent—as affectionate but ineffectual as a pet—that makes Dora dangerous. Nevertheless, she ultimately proves, like Betsey, to be a bountiful Fortune in her capacity as fairy-tale "donor": first by giving David his heart's desire (herself), and then, on her deathbed, by bequeathing her husband to Agnes (*DC,* 865). This final gesture ultimately deflects the danger posed by Dora and restores the novel's essentially providential trajectory. In short, *David Copperfield* offers two avatars of Fortune who, in their relation to David, metaphorically represent death and desire; but when the threat to David posed by the women turns out to be illusory in the first case and overcome in a timely fashion in the second, Fortune proves to be not the treacherous goddess of fatality that she was in *Dombey and Son,* but the kindly handmaiden of Providence.

The cover of *David Copperfield* does well to celebrate Fortune's power: sales of this most autobiographical of Dickens's novels made it the official fictional best-seller in England throughout the 1849–50 period of its serialization.[4] *Copperfield*'s popularity outstripped *Dombey*'s, and the fourteen-year track record of literary stardom that culminated with its publication caused a *Fraser's* reviewer, in a December 1850 article, to wax eloquent about the constancy of Dickens's good fortune:

> During these fourteen years kings have been tumbled from their thrones and set up again, unless killed by the fall; ministers have been ousted and reinstalled; demagogues have been carried on the popular shoulders, and then trampled under the popular feet; innumerable reputations have flared up and gone out; but the name and fame of Charles Dickens have been exempt from all vicissitude. One might suppose him born to falsify all the common-places about the fickleness of public favour, to give the lie to all the proverbs, to destroy the resemblance of all the similes. In his case this same public favour is a tide that never ebbs, a moon that never wanes; his wheel of fortune has a spoke in it, and his *popularis aura* is a trade wind.[5]

The reviewer makes clear that, considering the odds, given the accelerated turn of events that had come to characterize the Industrial Age, Dickens's good fortune was nothing less than miraculous—truly "inimitable," as his self-assigned epithet indicates. The reviewer's generalizations about the political upheavals of the era are not mere rhetoric, but reminders that the period of Dickens's rise to fame began with the death of a king and the accession of a queen in England, while 1848 was marked by revolution in almost every major city on the Continent. Although these revolutions, the outbreak of cholera in England, and the final (failed) efforts to ratify the People's Charter combined to make 1848, in the opinion of many, "the worst year in history,"[6] Dickens's fortune had suffered no such adversity, but had reached new heights with *Dombey,* as discussed in chapter 2. The incredible staying power of both Dickens's genius and his popularity would indeed have made it seem to anyone paying attention in 1850 as if "his wheel of fortune has a spoke in it": as if he had—like the prophecy implicit in the Rochester wheel of Fortune—so pleased the goddess as to stop her wheel in its tracks, thereby virtually erasing its waning side.

Part of Dickens's sustained popularity, as he knew, derived from keeping constantly before the public's eye, and in the spring of 1850 he took a decisive step toward maintaining such visibility for the rest of his life, so as to ensure the continued favor of a well-tempered Fortune reincarnated by Dickens as a household goddess. The inaugural issue of his long-considered periodical *Household Words,* published in late March of 1850, proclaims Dickens's ambition to enter the homes of and be on the most intimate domestic terms with his readers via the medium of a family magazine. In "A Preliminary Word" opening this first issue Dickens proudly announces: "We aspire to live in the Household affections, and to be numbered among the Household thoughts of our readers. We hope to be the comrade and friend of many thousands of people, of both sexes, and of all ages and conditions, on whose faces we may never look. We seek to bring into innumerable homes, from the stirring world around us, the knowledge of many social wonders, good and evil, that are not calculated to render any of us less tolerant of one another, less faithful in the progress of mankind, less thankful for the privilege of living in this summer-dawn of time."[7] This appeal shows that Dickens plans to reward his readers for letting him be their perpetual familiar by bringing them, quite literally, welcome news; and his confidence that such will be possible seems to reside in his feeling that the times themselves are blessed. For, even though the concluding sentence of this paragraph rather oddly backs into its social vision, the statement professes a belief in "the progress of mankind" and optimistically places the historical moment as "this summer-dawn of time," presumably foretelling a long sunny future for both Dickens and England.

Indeed, the summer of 1850 would see Joseph Paxton's stunningly innovative design for what would become known as the Crystal Palace published in the *London Illustrated News* and subsequently chosen by the royal commissioners as the structure that would house the Great Exhibition of the Industry of all Nations, to be held the following summer. The exhibition became the first and most spectacular of the many "social wonders" to be regularly covered in *Household Words,* and the magazine's reports leave a paper trail of the "good and evil" surrounding the planning and execution of this momentous international event. Beginning with R. H. Horne's appropriately titled article of July 20, 1850, "The Wonders of 1851," Dickens's new weekly was quick to criticize the commissioners' highhanded methods—their unwillingness to commit to any one of the many designs submitted for the great exhibition hall—just as Paxton's plan for a gigantic greenhouse was in fact being chosen. But *Household Words'* next article on the Crystal Palace, in the January 18, 1851, issue—a lively piece written by

Dickens's subeditor, W. H. Wills—was more laudatory. "The Private History of the Palace of Glass" traced the evolution of Paxton's design from its birth in the horticulturist's successful efforts to build a greenhouse large enough and with enough light-gathering capability to nurture the gargantuan *Victoria regia* water lily, discovered in South America by the British botanist Sir Robert Schomburgk in 1837 and named in honor of the then newly crowned queen.[8] The sheet-glass-and-iron structure that appeared by technological magic in Hyde Park the summer of 1851 served as a symbol for England's acknowledged place as the world's industrial leader, and the many wheels on display in the huge machinery and carriage sections must have made it seem as if Machiavelli's vision of the Palace of Fortune had at last been realized, with Victoria as the latest incarnation of the goddess. The queen would find herself as much at home in the Crystal Palace during the summer of 1851 as the exotic plant bearing her name had done in its own British glass house, and Victoria's delight in the Great Exhibition (she wrote that it "had quite the effect of fairyland") seemed to be a sure sign that Fortune had taken up residence in London.[9] And even though Dickens would confess to "an instinctive feeling against the Exhibition" and escape to his "watering-place" in Broadstairs to avoid its crowds, his "summer-dawn of time" image in *Household Words* proved to be prophetic of England's sense of its sunny superiority during the first two summers of the decade.[10]

If the initial optimism of *Household Words*' "A Preliminary Word" seems somewhat guarded, its closing paragraph demonstrates why Ruskin called Dickens the "leader of the steam-whistle party *par excellence*."[11] It leaves no doubt that Dickens viewed himself, in his role as the magazine's "Conductor," as Moses leading England to some sort of Promised Land:

> Thus we begin our career! The adventurer in the old fairy story, climbing towards the summit of a steep eminence on which the object of his search was stationed, was surrounded by a roar of voices, crying to him, from the stones in the way, to turn back. The voices *we* hear, cry Go on! The stones that call to us have sermons in them, as the trees have tongues, as there are books in the running brooks, as there is good in everything! They, and the Time, cry out

> to Go on! With a fresh heart, a light step, and a hopeful courage, we begin our journey. The road is not so rough that it need daunt our feet: the way is not so steep that we need stop for breath, and looking down, be stricken motionless. Go on, is all we hear, Go on! In a glow already, with the air from yonder height upon us, and the inspirating voices joining in this acclamation, we echo back the cry, and go on cheerily![12]

This passage is more noteworthy for its giddy confidence than its clarity: what exactly the metaphor of the uphill journey with Dickens as courageous pathfinder and guide has to do with the magazine and its readers is not really clear from the context. But the terms nevertheless seem to express Dickens's sense that England's victory march into the future had become inextricably bound up with his own pilgrimage of life. "In a glow already, with the air from yonder height upon us" suggests that Dickens's arrival at the top has in fact been accomplished; now his responsibility lies in inspiring others to follow his lead. David Copperfield has been transformed into Mr. Conductor.

That Dickens's ambition had long ceased to be driven entirely by a personal desire for fame and fortune is evident in his conception of the magazine's nature and purpose. As Forster explains, *Household Words* was to be both "entertainment and instruction" for "all classes of readers" as it assisted "in the discussion of the more important social questions of the time." But the useful was not to be separated from the sweet: it "was to be a cardinal point" that the magazine always include "something of romantic fancy."[13] Moreover, the general tone of the magazine would work to temper any "grim realities" that Dickens's active social conscience obliged him to report:

> No mere utilitarian spirit, no iron binding of the mind to grim realities, will give a harsh tone to our Household Words. In the bosoms of the young and old, of the well-to-do and of the poor, we would tenderly cherish that light of Fancy which is inherent in the human breast; which, according to its nurture, burns with an inspiring flame, or sinks into a sullen glare, but which (or woe betide the day!) can never be extinguished. To show to all, that in all familiar things, even in those which are repellant on the surface, there is Romance

> enough, if we would but find it out:—to teach the hardest workers at this whirling wheel of toil, that their lot is not necessarily a moody, brutal fact, excluded from the sympathies and graces of imagination; to bring the greater and the lesser in degree, together, upon that wide field, and mutually dispose them to a better acquaintance and a kinder understanding—is one main object of our Household Words.[14]

"A Preliminary Word" therefore reveals that the real task of *Household Words* was to provide a kind of spiritual leavening for all readers, but especially for those most in need of it because of the demands of their labor—those identified here as "the hardest workers at this whirling wheel of toil." The image recalls the "whirling wheels" described by Horne in the bluebook on child labor; Barrett's Ixionic wheel in "The Cry of the Children"; Blimber Academy's "mighty wheel" of studies in *Dombey and Son;* and the "whirlwind" of Mr. Toodle's working life as stoker and engine-driver for the railway. It is an image, in other words, that is drawn from and certainly evocative of the fate of the working class, the hapless drudges responsible for minding all those wheels that kept a prosperous, industrial England moving—"the wheels," as *Copperfield*'s Steerforth says, "on which the Ixions of these days are turning round and round" (*DC,* 324). But the inclusiveness implied by the phrase "this whirling wheel of toil," which indicates that Dickens identifies himself as a fellow laborer among these "hardest workers," suggests that he accepts at some fundamental level a working-class sense of felt time as well as an apprehension of its inherent cyclicality. If such is the case, then the giddy hilltop vision that ends "A Preliminary Word" cannot be seen as the ultimate conclusion of a linear journey, but as the high point in a cycle that inevitably precedes a fall. The more somber perspective hinted at by the image of the "whirling wheel of toil" therefore adumbrates the temporal view that pervades *Bleak House,* in which, for the first time in his career, Dickens articulates—in the voice of the unnamed narrator—a belief that time, history, and English civilization are not moving in a progressively linear fashion. Thus, despite *David Copperfield*'s confident, providential vision, its cover wrapper foreshadows Dickens's representation in *Bleak House* of the world as a wheel of Fortune: a world wholly governed by chance, one in which faith in providence is no better than a superstition. Nevertheless, in Esther Summerson's name Dickens renews the possibility that the historical moment may be "this summer-dawn of time," and in her voice he retains the determined optimism of *Household Words*' Mr. Conductor: "With a fresh heart, a light step, and a hopeful courage, we begin our journey. . . . Go on is all we hear, Go on! . . . [W]e echo back the cry, and go on cheerily!"

The Wheel of Chancery

As Robert Newsom has noted, Dickens's claim in *Household Words*' "A Preliminary Word" that "in all familiar things . . . there is Romance enough, if we would but find it out" anticipates the preface to *Bleak House,* in which Dickens similarly professes (after the fact) to have "purposely dwelt upon the romantic side of familiar things" as he wrote the novel (*BH,* xiv). Dickens's reiteration of terms reveals that *Bleak House* shares a common starting point with *Household Words* in its concern with domestic affairs, just as it espouses a similar philosophy regarding the treatment of subject matter. But, as Newsom explains, these terms embody contradiction: "familiar"—the real or ordinary—necessarily opposes the term "romantic"—the strange or fanciful—so that their relationship is not a synthesis or harmonious blending, but an "unsettling double perspective" that is evidence of a "profound conflict." And certainly, the apparently opposed social visions offered by the two narratives of *Bleak House* serve as an indication of a radically divided perspective. While Esther's narrative appears to move in a more or less linear progression because guided by a telos, her faith in divine providence, the other narrative, which arguably defines the larger structural frame for the whole novel, moves in circles but goes nowhere. The linearity of Esther's narrative is therefore illusory, a surface effect that is a function of her assertion, repeated at critical moments in the novel, of, as Newsom says, "a will to believe."[15]

Critics have repeatedly commented on *Bleak House*'s vicious circularity, varying the particulars of their metaphors but nevertheless agreeing on the shape that best describes the novel's narrative and thematic structure. Edgar Johnson's celebrated comparison of the novel's "movement" to a "whirlpool" is a prime example: "The movement of *Bleak House* becomes a centripetal one like a whirlpool, at first glance slow and almost imperceptible, but fatefully drawing in successive groups of characters, circling faster and faster, and ultimately sucking them into the dark funnel whence none will escape uninjured and where many will be crushed and destroyed."[16] This sense of centripetalism or "center-seeking," of being pulled involuntarily into an ever-narrowing circle, becomes most palpable in the second half of the novel. It begins with Esther's illness, accelerates when Esther learns that she is Lady Dedlock's daughter, and reaches maximum momentum as Bucket and Esther track Lady Dedlock to the novel's geographical and metaphorical center, the black hole of Captain Hawdon's grave. This centripetal momentum, which gathers force toward the end of the novel, thus counterbalances the centrifugal motion that broadcasts the plot following what Newsom calls the "suspended animation" of the novel's opening number.[17] H. M. Daleski begins describing the novel's narrative structure in similar terms, as radiation countered by concentration, explaining that *Bleak House*'s "movement, centring alternately in Esther and Lady Dedlock, is in both cases strongly centrifugal"; but after recounting how the "first-person narrative moves with increasing urgency to repeated meetings between Esther and Lady Dedlock," Daleski offers a corrective:

> This movement on the part of Esther and Lady Dedlock is, as it were, reciprocally centripetal, each moving toward the centre of the other's world, though to speak in such terms at once suggests the inadequacy of our initial conception of the structure. The narratives, we realize, not only overlap but converge; and the point at which they converge, the point at which the connection between Esther and Lady Dedlock is established, is seen to constitute the centre of a unified structure, of a circle that after all encompasses the "many circles within circles" of the two narratives in a single "round world."[18]

If the novel's circles ultimately resolve into one, then *Bleak House*'s divided perspective and its double narrative can both be seen as lenses designed by Dickens to create a sharper view of the object that provides the novel's motive power. Daleski's allusion to *Dombey and Son* gives us a clue that this object is Fortune's wheel, for such is the figure called to mind by the rest of the passage to which he refers. He reminds us of the conclusion to *Dombey and Son*'s chapter 34, entitled "Another Mother and Daughter," which compares the wretched, degraded Mrs. Brown and her daughter Alice Marwood to the aristocratic Mrs. Skewton and Edith using terms that anticipate the *Copperfield* cover wrapper's conflation of Fortune's wheel with a circular pilgrimage of life: "Were this miserable mother, and this miserable daughter, only the reduction to their lowest grade, of certain social vices sometimes prevailing higher up? In this round world of many circles within circles, do we make a weary journey from the high grade to the low, to find at last that they lie close together, that the two extremes touch, and that our journey's end is but our starting place?" (*DS*, 495–96). As discussed in chapter 2, the "weary journey from the high grade to the low" describes the descending movement that occurs on the waning side of Fortune's wheel, the fall from fortune to ruin of the *de casibus* tragedy; in the context of *Dombey and Son,* the "two extremes" are positions on the wheel represented by the upper-class Mrs. Skewton and Edith at the top and the destitute Mrs. Brown and Alice on the bottom. Viewed in this way the women portray good or ill fortune by representing Dame Fortune's victims or favorites rather than the goddess herself.

But Mrs. Skewton and Edith are also embodiments or avatars of Fortune in their role as dual personifications of the goddess who controls Dombey's fate: the young, beautiful, and proud daughter depicts Fortune in her desirable aspect, whereas the mother functions as a warning about desire's consequences, a fearful reminder that men who succumb to Fortune's power ultimately fall and risk death when she chooses to turn her wheel. Thus Mrs. Skewton can be considered as at once a personification of Fortune and a harbinger of ill fortune, because her fatal potential can be read in her face and general appearance. In *Dombey and Son,* however, the soothsaying dimension of Fortune's role finds expression most obviously (if melodramatically) in Mrs. Brown and Alice, who double and balance their aristocratic relatives and counterparts in a fearfully symmetrical fashion. They reify Dame Fortune's connection to fortune-telling and witchery with their stagey fist shaking and execration shouting, their vociferous threats, oaths, and fatal predictions for the future, specifically regarding Carker and his kin. We could say that Alice and Mrs. Brown are like the photographic negative or shadow versions of Edith and Mrs. Skewton;

the impoverished pair speak or tell a curse on the life of Carker like specters from the shadowy margins of the novel, just as their "betters" enact or effect a curse on Dombey at center stage, the difference in effectiveness between telling and acting being a function of power in quite realistic social terms—literally in terms of fortune. The relevance, then, of *Dombey and Son*'s circle metaphor to *Bleak House* has to do with Dickens's use in the later novel of Fortune's wheel as the controlling metaphor, as well as his representation of Dame Fortune as another mother-and-daughter pair representing death and desire. In fact, Lady Dedlock and Esther Summerson are Dickens's most intricately developed and ultimately most fascinating "realization" (using Martin Meisel's term) of this composite goddess.[19]

The Fortune's wheel motif of *Bleak House* shapes a kind of metanarrative to create Dickens's first truly spatial novel, one operated by a plot that could equally well be understood as a cosmology—an investigation of time, space, causality, and freedom as they relate to mid-nineteenth-century England's conflicted passion for fortune. Moreover, *Bleak House* is the first of Dickens's novels to make repeated references to the goddess Fortune and to specify the wheel as its central or controlling metaphor. As the novel proceeds, the Fortune and wheel references become more clearly and suggestively linked. Just over halfway through the novel, when Esther narrates her illness and recovery, she reports her reunion with Mr. Jarndyce, who bemoans his increasing estrangement from Richard, because of their Chancery lawsuit, using provocatively vivid terms that highlight the Fortune's wheel motif: "I would rather restore to poor Rick his proper nature, than be endowed with all the money that dead suitors, broken, heart and soul, upon the wheel of Chancery, have left unclaimed with the Accountant-General—and that's money enough, my dear, to be cast into a pyramid, in memory of Chancery's transcendent wickedness" (*BH*, 492). Mr. Jarndyce's punning image of "the wheel of Chancery" on which suitors are "broken, heart and soul," metaphorically transforms the court into a Fortune's wheel conceived as, in James M. Brown's terms, a "cruelly indifferent and inhuman machine";[20] it is both a roulette wheel and an instrument of torture—a conflation of functions familiar in the icon's history from Boethius through the Middle Ages to Hogarth. The emblematic topography of this image—a wheel torturing and killing victims who cannot resist trying their fortune on it while the fortune itself piles up in a pyramid out of their reach—is especially Hogarthian and particularly reminiscent of *The South Sea Scheme* (plate 10), with its carnival setting featuring a gigantic merry-go-round swarmed by Londoners eager to risk their money for a ride, and its rack on which the personified figure of Honesty is broken by the personification of Self-Interest. Dickens conveys the satirical and allegorical nature of Jarndyce's image in his evocation of emblematic, fanciful, theatrical props set incongruously against the realistic, contemporary London background that otherwise characterizes the general thrust of the narrative. The anonymous narrator's earlier description of workaday London as "the great tee-totum . . . set up for its daily spin and whirl" (*BH,* 221) similarly evokes—by shorthand and caricature—the image of a giant toy and gaming device in a realistic setting to assert that Fortune, rather than Justice, is the ruling goddess, not only in the Court of Chancery, but in all courts, in the City, and in England herself. That Justice has taken flight is emblematically expressed by Dickens in the character of Miss Flite, the "little mad old woman" and Chancery suitor who always "expect[s] a judgment. Shortly. On the Day of Judgment" (*BH,* 3, 33). In this most emblematic of Dickens's novels, the emblematical Miss Flite is just one of many fanciful characters and effects poised on the romantic side of Dickens's too-familiar contemporary England, with its antiquated government and legal system that are ill-equipped for tackling the problems of a new industrial age.

Jarndyce's "wheel of Chancery" image becomes the focal point for a network of references to Fortune and her wheel that not only serve as an organizing principle throughout the novel, but also reinforce the double meaning of "court" and "suitor."[21] In chapter 13, when Richard and Ada first openly declare their love for each other, Mr. Jarndyce's advice to Richard identifies the cause of Richard's eventual demise as a disregard for the ominous power of Fortune, using terms that equate courts with courtship and suitors in law with suitors in love: "Trust in nothing but in Providence and your own efforts. Never separate the two, like the heathen waggoner. Constancy in love is a good thing; but it means nothing, and is nothing, without constancy in every kind of effort. . . . If you entertain the supposition that any real success, in great things or in small, ever was or could be, ever will or can be, wrested from Fortune by fits and starts, leave that wrong idea here, or leave your cousin Ada here" (*BH,* 180). Jarndyce seems to be speaking for Dickens in this passage, for Richard's "wrong idea" concerning the degree to which Providence, personal effort, and Fortune might reasonably be expected to influence results does indeed ultimately bring about his downfall. Providence and one's "own efforts" are balanced as equally salutary in this formula, whereas personified Fortune is presented in an adversarial relation to the suitor, as possessing something which must be taken by force. In other words, Jarndyce presents Fortune as a necessary evil, not denying her eminently attractive and powerful role in any successful venture, but not quite approving it either. That Jarndyce's position originates with the Christian tradition's distrust of Fortune—a tradition that begins with Boethius and returns with a vengeance in Francis Quarles's *Emblems*—is clear from Jarndyce's continued, if qualified, faith in Providence, even though the idea that success must be "wrested from Fortune" is more reminiscent of the secular, Machiavellian strategy of winning the goddess's gifts by beating her at her own ruthless game.[22]

The source of Jarndyce's wise words sheds even more light on Dickens's development of the Fortune's wheel motif. Jarndyce's injunction to "Trust in nothing but in Providence and your own efforts. Never separate the two, like the heathen waggoner" alludes to the Aesop fable popularized in England by Robert Burton; his mention of it in *The Anatomy of Melancholy* helps to explain its relevance to *Bleak House.* As one of the "lawful cures" for melancholy, Burton recommends prayer, but cautions against depending on it to the exclusion of everything else: "To pray alone, and reject ordinary means, is to do like him in Aesop, that when his cart was stalled, lay flat on his back, and cried aloud, 'Help, Hercules!' but that was to little purpose, except (as his friend advised him, *Rotis tute ipse annitaris* [put your shoulder to the wheel yourself]) he whipped his horses withal, and put his shoulder to the wheel" (partition 2, section 1, member 2, Burton's translation).[23] Burton's gloss on this fable first of all explains the "heathen" status of Jarndyce's waggoner, so identified because he prays to Hercules after the hero's immortalization by the Olympian gods. But the waggoner's heathenness is not the issue here: his mistake comes from placing all his hopes in supernatural powers rather than trying to solve the problem himself. Thus it is the friend's advice to "put your shoulder to the wheel yourself" that informs *Bleak House*'s Fortune-and-wheel motif. Dickens introduces the phrase comically early in the novel when describing Mrs. Rouncewell's precocious son—the "ironmaster" as a child—who revealed his engineering genius by "constructing steam-engines out of saucepans and setting birds to draw their own water" so "that a thirsty canary had only, in a literal sense, to put his shoulder to the wheel, and the job was done" (*BH,* 84). The phrase's thematic importance becomes clear when Richard, rather than apply himself to learning a profession, puts his faith in Chancery and Mr. Vholes, the ghoulish lawyer whose repeated insistence that he has his "shoulder to the wheel" on Richard's behalf becomes a litany in the latter half of the novel (*BH,* 550, 554, 617, 621, 691, 817). Like all those other lawyers committed to the English legal system's "one great principle," which is, as the unnamed narrator tells us, "to make business for itself" (*BH,* 548), Vholes helps to turn the "wheel of Chancery" by proxy for his client, bringing Jarndyce's image full circle by contributing to Richard's ruin and death. Vholes's shoulder is to the wheel to wrest success from Fortune for himself; Richard is merely a convenient sacrifice, and Richard's realization early on in their relationship that the wheel goes round "with Ixion on it" does nothing to prevent the inevitable outcome (*BH,* 550).

Richard is clearly intended by Dickens to be the most tragic of *Bleak House*'s "dead suitors, broken, heart and soul, upon the Wheel of Chancery," as he actively (even if "by fits and starts") courts Fortune and disaster—to Mr. Vholes's profit and at Ada's expense. In one highly emblematic vignette that could easily be a variant of Quarles's "mad-brain world" driven to destruction in a chariot with Satan as its "furious groom" (plate 7), Dickens allows Esther to foreshadow the inevitable end of Richard and Vholes's attorney-client relationship: "I never shall forget those two seated side by side in the lantern's light; Richard, all flush and fire and laughter, with the reins in his hand; Mr. Vholes, quite still, black-gloved, and buttoned up, looking at him as if he were looking at his prey and charming it. I have before me the whole picture of the warm dark night, the summer lightning, the dusty track of road closed in by hedgerows and high trees, the gaunt pale horse with his ears pricked up, and the driving away at speed to

Jarndyce and Jarndyce" (*BH,* 535). Although the apocalyptic "gaunt pale horse" substitutes for Quarles's sheep and goat, and Richard is the driver of this ill-fated vehicle rather than the satanic Vholes, Richard's "flush and fire and laughter" and the speed at which the gig moves toward London and Chancery convey the same sense of hell-bent inevitability as Quarles's emblem. Finally, near the end of the novel, in a chapter appropriately titled "Perspective," Esther becomes even more explicit about Mr. Vholes's connection to the novel's wheel imagery: "That the money Ada brought him was melting away with the candles I used to see burning in the dark in Mr. Vholes's office, I knew very well. It was not a large amount in the beginning; he had married in debt; and I could not fail to understand, by this time, what was meant by Mr. Vholes's shoulder being at the wheel—as I heard it still was. My dear made the best of housekeepers, and tried hard to save; but I knew they were getting poorer and poorer every day" (*BH,* 817). Esther's comment implies that Vholes's wheel, the wheel of Chancery, and Fortune's wheel are one and the same. Moreover, any movement of this wheel is not a progress, but a vicious grinding that merely accelerates Richard's destruction, for with each turn Richard and Ada's already meager fortune turns into Vholes's fortune. What Richard would have "wrested from Fortune by fits and starts," Vholes pursues relentlessly, thereby breaking his client and taking his fortune in the process.

The grim reality behind Dickens's portrayal of Chancery's wheel-like operation is tempered by his more fanciful treatment of the goddess Fortune, who appears by name and by implication throughout the novel. Jarndyce's adversarial personification of Fortune in his courtship advice to Richard—that nothing can be "wrested from Fortune by fits and starts"—foreshadows Skimpole's thoroughly romantic view of Richard's legal "courtship," which interprets Richard's tragic involvement in the Jarndyce and Jarndyce lawsuit as pastoral poetry, casting Fortune explicitly as a goddess of celebration, music, and dance, and implicitly as a goddess of gaming and venery, in both its senses—the chase and the gratification of sexual desire. Skimpole tells Esther: "here is our friend Richard . . . full of the brightest visions of the future, which he evokes out of the darkness of Chancery. Now that's delightful, that's inspiriting, that's full of poetry! In old times, the woods and solitudes were made joyous to the shepherd by the imaginary piping and dancing of Pan and the Nymphs. This present shepherd, our pastoral Richard, brightens the dull Inns of Court by making Fortune and her train sport through them to the melodious notes of a judgment from the bench. That's very pleasant, you know!" (*BH,* 522).

And later: "If [Richard] takes me by the hand, and leads me through Westminster Hall in an airy procession after Fortune, I must go. If he says, 'Skimpole, join the dance!' I must join it. Common sense wouldn't, I know; but I have *no* common sense"(*BH,* 531). These two passages make it clear that, disclaimers aside, Skimpole himself has no illusions about the serious nature of Richard's pursuit, about the "darkness of Chancery." Nevertheless, Skimpole's whimsical vision of "Fortune and her train," who have replaced "Pan and the Nymphs" as they "sport" in "airy procession" through the courts in a sort of Dionysian revel, suggests that what solicitors and suitors alike are really after is not justice at all, but the sense of freedom and power associated with wealth, the possession of which is figured as the illicit gratification of desire.This desire is identifiable in any number of ways, yet appropriately personified by a goddess presumably imagined as a beautiful, sexually desirable, and by definition uncontrollable woman—a woman more suited to the wilds, to "woods and solitudes," than to the domestic felicities of hearth and home. Skimpole has a gift for speaking emblematically (he identifies Esther as the incarnation of "responsibility" and even produces a wonderfully vivid personification of "Common Sense" [*BH,* 531]), and his identification of the court's goddess as Fortune rather than Justice reiterates Dickens's major point in employing the Fortune's wheel motif in *Bleak House.* But Skimpole's representation of this goddess using only thinly disguised sexual terms also reminds us that, in Dickens's midcentury novels, as in Fielding's *Tom Jones,* Fortune and sexual desire are rarely far apart, both being usually understood as an illicit or excessive desire for money, class, and power, a wanton kind of chase after riches. Esther's supposition that the suit's "influence" on Richard has weakened his feelings for Ada reinforces this interpretation (*BH,* 523). Richard's obsession transforms the goddess into a rival who will destroy the couple's bond despite Ada's being "the best of housekeepers," for no effort on the part of this young wife can "save" the marriage when the domestic economy is disrupted by the desire for fortune.

Fortune and Her Train

Jarndyce's personification of Fortune as a powerful adversary from whom success must be "wrested" and Skimpole's Dionysian portrayal of the goddess combine many features from her literary and iconographic history; moreover, these personifications serve as prime indicators that, according to Dickens's emblematic method in *Bleak House,* Fortune exists in the novel not just as a lively figure of speech, but as a living presence simultaneously cast as an iconographic symbol. Like *Tom Jones*'s Fortune, *Bleak House*'s goddess is a personage supple enough to move easily from idea to imagery to identifiable form as a flesh-and-blood character. Indeed, Skimpole's reference to "Fortune and her train" could also be a retrospective glance at the Fortune and wheel motifs of *Dombey and Son,* in which the avatars of Fortune and the spectacular wheel imagery associated with the railway are linked by Mrs. Skewton's emblematically suggestive debut in the novel as Fortune in a Bath chair. Instances of such patterns originating in one novel to be creatively expanded in a later work are frequent throughout Dickens's career and especially noticeable from its midpoint on. Alexander Welsh and Michael Slater are both eloquent on the subject of Dickens's use of related patterns or archetypes in his portrayal of women, just as they are both quick to recognize larger thematic patterns and representational connections among female characters across the whole of Dickens's works.[24] And although this critical method admittedly risks either separating women characters from the larger movement of the novels in which they appear or seeing these women less as characters and more as representations of theme, I hope to emphasize the subtlety and richness of Dickens's adaptation of traditional female types to suit locally important thematic concerns, while still acknowledging how Dickens ties these characters—with equal skill and subtlety—to a central iconographic vision. It is perhaps because of the very seamlessness of Dickens's presentation that his innovative handling of Fortune as theme, personified abstraction, and fully realized character has been regularly overlooked.

In any case, given Fortune's attributes, as outlined above, *Bleak House*'s most obvious incarnation of the goddess will be fascinating, mysterious, elusive, formidable, and unmanageable. The character of desirable Fortune is of course assigned to Lady Dedlock, the novel's most elegant, powerful, and apparently fortunate woman, who, as the wife of Sir Leicester and the reigning embodiment of the Dedlock family fortune, serves as the living symbol of wealth and aristocratic privilege in *Bleak House.* Lady Dedlock's position "at the centre of the fashionable intelligence, and at the top of the fashionable tree" helps to establish her identity as both goddess and icon (*BH,* 10). The ambiguity of this location—both at the "centre" and the "top"—makes more sense if we think iconographically, in terms of Fortune's connection to her wheel: a place at the top suggests her ascendancy and authority whereas the center suggests Fortune's office, as it were—her site of operation. The goddess—like the Fortunes on the *Nickleby* and *Copperfield* cover wrappers—holds sway over all in Dickens's world, but, considered as the unmoved mover of the wheel that controls the changing fortunes of others, she must be at the hub or center around which the rest revolve, as Fortune had been depicted on the fresco in Rochester Cathedral or would come to be in Burne-Jones's several paintings of the goddess. Thus, when Inspector Bucket says of Lady Dedlock, "She is the pivot it all turns on," the description locates the lady not only as the key to the mystery of Tulkinghorn's murder, but as the personification of the deity inextricably linked to the novel's motive power (*BH,* 727). Moreover, the ambiguity or confusion about where to locate Lady Dedlock, which runs as a theme throughout the novel, reinforces her divine (and her untamed) status, for the ability to appear and disappear at will—to travel swiftly and easily from Chesney Wold to the house in town or to Paris on a whim as well as to manage more clandestine movement in disguise—is one of the time-honored prerogatives associated with godhood.

That Lady Dedlock is a goddess is certainly not in question. The unnamed narrator refers to her as "an exhausted deity, surrounded by worshippers, and terribly likely to be bored to death, even while presiding at her own shrine" (*BH,* 166). She is so inured to her transcendent state that "[i]f she could be translated to Heaven tomorrow, she might be expected to ascend without any rapture" (*BH,* 10). And her mastery of disguise carries over to a godlike power to mask her emotions, described in curiously supernatural terms that—like the last two examples—emphasize the lady's world-weariness: "As if all passion, feeling, and interest, had been worn out in the earlier ages of the world, and had perished from its surface with its other departed monsters" (*BH,* 652). This final not-so-oblique suggestion that the lady is a "monster" resurrected from the distant past reiterates Lady Dedlock's role (like Mrs. Skewton's) as the latest avatar of an ancient goddess, in this case one so plagued by the constant attention of suitors that she is eager and finally desperate to escape their attempts to seek her out. She is "hotly pursued by the fashionable intelligence" (*BH,* 10–11), whom she deftly eludes on several occasions; hounded by Guppy and stalked by Tulkinghorn, who both succeed in wresting her interest and fear; and ultimately tracked down by Bucket and her daughter to be destroyed at her ex-lover's grave. Over and over again Dickens displays Fortune-seeking in the novel as the pursuit of Lady Dedlock, but the identification of character and goddess is so narratively appropriate that we hardly notice its thematic resonance.

Lady Dedlock is both goddess and icon; like a figure from Ripa's *Iconologia,* she is portrayed in this latter capacity as cold, "bloodless," etiolated statuary—nevertheless she sees very clearly how she is imprisoned by her own meaning. Like Edith Granger's, Lady Dedlock's desirability works to deprive its possessor of personhood, because it transforms her into a repository for other people's desires. The character most resentful of this power of signification, so to speak, is Lady Dedlock's most vicious rival, Tulkinghorn, who is also cast as a "silent repository" of "family confidences" (*BH,* 11), but who capitalizes on his power by brokering the kind of information that Lady Dedlock epitomizes. Appropriately, Tulkinghorn's wresting of her secret prompts Lady Dedlock to admit that she is "tied to the stake" and "stuck on a 'gaudy platform'" (*BH,* 580). And just as the worship of Fortune in Hogarth's *The South Sea Scheme* results in the statue-goddess's mutilation by the Devil, who "cuts out" her "Golden Haunches" to toss to the crowd clamoring below the stage, so the deification of Lady Dedlock leads to her being sacrificed to the novel's version of the mob: Smallweed, the Chadbands, and Mrs. Snagsby.

Lady Dedlock's only escape from iconographic imprisonment is to divest herself of both Fortune's role and power; but even the goddess's fall from fortune must be rendered by way of an iconographically conventional narrative—the narrative outlined by Dickens in *Dombey and Son* as the fate of "Another Mother and Daughter" and illustrated by Phiz on the *Copperfield* wrapper. Thus the last "weary journey" of Lady Dedlock "from the high grade to the low"—to a site where the "two extremes" of "end" and "starting-place" finally "touch" as they bring together grave, lover, and daughter—is patently symbolic and treated as such by all critics of the novel. Marcia Renee Goodman interprets this symbolic journey as "the anger the novel directs at the mother figure," explaining that "the subtext tells a tale of primary love that cannot be trusted, of connection that is dangerous; and the novel offers the fantasy of completely separating oneself from it."[25] Goodman's reading suggests that the pursuit of Lady Dedlock and her subsequent death afford a kind of exorcism, but its meaningful potential can be extended if we think of the lady also as Fortune and "primary love" as desire—as love stripped of association with maternal affection or sympathy. In other words, Bucket's motives for pursuing Lady Dedlock must be considered as well as Esther's, and Dickens makes clear that Bucket understands his mission completely in terms of fortune (*BH,* 763, 766). Indeed, his name indicates the depth of his perspicacity and of his willing capacity for fortune: "Bucket" reinforces the fact that he, like Richard, Skimpole, and Tulkinghorn, is a Fortunatus's purse of desire and perhaps Fortune's most successful suitor.[26] Captain Hawdon, of course, plays the original suitor forsaken by Fortune, emasculated to the point of becoming "Nemo" and left to die as "Poverty" takes hold of his room, while "famine" stares through the "two gaunt holes" in the shutters like his "Banshee" (*BH,* 136).[27] Such an image is a graphic reminder that love of Fortune is the root of all evil in *Bleak House;* Fortune, as Lady Dedlock, therefore must be destroyed.

Yet Dickens's romantic treatment of Fortune—apparent in his allowing the uncontrollable version of the goddess to disappear, only to surface elsewhere in a more manageable, domesticated form—casts the goddess's demise in a more sympathetic light. The text's atmospheric darkness adumbrates Lady Dedlock's martyrdom in such a way as to suggest that she too is a victim:

> Where is she? Living or dead, where is she? If, as he folds the handkerchief and carefully puts it up, were it able, with an enchanted power, to bring before him the place where she found it, and the night landscape near the cottage where it covered the little child, would he descry her there? On the waste, where the brick-kilns are burning with a pale blue flare; where the straw roofs of the wretched huts in which the bricks are made, are being scattered by the wind; where the clay and water are hard frozen, and the mill in which the gaunt blind horse goes round all day, looks like an instrument of human torture;—traversing this deserted, blighted spot, there is a lonely figure with the sad world to itself, pelted by the snow and driven by the wind, and cast out, it would seem, from all companionship. It is the figure of a woman, too; but it is miserably dressed, and no such clothes ever came through the hall, and out at the great door, of the Dedlock mansion. (*BH,* 767)

In this incredible passage visualized from the "high tower in [Bucket's] mind" as he folds the handkerchief like a gothic villain (or the detective he is; *BH*, 767), we move to the scene itself as by an "enchanted power"—a clue that we are dealing with primal and highly symbolic images here. And so we are: birth and death are evoked by reference to the brickmaker's child, who died while Esther and Ada looked on (in chapter 8), and by the dark and wasted site of the child's death, a lonely brickyard in winter where the "clay and water"—the material of creation and the very stuff of life—"are hard frozen." More particularly relevant, "the mill in which the gaunt blind horse goes round all day" and "looks like an instrument of human torture" describes in Dickenspeak another "wheel of Chancery," reminding us of the apocalyptic "gaunt pale horse" that carried Richard and Vholes "at speed to Jarndyce and Jarndyce" (*BH,* 535). In this case, however, the victim must be the outcast woman, the only human being mentioned as part of the scene. By implying that this woman is not Lady Dedlock, Dickens in effect tells us that she is; by identifying her with the image of Poverty, Dickens tells us she is Fortune, the goddess who abandoned the dead lover whose pauper's grave she now seeks.

Concomitantly, Phiz's illustration "The lonely figure" (plate 22) captures not only the details of Dickens's text but a visceral feel for Dickens's motif that communicates the danger inherent in Fortune and her wheel as well as the romantic foreboding always associated with the motif. Michael Steig considers "The lonely figure" the most "extraordinary" of the so-called dark plates for conveying what he considers to be *Bleak House*'s "iconography of darkness," which works in both the visual and verbal medium essentially as a reversal of tone.[28] Just as the ominous darkness of the text arouses our sympathy for Lady Dedlock as a shadowy and sorrowful character from the genre of romance, so Phiz's illustration translates this information by using the darkness surrounding "the lonely figure" to set the mood for tragedy. The fleeing woman almost at the scene's center seems to be heading for the plank precariously positioned over a pit at bottom center while she moves in front of one of the straw-roofed "wretched huts," which, seen at a distance on the left, look like graves. The foreground hut, however, looks more like a manger, reminding us of "the little child" mentioned in the text, of Christ, of Esther, and of birth itself, as well as of the text's cradle-grave association. The foreground scene can therefore be read as a variation on the scene at the bottom of the *Copperfield* cover wrapper, which is also the bottom of Fortune's wheel, where death and birth, the final end and starting-place, are yoked together; but here the composition forces us to read cradle and grave from the "traversing" figure's point of view—as if somehow, death and birth refer primarily to her. Images of death predominate—including the kilns on the far left that look like pyramids, reminding us of Jarndyce's other monumental image from his wheel of Chancery speech and of the dead Nemo's looking as "dead as Pharaoh" (*BH,* 140). Most dramatically, the toothed wheels of the machine at the top right of the plate are poised ominously above the figure to suggest the instrument that will bring the woman down. Instead of "The lonely figure," the illustration could have been titled "The Martyrdom of Fortune by Her Own Device," for we can read the woman as a tragic heroine whose feigned anonymity merely increases our interest, just as it reminds us of the other outcast or wild women in the novel, women with whom Lady Dedlock is associated: principally, the brickmakers' wives and Hortense, the novel's murderess. We are not fooled by the woman's humble clothing, for the disguise of Poverty in fact reveals what Lady Dedlock has become—the personification of ill fortune.

Phiz's threatening placement of the wheels in "The lonely figure" may have been inspired by a much earlier passage from Esther's narrative. Moving toward the same landscape on the night when she contracts her own life-threatening illness, Esther offers us one of the most haunting and cryptic paragraphs in the novel, one that may be profitably read as part of the Fortune's wheel imagery: "I had no thought, that night—none, I am quite sure—of what was soon to happen to me. But I have always remembered since, that when we had stopped at the garden-gate to look up at the sky, and when we went our way, I had for a moment an undefinable impression of myself as being something different from what I then was. I know it was then, and there, that I had it. I have ever since connected the feeling with that spot and time, and with everything associated with that spot and time, to the distant voices in the town, the barking of a dog, and the sound of wheels coming down the miry hill" (*BH,* 429). This is a moment of presentiment or prophecy, for it describes a view of the future, not in any way predictable at the time, to provide a major clue regarding Esther's identity, which shares the ambiguity, complexity, and elusiveness that characterize Lady Dedlock, although with Esther these mysterious qualities find expression in a different form. The strange feeling that Esther describes here of course comes through the lens of the past, but it speaks of an essential change in state of being which presumably has not yet occurred: "I had for a moment an undefinable impression of myself as being something different from what I then was." In other words, Esther is telling her own fortune here; for shortly afterward she will be stricken down by a near-fatal illness that leaves her face scarred and will learn what her mother has learned just two chapters earlier—that she is Lady Dedlock's child. Because both mother and daughter had assumed the other was dead, it is as if there can be only one life—one Fortune—between them; this knowledge of the other's living existence, then, is more than the solution to a mystery. It replaces an idea with a visible image, turning word or perhaps spirit into flesh that must be reckoned with, as Dickens has done through his emblematic technique and his goddess imagery. Esther's "undefinable impression" that she is "something different" can therefore be interpreted not just as presentiment or prophecy, but as an apprehension of her role as an incarnation of Fortune, the heir to her mother's very identity. Appropriately, when Esther reaches her fateful destination that night, the brick maker's cottage where Jo lies ill, he mistakes her for Lady Dedlock, whom he describes in terms that suggest both women's association with Fate or Fortune: "She's come to get me to go along with her to the berryin ground. I won't go to the berryin ground. I don't like the name on it. She might go a-berryin *me*" (*BH,* 430). For Esther to assume her mother's role as Fortune, however, means that Lady Dedlock must die, so that Esther can succeed her as the goddess who brings order, rather than destruction, to the domestic scene. Read in this way, the last image of the paragraph—"the sound of wheels coming down the miry hill"—must be interpreted as it is represented in Phiz's illustration "The lonely figure." It is part of the Fortune's wheel motif, adumbrating the "whirling" of the carriage's "monotonous wheels" that forever claims Esther's memory of her winter ride with Bucket in pursuit of Lady Dedlock, cast at last as ill fortune and destined to die at her journey's end (*BH,* 771).[29]

Good Housewife Fortune

As mentioned earlier, *Bleak House*'s most significant variation in Dickens's representation of Fortune as another mother-and-daughter pair derives from the fact that in this novel the mother and daughter reverse roles: indeed, since Lady Dedlock is desirable Fortune, it would seem to be almost by default that Esther is left to represent the alternate face of the goddess, Fortune in her deathly aspect, formerly depicted as a crone—whether comic, horrific, or some combination of both. But just as Dickens works hard to transform Lady Dedlock from cold, formidable statuary into a truly desirable, flesh-and-blood woman, so he is equally intent on fleshing out Esther as a character of complexity and contrast: she must first be an attractive, sympathetic, appealing heroine/narrator like Jane Eyre before fulfilling her more symbolic function, as a tempered version of the Fortune who represents death and as the visible manifestation of Fortune's dark side. The striking complexities and innovations in Dickens's characterization of Esther, then, can be explained by the need to present her as a new kind of Fortune: as a desirable woman like her mother, but also as a domesticated, chastened embodiment of Fortune's deathly nature.

Esther's identification with death is apparent by way of her connection to the above-mentioned motif of the dead child. Early in her narrative we learn that Esther herself was left for dead, was thought dead by her mother, and was taught to think of herself as better off dead by her cruel godmother, Miss Barbary, whose gloomy message, "It would have been far better, little Esther, that you had had no birthday; that you had never been born!" (*BH,* 17), serves as the defining moment of Esther's coming into self-consciousness, one that leaves her emotionally scarred. Although the identity of Esther's mother is a secret, the daughter's illegitimacy is common knowledge; as a consequence of her relation to her mother, Esther embodies deathly ill fortune, for which her scarred face after her near-fatal illness appropriately serves as attribute. Concomitantly, the circumstances of Esther's birth place her at the absolute bottom of Fortune's wheel, where she is forced by her situation and her own nature continually to replay the cradle/grave cycle until she can be released from this state by the death of her mother. Nevertheless, Esther's apprehension of her degraded position does not lead to embitterment, but to sympathy for everyone in unfortunate circumstances—a trait that promises to turn Esther into the image of "Good Housewife Fortune" that she will become by the novel's conclusion.

The precariousness of Esther's sense of self—unmistakably the defining feature of her character, as revealed through her narrative voice, and the trait that has been the focus of most critical attention[30]—originates in her initial and ongoing identification with nonbeing. Esther's early representations of herself are noticeably characterized by self-effacement or self-deprecation, by such a shadowy sense of selfhood that they everywhere express her disbelief in her own existence. This ghostly quality accounts for her habitual use of the subjunctive mood at moments of highest self-consciousness: it is "as if" the vital part of her identity exists only in a hypothetical state, somehow detached from another self who goes through the motions of life but has no claims whatsoever on anyone or anything living.[31] Esther asserts a zenlike absence of desire, expecting no rewards, only duties; and even though her efforts succeed in helping her to "win some love to [her]self" (*BH,* 18), her lover must also exist (through most of the novel) in a subjunctive state, as his name, "Woodcourt," implies—unlike Ada's fully realized and openly declared lover, Richard. In *Bleak House*'s psychological topography Esther's consciousness of her own identity is as the shadow or subjunctive version of Ada, who in turn must "realize" Esther's beauty as well as the romance of Esther's life, history, and narrative. But if Esther is Ada's good Fortune, she remains ill fortune in relation to her mother until Lady Dedlock assumes this role herself, as discussed previously. In the larger structural economy of the novel, Lady Dedlock's self-possession is bought at the cost of Esther's benevolent selflessness: if Lady Dedlock will be high, then Esther must be low; if Lady Dedlock embodies desire, then Esther can have none of it. And it is this quality of negation that turns Esther into a comically grotesque Fortune: her absolute self-denial has effected a wizening of spirit, a premature aging of the psyche symptomatic of the sense that her right to human sexuality and even to her very existence has been forfeited. Esther's womanhood has been broken on the wheel before its time, scarred and atrophied by the burden of the past because her mother has consumed all the good fortune they share.

Moreover, Esther, never having known this mother, forms her identity through her early experience with the mother's sister and surrogate, the stern godmother who also negatively defines herself in reaction to Lady Dedlock's status as Fortune and who curses the child for the mother's sin. Miss Barbary takes over the role of Fortune as fortune-teller/fairy godmother played in *Dombey and Son* and *David Copperfield* by Mrs. Brown and Betsey Trotwood, respectively; but otherwise, she bears little resemblance to these two characters. Instead, Dickens's brilliant treatment of Miss Barbary makes her one of the most realistically malevolent women in all his novels, one whose self-pity turned to vindictiveness compares only with Mrs. Clennam's, to come two novels later in *Little Dorrit.* Like Mrs. Clennam (but unlike Mrs. Brown and Betsey Trotwood), Miss Barbary is a woman given to dire prophecies, not because she knows the future, but because she has a vengeful spirit, which she rationalizes as Christian piety.

Her last words, from Mark 13:35–37, which repeat Christ's exhortation to his disciples to prepare for the Second Coming ("Watch ye therefore! lest coming suddenly he find you sleeping. And what I say unto you, I say unto all, Watch!" [*BH,* 19]), indicate that Miss Barbary considers herself a seer; nevertheless, she is blind to the possibility that God's will might be different from her own. In the legalistic world of *Bleak House,* there is no law so rigid, no judgment so harsh, as those of this barbarous godmother, whose dark words and looks "hold such power over" Esther that the child indeed takes what she says as the word of God. Thus Esther accepts without question Miss Barbary's characterization of her as an "unfortunate girl, orphaned and degraded from the first," just as she resigns herself to the life sentence of nunlike mortification that her godmother hands down: "Submission, self-denial, diligent work, are the preparations for a life begun with such a shadow on it. You are different from other children, Esther, because you were not born, like them, in common sinfulness and wrath. You are set apart" (*BH,* 17–18). As this pronouncement indicates, Miss Barbary is only too willing to predict a gloomy fate for Esther based on the circumstances—the accident—of her birth. This punitive sensibility transforms what should be the religious counsel of a "god"-mother into a curse, for being "set apart" is tantamount to being erased from the book of life, condemned to a shadowy, subjunctive, it-would-have-been-better state of darkness and nonexistence with no claims on the interests and affairs of the world. And even though Dickens makes it clear that Miss Barbary has no inherent gift for divination, Esther's acceptance of her godmother's sacred office and authority causes these cruel words to become a self-fulfilling prophecy: for Esther, feeling at home and at ease with herself comes to mean being anonymous and invisible, an observer from the margins rather than a privileged participant in the middle of things. Ironically, then, it is Esther's faith that invests her godmother's words with their supernatural power, so that they work on her estimation of self and life like a magical spell.

Miss Barbary's role as the forecaster of Esther's destiny helps to establish early on that fortune-telling is one of Dickens's chief preoccupations in *Bleak House.* In all the competing arguments put forward for the many causes in the novel, belief, superstition, and self-interest are so hopelessly entangled that Truth, like Justice, seems to have vanished; but claimants to truth abound, and those who consider themselves privy to divine sources of information are among the most dangerous. Thus Miss Barbary, as the self-appointed solicitor and judge for the "cause" of a harsh religion and morality, bears comparison not only with the officials and lawyers of the Court of Chancery, but with the multitude of suspect and equivocal preachers, prophets, enthusiasts, prognosticators, visionaries, gossips, busybodies, and proselytizers who proliferate in *Bleak House* and whose presence in the novel challenges any notion that a providential design is now at work for the glory of God and England. Dickens peoples this novel with do-gooders and evildoers (with Miss Barbary being a fine example of both) who alike believe they have privileged access to Truth, when in most cases their pronouncements are no more reliable (but far more capable of damage) than the madwoman Miss Flite's. With the notable exception of Jo (who "don't know nothink" [*BH,* 219]), Nemo, and the other characters whose fortunes have been permanently ruined, almost everyone in *Bleak House* seems to be a fortune-teller of sorts. Krook, Chadband, Turveydrop, Skimpole, Smallweed, Bucket, Tulkinghorn, Sir Leicester, and even Guppy and Jarndyce—each in his way sees himself as somehow chosen to tell the fortunes of others; but women wield an incredibly wicked, witchlike power. Mrs. Rachel (a.k.a. Mrs. Chadband), Mrs. Jellyby, Mrs, Pardiggle, and Mrs. Snagsby are, like Miss Barbary, versions of the "sage women" who botched their prediction of David Copperfield's destiny, but who nevertheless exercised control over domestic opinion in "the neighborhood" of Blunderstone Rookery. Most explicitly, Esther's future mother-in-law, Mrs. Woodcourt, plays fortune-teller in a little scene with Esther, predicting that "the fortune yet to come" for the younger woman is a happy marriage to a "very rich and very much older" man—of course suggesting Mr. Jarndyce (*BH,* 414). Thus Miss Barbary's witchiness—her power to cast a spell on Esther—not only works to form Esther's identity; it also introduces the theme of fortune-telling, which Dickens more particularly addresses through the character of Esther herself.

The nicknames that Esther takes on when she assumes her place as housekeeper and Ada's companion at Bleak House are the most substantial clues to her alter-identity as a comically grotesque Fortune, an avatar of the cronelike witch/fortune-telling goddess who has more in common with Betsey Trotwood and the Fortune on the *Copperfield* cover wrapper than with the Fortune-as-Venus type represented by Lady Dedlock. Almost immediately after Esther's first arrival at Bleak House, when Mr. Jarndyce compares her to the "little old woman of the Child's . . . Rhyme" whose job is "[t]o sweep the cobwebs out of the sky," Esther is typed as an old maid "housewife" connected with brooms and webs, sweeping and spinsterhood (*BH,* 97). She tells us: "This was the beginning of my being called Old Woman, and Little Old Woman, and Cobweb, and Mrs. Shipton, and Mother Hubbard, and Dame Durden, and so many names of that sort, that my own name soon became quite lost among them" (*BH,* 98). Even though the tone of Mr. Jarndyce's remark and the names themselves—like the Fortune atop the *Copperfield* wrapper—are comic, the fanciful stuff of fairy tales and nursery rhymes, the act of renaming Esther reasserts her unfortunate identification with her godmother. William Axton noted some time ago that these nicknames serve to identify Esther not only as keeper of the house, but as a defeminized woman, an old crone past the possibility of anyone's sexual interest, including her own.[32] These names obviously assist in contrasting Esther with her mother, whose perennial desirability, even in middle age, seems almost as incongruous (in Dickens's world) as a beautiful young woman transformed into a household hag. Moreover, one of these names, "Mrs. Shipton," particularly links Esther to Dickens's Fortune's wheel motif and helps to establish Esther in her role as the morbid, comically grotesque, domestic, fortune-telling aspect of her desirable, fashionable, but formidable and feral, goddess-mother.

Axton designates "Mrs. (Mother) Shipton" as the "most temptingly allusive" among Esther's nicknames, because this legendary sixteenth-century Yorkshire witch "has been remembered chiefly for three qualities relevant to Esther": "her phenomenal ugliness, her reputation as a literal offspring of Satan, and her remarkable prophetic gifts (she was popularly supposed to have foretold the onset of the English civil wars and the great London fire)." The relevance of the first two qualities is clear: Mother Shipton's ugliness can be easily related to Esther's scars, and Esther's being born in more than "common sinfulness and wrath" makes her at least the metaphorical, if not "literal offspring of Satan" (*BH,* 18). Moreover, Mother

Shipton's pronouncements, which included telling the private fortunes of public figures among her contemporaries during the reign of Henry the Eighth (most notably Cardinal Wolsey), as well as predicting the major national catastrophes of a century later, link her—if rather loosely—to Esther in the latter's role as narrator. Thus Axton's supposition that "Esther, as Mother Shipton, bears a delicate and oblique relationship to a strain of apocalyptic imagery running through *Bleak House*" seems justifiable; but, beyond citing the novel's apocalyptic moments and pointing out the connection between Esther and the Dedlock ghost, Axton leaves the details of Esther's role as prophetess rather vague. Indeed, the primary prophecies of "the doom awaiting old evils such as Chancery and a moribund aristocracy" that Axton mentions are mostly voiced by the unnamed narrator.[33] Esther, by contrast, dutifully reports Miss Barbary's and Miss Flite's portentous proclamations, but acknowledges foresight of only one disaster—Richard's—during the course of her retrospective narrative. In short, Esther's connection to the novel's apocalyptic imagery via Mother Shipton is so "delicate and oblique" that another interpretation of the nickname's relevance seems warranted.

Although Mother Shipton was a well-known figure throughout the nineteenth century (with her reputation no doubt peaking in 1881, when her alleged prophecy that the world would end that autumn did not come to pass),[34] there is evidence to indicate that, at the time Dickens wrote *Bleak House*—in the early 1850s—she was best known to the general public as a more or less disembodied name for a fortune-teller, whose prophecies about "domestic" matters referred not to national affairs, but to the private sphere of "familiar things" and to women's more or less "romantic side" of these domestic concerns—finding a husband, setting up housekeeping, dealing with a spouse, taking care of a family, and enduring the misfortunes of sickness and death. Dudley Costello's article in the August 30, 1856, issue of *Household Words*, appearing only a few years after *Bleak House*'s publication, notes how well known Mother Shipton's name was, but suggests that the particulars of her prophecies were not so important as the fact of her soothsaying skill: "There are some names which attain a national celebrity without posterity knowing exactly why or wherefore. That of Mother Shipton is one of the most noted in the traditionary annals of this country. Her fame as a prophetess has extended throughout the land; and her sayings have become, in the remotest corners, Household Words." Costello goes on to identify Mother Shipton's celebrity as an instance of "concentrated reputation," a felicitous term whose definition can be easily grasped in Costello's description of how it works: "Undoubtedly there have been witches—for in that category must Mother Shipton be classed—who have played the oracle as well as she; but, as generally happens the multitude are lost sight of in the course of time, and the wisdom of many is eventually ascribed to one."[35] In other words, by midcentury Mother Shipton had become a rather composite prophetess figure whose name was virtually a synonym for "fortune-teller." The actual record of her celebrity, as Keith Thomas relates in *Religion and the Decline of Magic,* is as follows: after posthumously rising to national fame in 1641, when her "murky predictions" were first published, Mother Shipton became one among a host of prognosticators included in numerous "prophetic anthologies" that were printed over the next twenty years, thereby establishing a new popular genre.[36] Credit for predicting the Great Fire of 1666 undoubtedly bolstered Mother Shipton's reputation, which continued through the eighteenth and into the nineteenth centuries among a literate and semiliterate audience by way of several chapbook versions of her "history," all agreeing in their depiction of her unusual parentage and birth, her aforementioned ugliness, her marriage at the age of twenty-four to the Yorkshire carpenter Toby Shipton, and her prophecies.

Like that of the legendary personage and chapbook hero Fortunatus, the history of Mother Shipton was no doubt read primarily for its entertainment value. One version, which was certainly extant during the first part of the nineteenth century—and thus known to Dickens in his childhood—is described by John Ashton in *Chap-Books of the Eighteenth Century.* Ashton's summary of *The History of Mother Shipton,* which briefly recounts this version's description of her birth, extraordinary ugliness, and life, communicates a sense of the general mood of comedy that had come to surround the legend of the good Yorkshire witch. As Ashton comments: "The wonders she worked are all jocular, and some rather broad in their humour, but it is by her prophecies that she is more generally known. Many are attributed to her, which she probably never uttered, and those in the Chap-book are mainly local." Ashton offers a sampling of her prophecies (including the cryptic statement taken as the prediction of the London Fire) and reproduces three woodcuts that—with their naive, cartoonlike flatness—help to establish the essentially "jocular" tone of the whole publication. The cover illustration (plate 23), especially, presents Mother Shipton as a rather kindly-looking, comic figure, certainly not what one would expect as the grown-up version of the infant who "frighted the gossips" at her birth with her "strange physiognomy."[37]

Another early-nineteenth-century chapbook, "Printed and Sold by Dean and Munday, Threadneedle-Street" (as the title page acknowledges) circa 1825, is obviously a variant covering the same material as Ashton's summary, as its rather exhaustive title suggests: "The Life and Death of the Famous Mother Shipton containing, an account of her Strange Birth, and the Most Important Passages of her Life; also her Prophecies, now newly collected and explained, and illustrative of some of the most wonderful Events that have happened, or are come to pass." This version, which claims to be "Taken from a very scarce Copy, published upwards of Two Hundred Years since, and embellished with a Likeness of Mother Shipton, and several curious Scenes from her and her Mother's life," is most notable for the apparent delight it takes in Mother Shipton's awful appearance. The luridly colored foldout frontispiece displays a hunchbacked and lumpy-nosed Mother Shipton as a bust, surrounded by four scenes related to her birth: (1) the Devil appearing in the form of a gentleman to her mother, Agatha; (2) Agatha entertained by the devil; (3) persons bewitched by Agatha; and (4) demons playing pranks on the daughter Ursula's nurse. The text goes to great lengths to convey Ursula's ugliness in vivid detail, even after prefacing the description with the disclaimer "that it is altogether impossible to express it fully in words, or the most ingenious to limn her in colours, Though many persons of eminent qualifications in that art have often attempted it, but without success."[38] Even so, the exact repetition of key terms (Ursula's "big-boned" body, her "great goggling but sharp and fiery eyes," and her "unproportionable," light-emitting nose) suggests that the text of this chapbook and *The History of Mother Shipton,* quoted in Ashton, derive from the same source, with Ashton's being a later, more abbreviated version. Both versions, however, reveal a greater fascination with Mother Shipton as that phenomenon which the *Household Words* article describes as "a "strong-minded woman"—one whose "understanding" was "extraordinary"—rather than with the particulars of her prophecies. In any case, Costello refers to such "pamphlets" as "now somewhat scarce," indicating that the name "Mother Shipton" must have been kept alive to midcentury through other channels.

One channel was, in fact, a chapbook entitled *Mother Shipton's Wheel of Fortune*, which was part of another category of ephemeral literature, books concerned with predicting the future, which seem to have had particular appeal to women. Like Zadkiel's Almanacs and astrological publications, *The Compleat Fortune-Teller,* and numerous ladies' "dreamers," *Mother Shipton's Wheel of Fortune, by which you may learn your Future Destiny* offered its readers a method for do-it-yourself divination, focusing primarily on matters such as courtship, marriage, and other domestic or women's concerns. These popular chapbooks gave instructions for employing every kind of divining medium, from casting horoscopes to reading palms to determining the signification of moles to interpreting dreams, cards, and even coffee or tea grounds. In the case of *Mother Shipton's Wheel of Fortune,* the divining medium is the title-page illustration (plate 24), a wheel with a perimeter band of alternating heart and triangle shapes containing randomly arranged numbers and symbols matched to the fortunes listed on the next page. The very specificity of the instructions helps to lend an air of credibility to the divining process and its results: "*The Party consulting the Oracular Wheel of Fate, must Prick through the back of the wheel blind-fold, for a number: if at the hour of twelve the answer may be depended on.*" The numbers correspond to a full range of personal fortunes—some phrased more enigmatically than others—as the following examples reveal:

> No. 1, A life full of changes, die rich.—2, Early marriage, and a handsome family.—3, Many lovers; but die single.—4, A speedy journey of great importance to others.—5, Become rich, through a legacy.—6, Hours of pleasure, years of care.—7, Your present lover is false.—8, You will marry your present choice.—9, Wed thrice, and die in widow-hood.—10, You will travel over land and sea.—11, If

> not already wed, you never will.—12, Gambling will be the ruin of your family.—13, You will be happy in marriage . . .—34, A serious quarrel.—35, A disgraceful intrigue.—36, A run of ill luck.—37, Denotes ill health.—38, News from distant friends.—39, Trouble and deception.—40, Backbiting and scandal.

As with the numbers, the symbols run the gamut of personal fortunes and are often phrased cryptically, although the design does have some connection to the prediction. For example, "The Crown denotes an rise in life"; the "Coffin" indicates "much sickness, a death in your family"; the "Ring," "an approaching wedding"; the "Cross," "a religious partner, but deceitful"; and the "Key," "much treasure, attended with trouble."[39] But regardless of the cryptic phrasing, the obvious concern with fortune as it relates to love and marriage suggests that *Mother Shipton's Wheel of Fortune* was devised with a female audience—and a relatively young one—in mind. This idea is reinforced by the emphasis in the rest of the chapbook on charms and spells mostly designed for women, to determine their future husbands or lovers. In short, *Mother Shipton's Wheel of Fortune* in particular and chapbooks devoted to divination in general passed along formulas and rituals to assist maidens—like Keats's Madeline in *The Eve of St. Agnes*—in conjurations of a romantic nature. And Mother Shipton's name, attached to this "Oracular Wheel of Fate," further evidences that such methods of divination were commonly believed to have originated in old dames' lore as part of a body of knowledge traditionally considered to be female.

Mother Shipton's connection to the wheel of Fortune is asserted rather than explained, but the title page's illustration tacitly insists on her pivotal role. Wearing a conical witch's hat and riding a broom, the good mother occupies the center of the wheel, thus indicating that she is the old dame who controls the wheel's movement and ordains its prognostications. Moreover, this image of Mother Shipton, not as the prophet of doom, but as the comically grotesque guardian and purveyor of female wisdom and the woman in charge of the wheel of Fate, resembles the Fortune of the *Copperfield* cover wrapper, perhaps revealing a visual source for Phiz's design. In any case, *Mother Shipton's Wheel of Fortune* has an important connection to Esther in her role as female narrator and housekeeper of

Bleak House, for Dickens depicts Esther as the novel's primary fortune-teller: the medium through which dames' lore not only is received and transmitted, but also is sanctified, making her a "diviner" in the highest sense of the term. It is Esther's narrative responsibility to tell the "woman's" story of the novel—to narrate events specifically concerned with domestic matters and the private sphere in a way that women would find familiar, appealing, and, most of all, convincing. Dickens's correspondences with Mrs. Richard Watson, Mary Boyle, Mary Cowden Clarke, and Grace Greenwood, as well as his personal and literary relationship with his sister-in-law Georgina Hogarth, clearly indicate that writing in a "womanly" way was a central creative concern of *Bleak House,* as Michael Slater and Suzanne Graver have shown.[40] Consequently, Esther's narrative is primarily and deeply concerned with a female epistemology—with women's ways of knowing and the limits of their understanding—which includes their typical (in Dickens's view) belief in God and acceptance of a providential vision. Like Jane Eyre's narrative, Esther's must be not only a romance, but a spiritual autobiography, one that demonstrates that Esther—in the time-honored tradition of English Puritanism—can "detect the hand of God in daily events."[41] Thus the dames' lore that Esther inherits—which comes from her godmother—is steeped in Miss Barbary's Christian faith, and, more specifically, in the belief that suffering is the special province (indeed, providence) of women. As Esther recalls her godmother saying, "'Your mother, Esther, was your disgrace, and you were hers. The time will come—and soon enough—when you will understand this better, and feel it too, as no one save a woman can. I have forgiven her;' but her face did not relent; 'the wrong she did to me, and say no more of it, though it was greater than you know—than any one will ever know, but I, the sufferer'" (*BH,* 17). Miss Barbary here gives lip service to the "suffer and be still" female code of belief and behavior espoused by Sarah Stickney Ellis in *The Daughters of England.*[42] In actuality, of course, Miss Barbary's idea of suffering is to inflict it on someone else, and she uses this female code as a weapon to inflict punishment on Esther, who immediately experiences the unspeakable pain that her godmother wishes to communicate. Esther's suffering, therefore, is really a double inheritance: it comes reputedly from her mother, but most directly from the godmother who delivers this terrible accusation. But even as Esther dutifully believes what her godmother tells her, accepting the burden of guilt and pain as her womanly due, she also assimilates the ideas of mercy and salvation that are part of the Christian teachings to which Miss Barbary exposes her but does not herself (in reality) subscribe. Esther's divinations are therefore less prophecies than professions of faith: she sees almost everything except herself in the most positive light, but even in her darkest moment considers her own life as one in which "many things had worked together, for [her] welfare" (*BH,* 516). Esther considers her personal "history" to be "benignant" even before its last upward turn (*BH,* 611), further indication that her relentless optimism stems from her will and not from circumstances as they present themselves.

That Esther could embrace the Christian ideals of forgiveness and charity under the tutelage of Miss Barbary, could manage to develop and sustain a faith in God after such an exposure to (presumably) his wrath, is—in Dickens's view—the acid test of her skill at divination and the supreme proof of her true womanhood. As Michael Slater notes, Dickens was convinced that women were by nature more "spiritual" than men;[43] thus part of Dickens's narrative strategy is to give Esther the voice of Providence and progress in *Bleak House,* while framing her voice in such a way that Dickens himself is distanced from these beliefs. The early Dickens, the author of *Dombey and Son* and *David Copperfield,* and even the Conductor who penned a "Preliminary Word" for the first issue of *Household Words,* apparently upheld a providential vision like Esther's; but the impersonal narrator of *Bleak House*'s other story shows no evidence of espousing such beliefs. And even though Esther is, like the Mother Shipton of the *Household Words* article, a "strong-minded woman" with an "extraordinary" "understanding" (the addition of "Minerva" to her list of nicknames is relevant here), she is also portrayed as truly feminine and thoroughly domesticated. By gender, nature, and disposition, therefore, Esther is obedient, benevolent, and faithful. Thus Esther "divines" in true womanly fashion: she assimilates the teachings of the Bible that she learns through her godmother, but understands these beliefs in a distinctly female light, so that

Esther's humble sense of self is of a piece with her unquestioning faith in God's goodness and providential care.

Indeed, Esther is the most reliable source in the novel for what can surely be called "home truths": she sees through the willful blindnesses of characters like Mrs. Jellyby, Mrs. Pardiggle, Richard, and Skimpole, because her vision is grounded in a "homely" philosophy—an understanding and acceptance of the limits that circumscribe the private sphere. She articulates this philosophy when Mrs. Pardiggle attempts to force her into service as an assistant charity worker and "moral Policeman": Esther refuses, telling her, "I thought it best to be as useful as I could, and to render what kind services I could, to those immediately about me; and to try to let that circle of duty gradually and naturally expand itself" (*BH*, 104). Esther's clear-sighted apprehension of her "circle of duty" is based on the womanly domestic ideology that charity must begin at home—which is another way of saying that, in Dickens's view, the best Fortune is a woman who brings happiness and order to the domestic scene. The other good housekeepers in the novel—Mrs. Bagnet, Mrs. Rouncewell, Charley, and, later, Caddy and Ada—serve as reminders of this central theme.

Like Mother Shipton (and like Dame Durden, whose name she is given most frequently),[44] Esther is the good Fortune at the center and in control of her own wheel of destiny: she is the little woman who serves as the benevolent principle and the motive power for the round of domestic existence in (at least) three "Bleak Houses": the microcosmic homes in St. Albans and—finally and appropriately—in Yorkshire, as well as the macrocosmic Bleak House that is England and the novel. As Skimpole rightly observes, Esther is "intent upon the perfect working of the whole little orderly system of which [she] is the centre" (*BH*, 531). She is the prime example in the novel of a character who, as Jarndyce advises, always combines a "trust in Providence and [her] own efforts," shouldering the wheel of responsibility for all who fall within her domestic sphere (*BH*, 180). Her "real" name, "Esther Summerson," further identifies her as a radiant center around which others revolve, using positively cosmic terms: she is a "star," a "sun" in its finest season from an earthly point of view, a Persian queen and savior of the Jews. Esther's exchange with Inspector

Bucket on their wintry carriage ride to find her mother sums up her role as the domesticated version of Fortune. Bucket begins,

> "Lord! You're no trouble at all. I never see a young woman in any state of society—and I've seen many elevated ones too—conduct herself like you have conducted yourself, since you was called out of your bed. You're a pattern, you know, that's what you are," said Mr. Bucket, warmly; "you're a pattern."
>
> I told him I was very glad, as indeed I was, to have been no hindrance to him; and that I hoped I should be none now.
>
> "My dear," he returned, "when a young lady is as mild as she's game, and game as she's mild, that's all I ask, and more than I expect. She then becomes a Queen, and that's about what you are yourself." (*BH,* 801)

Esther may not be the assertive protofeminist that Jane Eyre is credited with being, but she is wonderfully real as a type of intelligent, generous-hearted, thoroughly domesticated, "pattern" Victorian woman who has been broken on the wheel of Fortune but has risen from defeat to tell her story. After she has undergone so much suffering, Esther's continued faith in a grand providential design and in forward progress is nothing short of miraculous. Dickens thus presents this kind of faith as an illusion, a quaint, old-fashioned fiction of domestic happiness handed on by simple wives and old dames, but also as the only hope for salvation in what was looking to him increasingly like a dark time. Robert Newsom calls *Bleak House* a novel of mourning,[45] and Esther, while living happily in the present, nevertheless carries with her the burden of a mournful past that inevitably casts a shadow over her story and her life; yet her psychology is such that the weight and the darkness she bears throw the present and even the future into what can be called high relief—into hopeful, refreshing light. Her relentless effort to make the best of everything is not a denial but an acknowledgment of the noble truth of suffering. Her concluding "—even supposing—" and the silence that follows mark the humble limits of her knowledge of self and life, but they also open out toward a seemingly infinite expanse of womanly love and compassion, Christian charity and duty.

Suzanne Graver seems generally correct when she asserts, "The dual narration of *Bleak House* replicates the nineteenth-century ideology of a male public and a female private sphere," which held that "[t]he values of . . . women's domestic sphere, were to counteract the negative psychic and moral effects of aggressive, competitive, marketplace individualism." Yet it is not quite true that "Dickens's own social vision, as figured in the overall narrative structure of *Bleak House,* maintains a separation between public and private, male and female, that works against integrating the positive values Esther represents into the public sphere."[46] It seems more to the point to emphasize how Esther's narrative reveals Dickens's growing disenchantment with "marketplace" values in general and, further, demonstrates his increasing skepticism that such a thing as a "male public sphere" still existed. Dickens's portrayal of Mrs. Jellyby, Mrs. Pardiggle, and legions of other "Ladies of a hundred denominations" who lead "feverish lives" as highly visible community figures (*BH,* 100)—not to mention his portrayal of Lady Dedlock, who, as queen of the world of fashion, holds sway in the widest orbit of social life—suggests that the public sphere, in Dickens's view, could not be considered an exclusively male realm. Moreover, despite his criticism of women with "missions," Dickens seems less interested in advocating that women stay out of the public sphere than in reminding both women and men that the values of the two spheres are not discontinuous. Ultimately Dickens intends to show that the relentless pursuit of one's own "fortune"—construed in its "marketplace" sense of money and power—without regard to the "fortunes"—construed as happiness and well-being—of others would result in disaster for everyone concerned. Being forced to "move on" for the sake of other people's interests, as Dickens demonstrates in *Bleak House,* and as even Jo knew, is finally a sentence of death.

Dicken's article "Our [English] Watering-Place," which appeared in the August 2, 1851, issue of *Household Words,* describes the sleepy, "old-fashioned" coastal town of Broadstairs as "indeed a blessed spot" when one desires to escape all that is "disturbing and distracting" in "the great metropolis" of London; and he goes on to detail with obvious affection the numerous indications of the resort's being outdated, "left somewhat high and dry by the tide of years." Included in his inventory of the town is a "bleak chamber" called the "Assembly 'Rooms'" (where no one assembles anymore), whose library contains "a wheel of fortune" that is "rusty and dusty, and never turns," even though there is a lottery still in progress. Dickens wryly explains: "A large doll, with moveable eyes, was put up to be raffled for, by five and twenty members at two shillings, seven years ago this autumn, and the list is not full yet. We are rather sanguine, now, that the raffle will come off next year. We think so, because we only want nine members, and should only want eight, but for number two having grown up since her name was entered, and withdrawn it when she was married" (*UT,* 391–93). This nostalgic commemoration of a "wheel of fortune" that "never turns," of a "raffle" that (evidently) will never "come off," and, ultimately, of the ongoing process of human life outwearing commercial enterprises can be seen as an anticipation of *Bleak House* and its "wheel of Chancery" motif. Even as London that summer was all aglow with its Crystal Palace, Dickens was starting to view the city and nation as a Bleak House, a place whose worship of Fortune subjected all its inhabitants to the dangerous movement of the goddess's constantly whirling wheel. Thus, by a fictional strategy akin to sympathetic magic, Dickens created Jarndyce's and finally Esther's "Bleak Houses" as lighter, if smaller, habitations designed to illuminate the larger darkness he envisioned and thereby reverse its effects. In the same fashion he turned Esther into the good housewife Fortune, whose charge over a small wheel of Fate in Yorkshire might just serve as the much-needed brake for the large wheel of Fortune, whose operation, in Dickens's view, had begun to spin out of control.

ILLUSTRATIONS

Plate 1. "Ludgate Hill—A Block in the Street" by Gustave Doré. From Gustave Doré and Blanchard Jerrold, *London: A Pilgrimage* (London: Grant & Co., 1872), 118.

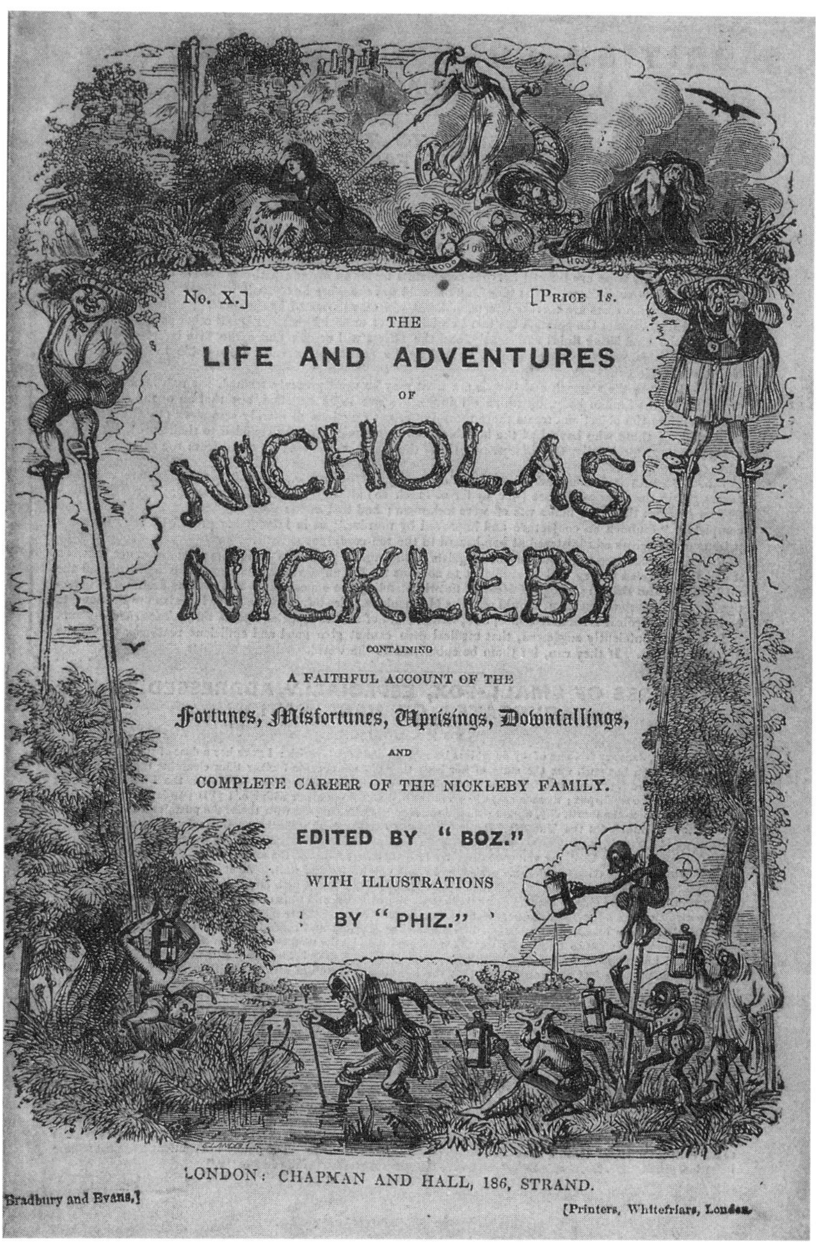
No. X.] [Price 1s.

THE

LIFE AND ADVENTURES

OF

NICHOLAS NICKLEBY

CONTAINING

A FAITHFUL ACCOUNT OF THE

Fortunes, Misfortunes, Uprisings, Downfallings,

AND

COMPLETE CAREER OF THE NICKLEBY FAMILY.

EDITED BY "BOZ."

WITH ILLUSTRATIONS

BY "PHIZ."

LONDON: CHAPMAN AND HALL, 186, STRAND.

Bradbury and Evans,] [Printers, Whitefriars, London.

Plate 2. *Nicholas Nickleby* cover wrapper by Hablot K. Browne. Courtesy Lilly Library, Indiana University, Bloomington, Indiana.

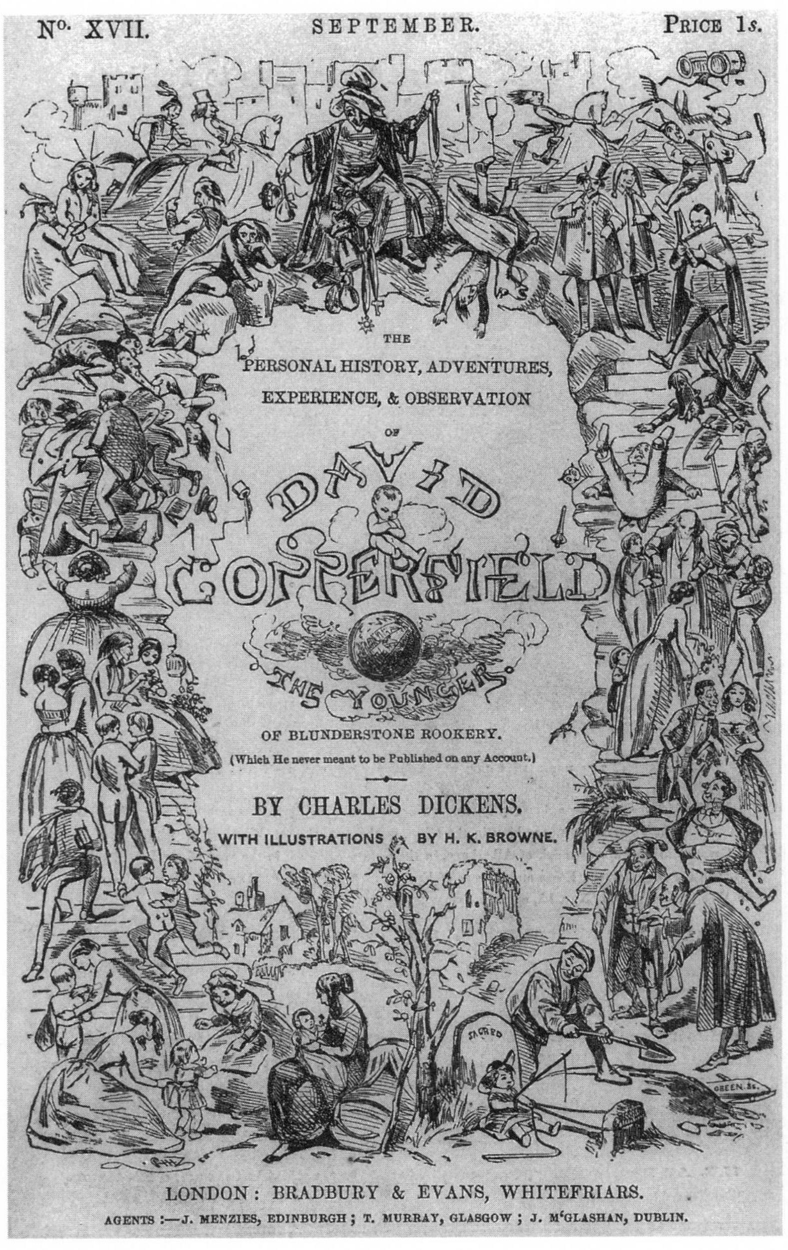

Plate 3. *David Copperfield* cover wrapper by Hablot K. Browne. Courtesy Lilly Library, Indiana University, Bloomington, Indiana.

In occaſionem.

To my Kinſman M. Geffrey Whitney.

Plate 4. "Occasion" by Geffrey Whitney. From Henry Green, ed., *A Choice of Emblems* (London: Lovell Reeve & Co., 1866), 181.

IX.

Frustra quis stabilem figat in orbe gradum.

Plate 5. Emblem 1.9 by Francis Quarles. From Quarles, *Emblems, Divine and Moral* (New York: Robert Carter & Brothers, 1854), 49.

X.

Utriusque crepundia merces.

Plate 6. Emblem 1.10 by Francis Quarles. From Quarles, *Emblems, Divine and Moral,* 53.

XI.

Mundus in exilium ruit.

Plate 7. Emblem 1.11 by Francis Quarles. From Quarles, *Emblems, Divine and Moral,* 57.

XII.

In cruce stat securus amor.

Plate 8. Emblem 2.12 by Francis Quarles. From Quarles, *Emblems, Divine and Moral,* 121.

Plate 9. *Benefit Ticket for Spiller* by William Hogarth. Courtesy Print Collection, Miriam and Ira D. Wallach Division of Art, Prints and Photographs, The New York Public Library, Astor, Lenox and Tilden Foundations.

Plate 10. *The South Sea Scheme* by William Hogarth. Courtesy Print Collection, Miriam and Ira D. Wallach Division of Art, Prints and Photographs, The New York Public Library, Astor, Lenox and Tilden Foundations.

Plate 11. *The Lottery* by William Hogarth. Courtesy Print Collection, Miriam and Ira D. Wallach Division of Art, Prints and Photographs, The New York Public Library, Astor, Lenox and Tilden Foundations.

Plate 12. *The Industrious 'Prentice a Favourite, and entrusted by his Master* by William Hogarth. Courtesy Print Collection, Miriam and Ira D. Wallach Division of Art, Prints and Photographs, The New York Public Library, Astor, Lenox and Tilden Foundations.

THE

HISTORY OF FORTUNATUS

CONTAINING

Various Surprising Adventures.

AMONG WHICH HE ACQUIRED A PURSE THAT COULD NOT BE EMPTIED.

And a Hat that carried him wherever he wished to be.

PRINTED AND SOLD IN ALDERMARY CHURCH YARD, BOW LANE, LONDON.

Plate 13. Cover for *The History of Fortunatus.* From John Ashton, *Chap-Books of the Eighteenth Century* (London: Chatto & Windus, 1882), 125.

Plate 14. Wheel of Fortune from Rochester Cathedral. Illustration from *Gentleman's Magazine,* n.s., 14 (August 1840): 137. Courtesy Special Collections, Michigan State University Libraries.

Plate 15. "The Child in her Gentle Slumber" by Samuel Williams. From Dickens, *The Old Curiosity Shop.* Courtesy Lilly Library, Indiana University, Bloomington, Indiana.

Plate 16. "At Rest" by George Cattermole. From Dickens, *The Old Curiosity Shop.* Courtesy Lilly Library, Indiana University, Bloomington, Indiana.

Plate 17. Frontispiece by Hablot K. Browne. From Dickens, *Dombey and Son.* Courtesy Lilly Library, Indiana University, Bloomington, Indiana.

Plate 18. *Dombey and Son* cover wrapper by Hablot K. Browne. Courtesy Lilly Library, Indiana University, Bloomington, Indiana.

Miss Tox introduces the Party

Plate 19. "Miss Tox introduces 'the Party'" by Hablot K. Browne. From Dickens, *Dombey and Son.* Courtesy Lilly Library, Indiana University, Bloomington, Indiana.

The Dombey Family

Plate 20. "The Dombey Family" by Hablot K. Browne. From Dickens, *Dombey and Son.* Courtesy Lilly Library, Indiana University, Bloomington, Indiana.

TO THE
PUMP RO
Major Bagstock is delighted to have that opportunity.

Plate 21. "Major Bagstock is delighted to have that opportunity" by Hablot K. Browne. From Dickens, *Dombey and Son.* Courtesy Lilly Library, Indiana University, Bloomington, Indiana.

Plate 22. "The lonely figure" by Hablot K. Browne. From Dickens, *Bleak House.* Courtesy Lilly Library, Indiana University, Bloomington, Indiana.

THE

HISTORY

OF

MOTHER SHIPTON.

PRINTED AND SOLD IN ALDERMARY CHURCH YARD, LONDON.

Plate 23. Cover for *The History of Mother Shipton.* From John Ashton, *Chap-Books of the Eighteenth Century,* 88.

MOTHER SHIPTON'S
WHEEL OF FORTUNE
by means of which, you may learn youı
FUTURE DESTINY.

Containing also, Fortune-telling by CARDS,
Lines in the HAND: as well as some strange
CHARMS, SPELLS, &c.

Published by J. March, 12, Webber Street, London.
Price One Penny.

Plate 24. Title page from *Mother Shipton's Wheel of Fortune* by Ursula Shipton, 1861. Courtesy Bodleian Library, University of Oxford. Shelf mark: 9390 e.8 (19).

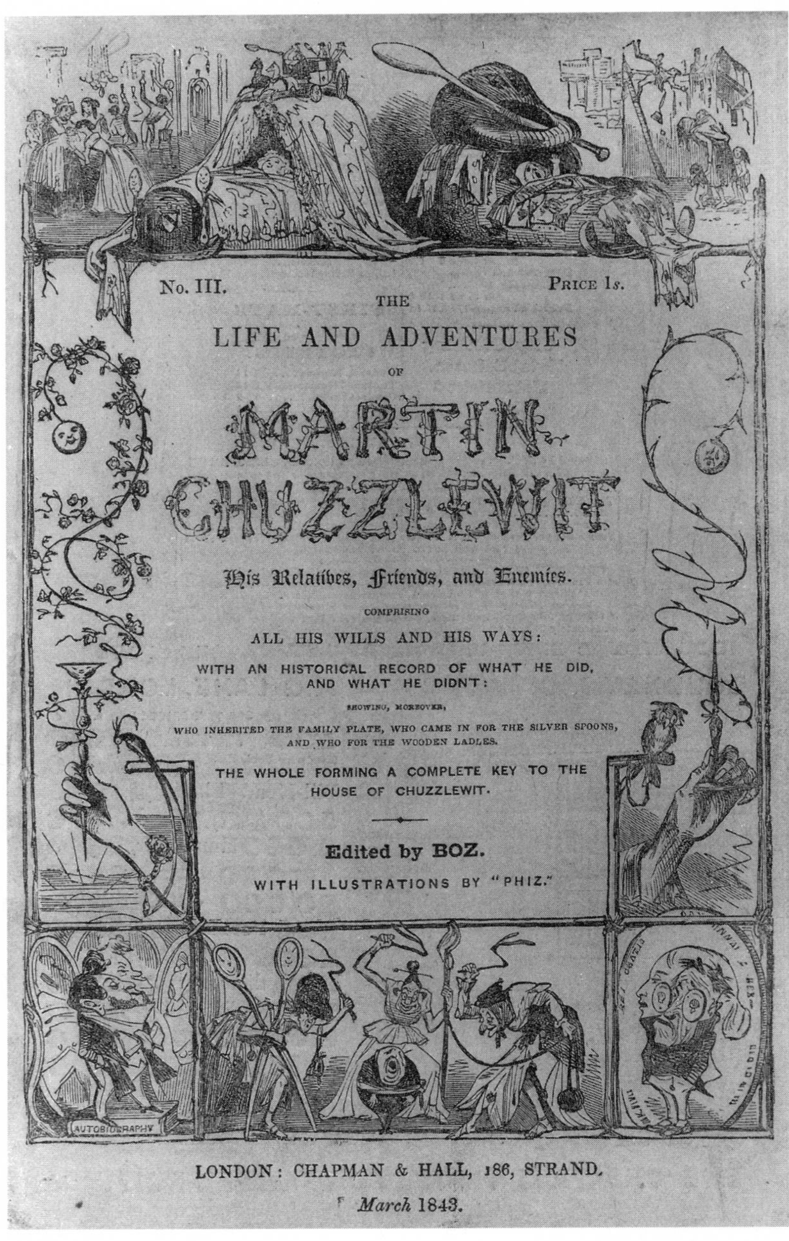

No. III. PRICE 1s.

THE

LIFE AND ADVENTURES

OF

MARTIN CHUZZLEWIT

His Relatives, Friends, and Enemies.

COMPRISING

ALL HIS WILLS AND HIS WAYS:

WITH AN HISTORICAL RECORD OF WHAT HE DID, AND WHAT HE DIDN'T:

SHOWING, MOREOVER,

WHO INHERITED THE FAMILY PLATE, WHO CAME IN FOR THE SILVER SPOONS, AND WHO FOR THE WOODEN LADLES.

THE WHOLE FORMING A COMPLETE KEY TO THE HOUSE OF CHUZZLEWIT.

Edited by BOZ.

WITH ILLUSTRATIONS BY "PHIZ."

LONDON: CHAPMAN & HALL, 186, STRAND.

March 1843.

Plate 25. *Martin Chuzzlewit* cover wrapper by Hablot K. Browne. Courtesy Lilly Library, Indiana University, Bloomington, Indiana.

Mr. Flintwinch mediates as a friend of the Family.

Plate 26. "Mr. Flintwinch mediates as a friend of the Family" by Hablot K. Browne. From Dickens, *Little Dorrit.* Courtesy Lilly Library, Indiana University, Bloomington, Indiana.

Plate 27. *Little Dorrit* cover wrapper by Hablot K. Browne. Courtesy Lilly Library, Indiana University, Bloomington, Indiana.

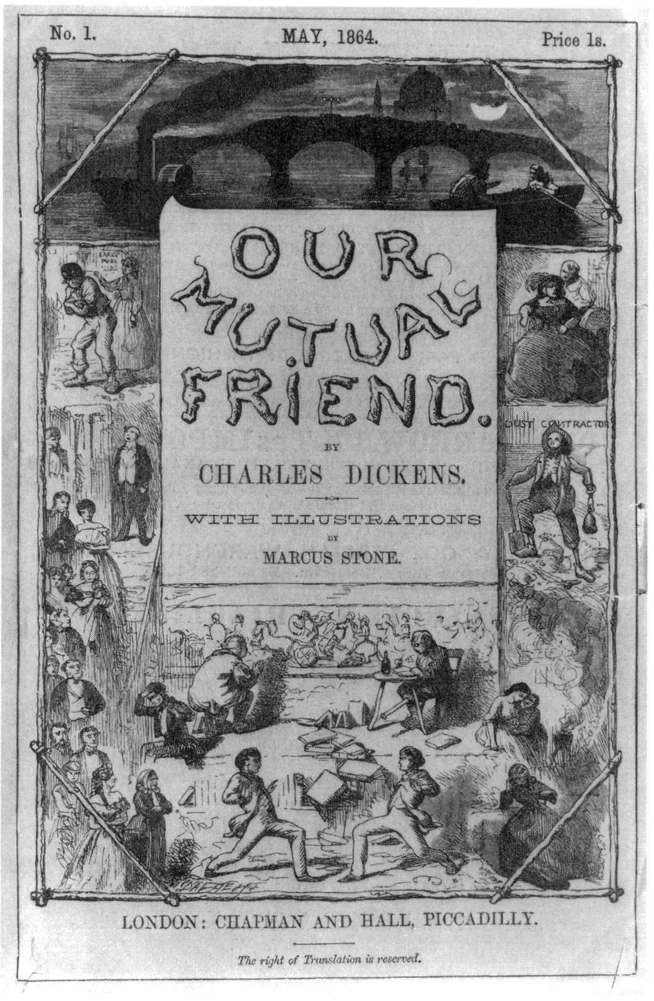

Plate 28. *Our Mutual Friend* cover wrapper by Hablot K. Browne. Courtesy Lilly Library, Indiana University, Bloomington, Indiana.

THE

WORLD

TURNED

UPSIDE DOWN

OR THE

FOLLY OF MAN

EXEMPLIFIED

IN TWELVE COMICAL RELATIONS

UPON

UNCOMMON SUBJECTS

Illustrated with Twelve curious Cuts
Truly adapted to each Story

PRINTED AND SOLD IN LONDON

SUN, MOON, STARS AND EARTH TRANSPOSED.

THE OLD SOLDIER TURNED NURSE.

Plate 29. Cover and three illustrations for *The World Turned Upside Down.* From John Ashton, *Chap-Books of the Eighteenth Century,* 265, 266, 268, 272.

Plate 30. *The Wheel of Fortune* by Edward Burne-Jones. Courtesy of London Borough of Hammersmith and Fulham.

Plate 31. Queen Victoria at her spinning wheel. Photograph ©Leeds Museum and Galleries (Temple Newsam House).

JOHN BROWN EXERCISING THE QUEEN.

Plate 32. "John Brown Exercising the Queen." Woodcut from Daniel Joseph Kirwin, *Palace and Hovel* (Hartford, Conn.: Belknap & Bliss, 1870), 53.

FALL 1854–1859

Minding the Wheel

4

O, fellow, come, the song we had last night.
Mark it, Cesario; it is old and plain.
The spinsters and the knitters in the sun,
And the free maids that weave their thread with bones,
Do use to chant it. It is silly sooth,
And dallies with the innocence of love,
Like the old age.

—SHAKESPEARE, *Twelfth Night*

I am moved by fancies that are curled
Around these images, and cling:
The notion of some infinitely gentle
Infinitely suffering thing.

—T. S. ELIOT, *"Preludes"*

Time's Threads Spun into a Woman: **Hard Times**

In "The Close of Esther's Narrative," set "Full seven happy years" after her marriage to Woodcourt, Esther records the fates of all those best-loved characters still connected to her domestic sphere, now centered in the idyllic Bleak House in Yorkshire. After expressing surprise that Charley could be "married to a miller in our neighborhood," Esther indulges in a moment of reverie as she watches "the very mill going round," which she can see "from [her] desk . . . early in the morning at [her] summer window." She concludes, "So far as my small maid is concerned, I might suppose Time to have stood for seven years as still as the mill did half an hour ago; since little Emma, Charley's sister, is exactly what Charley used to be" (*BH,* 877–78). This serene vision of human life moving unobtrusively—and presumably providentially—forward, but also replicating itself in a way that seems to nurture human existence and even redeem it from the ravages of time, is very familiar in Dickens's works—as is the expression of this vision via female form.[1] And even though the image of two young women "exactly" alike would seem to celebrate that mechanical principle of completely interchangeable parts so crucial to the technological innovations featured at the Great Exhibition,[2] its purpose in this context is to suggest a quality of nature rather than of the machine. From Esther's perspective the turning of the mill wheel evokes an impression of human work and life in harmony with each other and the natural world—what Patrick J. Creevy calls the "sacred tempo" of "healthy human (or organic) timing."[3] The mill, so reminiscent of the romantic naturalism of John Constable's rural landscapes, recalls an idealized preindustrial England, a time when, according to N. N. Feltes (and Adam Smith), the rural worker could "saunter" through a day occupied with seasonal and variable tasks rather than "hurry" through factory work of monotonous regularity[4]—in other words, a time when the machine served humankind and not the other way around. Thus, despite the linear-progressive trajectory of Esther's narrative, her perception of time is presented here as fundamentally cyclical, a temporality that calibrates growth and change in terms not of mechanical production but of organic reproduction—that is, in terms associated with female subjectivity, maternity, and therefore with women's time.[5] Even Esther Summerson's name—with its invocation of cosmic or celestial properties—connects her to the natural world, which is also traditionally associated with women's time by way of its inherent cyclicality. This natural cyclicality has to do with the round of the seasons and the orbit of planets, and, further, with the concept of eternal return derived from the ancient perception of the universe—as in Plato's Spindle of Necessity—as a great cosmic wheel.

Esther's happy association of a rural Yorkshire mill with the cycles of nature and women's time anticipates George Eliot's nostalgic dream-vision of Dorlcote Mill in the opening chapter of *The Mill on the Floss* (1860), a novel whose Fortune's wheel imagery may owe something to Dickens's use of the motif in his midcentury novels. Eliot lovingly depicts Dorlcote Mill as the salient feature in a rural landscape to recall an earlier epoch, before the coming of "steam," which now (in the neatly turned comment of Stephen Guest, as reported by Mr. Deane) "drives on every wheel double pace and the wheel of Fortune along with 'em." But the details of Eliot's mill imagery—"the rush of the water and the booming of the mill" and the "unresting wheel sending out its diamond jets of water"—nevertheless emphasize the mill's function as a source of energy and power, a noisy, mechanical genius loci causing anyone within its radius to experience "a dreamy deafness which seems to heighten the peacefulness of the scene" by creating "a great curtain of sound, shutting one out from the world beyond."[6] Eliot's imagery, in other words, attempts to place the reader in the scene to experience what it feels like to stand before a mill, whereas Dickens holds us at a distance from the mill so that we may view it as an icon or symbol. Esther's mill, therefore, is noticeably silent: although it shares the "dreamy" quality of Eliot's mill and serves as the requisite element for the "peacefulness of the scene," Dickens's emphasis is not on sound but on sight, the mill's ability to convey a visual impression of cyclicality—which is then explicitly and happily associated with the female, with Charley and Emma, marriage and sisterhood.

This final mill of *Bleak House* appropriately serves as a symbol of closure and a corrective for the novel's earlier mill and wheel imagery. It is in striking contrast to Esther's nightmarish simile describing the vicious circularity of her carriage journey with Bucket in search of Lady Dedlock: "We were again upon that melancholy road by which we had come; tearing up the miry sleet and snow, as if they were torn up by a waterwheel" (*BH*, 785). Here and elsewhere, *Bleak House*'s references to mills—whether actual or metaphorical—usually signal impending disaster, as in the case of the metaphorical "slow mill" of Chancery, in which Tom Jarndyce was "ground to bits" (*BH*, 53), and that other mill turned by "the gaunt blind horse" on a "blighted spot" near the brick kilns, which "look[ed] like an instrument of human torture" (*BH*, 767). Even though Dickens is evidently considering different types of mills in these examples,[7] all have in common an attempt to communicate a felt experience of time; and in every case—for good or for ill—that experience is cyclical. In contrast to the pastoral Yorkshire waterwheel, however, the "slow mill" of Chancery and the one drawn by the "gaunt blind horse" have both gothic and industrial associations, linking cyclical time with servitude, forced labor, and punishment—with work as endless repetition that grinds, wears down, and tears into bits, stripping labor of its pleasure and thereby reducing it to the dull monotony of a beast's existence. This punitive image of industrial time dominates in Dickens's next novel—appropriately named *Hard Times.* Thus the Yorkshire mill and the time it represents are left, like Esther, in a subjunctive mood, while the bleak image of the mill near the brick kilns provides the emblematic link to the character and philosophy of Thomas Gradgrind, the textile mills of Coketown, and the "deadly statistical clock" that serves as the controlling temporal standard in *Hard Times,* serialized in *Household Words* in 1854 (*HT,* 96–97).

Dickens's only venture into the genre of the industrial novel, *Hard Times* is less a criticism of specific industrial practices than of the dehumanizing, mechanistic philosophy of life that both informs and derives from these practices; consequently, Time, which Dickens explicitly personifies, takes on an essentially masculine, if also mechanical, character, as it does in *Dombey and Son,* Dickens's other novel exposing a masculine and mechanistic temporal philosophy. In chapter 14—as its title reveals—Time makes his most important appearance personified as "The Great Manufacturer," whose operations, appropriately, parallel those of the town's factories in many respects: "Time went on in Coketown like its own machinery: so much material wrought up, so much fuel consumed, so many powers worn out, so much money made." Obviously Coketown runs on "commodity time," which has value only insofar as it is productive and therefore profitable.[8] Yet, despite the mechanical regularity that characterizes the industrial world of *Hard Times,* Dickens indicates that Time writ large is not always so monolithic, that even in Coketown natural time will inevitably assert itself and bring change, providing variation within Time's repetitions: "But, less inexorable than iron, steel, and brass, [Time] brought its varying seasons even into that wilderness of smoke and brick, and made the only stand that ever *was* made in the place against its direful uniformity" (*HT,* 90). Time's variability, therefore, applies particularly to "his manufacture of the human fabric": as in the cases of young Tom Gradgrind and Sissy Jupe, he works quickly to complete the season of youth, but moves more slowly to effect changes in adulthood—as in the case of Mr. Gradgrind, "who seemed stationary in his course, and underwent no alteration" (*HT,* 92).

Finally, the complexities of Time's operations in this chapter are not limited to his role as the "Great Manufacturer"; Dickens transforms Time from capitalist to laborer at the chapter's conclusion, when Louisa Gradgrind wonders about what the future holds for her: "she tried to discover what kind of woof Old Time, that greatest and longest-established Spinner of all, would weave from the threads he had already spun into a woman. But his factory is a secret place, his work is noiseless, and his Hands are mutes" (*HT,* 95). Dickens's image of "Old Time" as a masculine "Spinner" suits the context of Coketown and its textile industry, just as it softens Time's image as the "Great Manufacturer" in the long temporal conceit of this chapter. "Old Time" is venerable, a hard worker whose epithet, "old," and whose status as laborer would seem to associate him more with Stephen Blackpool than with Mr. Bounderby, *Hard Times*'s obnoxious and blustering embodiment of a Captain of Industry. But the fanciful image of Time spinning his threads into a woman reminds the reader less of traditional—and male—iconic representations of Time and more of the three female Fates who were responsible for spinning, measuring, and cutting the thread of each person's life. Curiously, this idea of "threads . . . spun into a woman" is an interesting variation of the bottom scene on the cover wrapper of *Martin Chuzzlewit* (plate 25), which, except for its gender reversals, almost literalizes the image: three comically grotesque Fates are the "spinners," and a roly-poly man is being "spun," although not like a thread but like a top. That Phiz's cover illustration for *Martin Chuzzlewit* came to Dickens's mind when thinking about time, fate, and fortune as he wrote *Hard Times* is suggested also by his introduction of Stephen Blackpool in chapter 10. After noting that Stephen is "forty years of age," Dickens articulates a comparison that comes directly from the rose and thorn images flanking the left and right sides, respectively, of the *Chuzzlewit* title: "Stephen looked older, but he had had a hard life. It is said that every life has its roses and thorns; there seemed, however, to have been a misadventure or mistake in Stephen's case, whereby somebody else had become possessed of his roses, and he had become possessed of the same somebody's thorns in addition to his own. He had known, to use his words, a peck of trouble. He was usually called Old Stephen, in a kind of rough homage to the fact" (*HT,* 63). As this introduction and the rest of the novel reveal, Stephen seems to have been cruelly chosen to be the whipping boy of Fate; and even though he is the novel's representative "Hand," the weaver who works quietly "in the innermost fortifications of that ugly citadel" of Coketown (*HT,* 63), Stephen bears no further resemblance to Dickens's image of "Old Time" or one of his workers. Indeed, what makes the concluding passage describing "Old Time" as a "Spinner" so striking is the way the female emerges and takes over the metaphor: a woman spun from threads to be woven into the cloth of her destiny is richly suggestive that the woman is herself an image of fate; and the picture called to mind of a woman wrapped in threads resonates ominously throughout the novel. For example, Mrs. Gradgrind is really nothing more than a "bundle of shawls" (*HT,* 15); the "shawls drawn over their heads and held close under their chins" are all we see of Coketown's young factory women (*HT,* 64); Mrs. Sparsit disguises herself by "tumbl[ing] her shawl into a new shape" to pursue Louisa (*HT,* 213); Louisa herself fatefully runs away from her marriage "hastily cloaked and muffled" (*HT,* 213); and, most ominous of all, Stephen's wife appears in "tatters," "disgraceful garments," pointedly emphasizing her role as Stephen's disastrous fate (*HT,* 67, 82). The many images of shrouded women in *Hard Times* remind us of their fateful role as avatars of Fortune in *Bleak House;* and here again they reveal that, despite Dickens's refusal to reveal the "secret place" that is Time's "factory," it is evidently a place where women, by virtue of their association with Fate, Fortune, and spinning, are still Time's chosen operatives.

Nevertheless, *Hard Times* is primarily a novel about the evils of industrialism that begin and end with men who abuse their power over other men, not about the women who exercise symbolic power over them all. Consequently, the death of Stephen Blackpool, the Hand victimized by capitalists and fellow laborers alike, serves as the narrative's climax and as Dickens's final comment on industry's destructive effects—in this case, on the environment. In the chapter entitled "The Starlight," when we learn that Stephen has realized the fate foreshadowed in his surname by falling down an abandoned mine shaft, Dickens sets up the scene using what might be called postpastoral imagery to describe the countryside just beyond Coketown. Here the open fields, pockmarked with "deserted works" and "old pits," appear like a vast industrial graveyard: "the grass was fresh; beautiful shadows of branches flickered upon it, and speckled it; hedgerows were luxuriant; everything was at peace. Engines at pits' mouths, and lean old horses that had worn the circle of their daily labour into the ground, were alike quiet; wheels had ceased for a short space to turn; and the great wheel of earth seemed to revolve without the shocks and noises of another time" (*HT,* 265–66). This passage recalls the mill near the brick kilns in *Bleak House,* "where the gaunt blind horse goes round all day"; but the curious temporal frame of the final clause, employing the verb "seemed" and distancing what is actually the present into a nonspecific past with the phrase "of another time," is one of cosmic transcendence, transforming the somber moment into an Esther-like subjunctive. The effect, however, is to increase the somberness of the scene and render what, in *Bleak House,* had been merely gothic now deeply elegiac. By aligning himself sympathetically with the cosmic time represented by "the great wheel of earth," Dickens reiterates his growing disenchantment with the Victorian idea of progress: the wheels of industry produce only "shocks and noises," not the commodities and conditions necessary to nurture and sustain planetary life.

The Prison House of Fortune: Little Dorrit

The detached, universalizing perspective that Dickens assumes near the end of *Hard Times* when he ironically considers "the great wheel of earth" turning "without the shocks and noises of another time" anticipates the mature vision that informs the last novels, but it especially looks forward to the two controlling images of *Little Dorrit,* begun the following year. Both images—the first characterizing human experience as the "whirling wheel of life" and the second, as "the prison of this lower world"—are emphatically Boethian (and Dantean) in their apprehension of a fickle and powerful Fortune spinning the destinies of impotent mortals (*LD,* 720, 763); and, even though both occur when they are locally appropriate, after *Little Dorrit*'s hero Arthur Clennam is thrown into prison for debt, they are nevertheless applicable to a general state of affairs throughout the novel (*LD,* 711). Such a tragic view of life is foreshadowed in *Bleak House*'s Wheel of Chancery motif, but there the implication is that being broken on the wheel is avoidable—that it is possible for the wary to refuse to play Fortune's game and thereby escape her power. In *Little Dorrit,* however, there is no escape. In its thoroughly fortune-driven world, as James M. Brown has convincingly argued, society is presented as "one huge market-place" in which "[a]ll social relations, including marriage and friendship, are mediated through an economic frame of reference."[9] As K. Theodore Hoppen elaborates, *Little Dorrit* reveals a departure from the view, in Dickens's early novels, that "money remains most influential at an individual level"; here we see for the first time that "the fortunes of almost everyone hang upon the careers of big financial capitalists, the whole thing is an intricate *system,* the world of investment no longer bears any relation at all to the world of work."[10] In this environment, in which speculation plays the dominant role, the capricious revolutions of Fortune gain momentum and intensity in their disaster-producing potential, elevating a material circumstance into a tragic metaphysical condition. In R. Rupert Roopnaraine's terms, the novel's "controlling vision" is that "[h]uman lives, trapped on a great cosmic roulette wheel spun by a wanton fate, fall victim to fortuitousness and contingency." Roopnaraine associates this "metaphor of circularity" with "the tragic vision of the Greeks, where man is the plaything of the gods, a cipher to be juggled with and disposed of according to the caprice of some malevolent deity."[11] But his description applies more specifically—given the economic basis of this circularity—to the concept of the medieval wheel of Fortune, which appropriated the Roman Fortuna, goddess of random chance, and turned her into an image of an inexorable and tragic fate. Fortune herself is the capricious "malevolent deity" who holds everyone in the world of *Little Dorrit* hostage, and who therefore spins the "whirling wheel of life." Moreover, the goddess's sovereignty is suggested by the novel's division into two books whose titles represent the two extremes of Fortune—"Poverty" and "Riches." Not surprisingly, then, the wheel functions as both a local image and a structural principle, as in *Bleak House,* while Fortune once again exists in the abstract as well as in the flesh in the form of a dual goddess who governs both halves of a uniformly tragic wheel and world. Indeed, the supreme power exercised by women in *Little Dorrit* indicates that Fortune's world has fallen completely into the hands of women, operating everywhere under female rule and by a female temporal standard.

Dickens's apprehension of the world of *Little Dorrit* as a giant wheel of Fortune begins with his perception of the operations of Victorian capitalism, but the combination of several other influences—middle age, a deep disappointment in personal and national affairs, and the first signs of a new professionalism and sense of public responsibility in women, at last recognizable by Dickens in a way that he could admire—were probably equally responsible for his use of the wheel in *Little Dorrit* as an all-encompassing symbol for man's fate, subject to a higher—and female—power. That this wheel imagery had profoundly personal implications for Dickens is apparent in his description of the unusual restlessness he felt when trying to begin writing the novel. In a letter to Leigh Hunt of May 4, 1855, Dickens complains: "I sit down to work, do nothing, get up, go down a Railroad, find a place where I resolve to stay for a month, come home next morning, go strolling for hours and hours, reject all engagements to have my time to myself, get tired of myself and yet can't come out of myself to be pleasant to anyone, and so go on turning upon the same wheel round and round over and over again until it may begin to roll me towards my end."[12] This depiction of Dickens himself caught in a vicious circle of thought and work, "turning upon the same wheel round and round over and over again," indicates the tragic feeling of entrapment and defeat that had taken hold of him at this point of his life, a feeling largely attributable to a female cause. His spectacular successes as a writer, editor, and public figure were no longer sufficient to compensate for his growing dissatisfaction with his marriage, which he brought to an all-but-legal end three years later. This sense of failure in his personal life, after years of publicly and privately espousing family values, undoubtedly exacerbated his rage over what he considered to be the failure of the British government in its own handling of domestic affairs, and, most recently, in its inept management of foreign affairs as well.[13] According to Dickens, the British bureaucracy had bungled its involvement in the Crimean War; England had fostered only one hero, and she was a woman—Florence Nightingale, whose efforts to establish nursing as a female profession were duly praised in *Household Words* and later in *All the Year Round.*[14] The "warm tribute" of Sidney Godolphin Osborne, taken from his "Scutari and its Hospitals" and quoted at length in the April 1855 edition of *The Household Narrative,* ends with a high opinion of her efforts that undoubtedly reflects Dickens's own view: "Miss Nightingale . . . is the one individual who in this whole unhappy war has shown more than any other what real energy, guided by good sense, can do to meet the calls of a sudden emergency." Moreover, Osborne's description of Nightingale's "general demeanour [as] quiet, and rather reserved," with a "face not easily forgotten" and a way of speaking with "grave earnestness," closely parallels Dickens's later characterization of Little Dorrit. Most particularly, Osborne's visualization of Nightingale carrying out her nursing duties has a strongly Dickensian quality that must have registered on the novelist: "She has an utter disregard for contagion, and I have known her spend hours over men dying of cholera or fever. The more awful to every sense any particular case, especially if it was that of a dying man, her slight form would be seen bending over him, administering to his ease in every way in her power, and seldom quitting his side till death released him."[15] This image of a self-sacrificing woman's "slight form . . . seen bending over" the sick and dying to offer comfort "in every way in her power" could easily have been one inspiration for Dickens's portrayal of Little Dorrit, whose ministerings to her father, her brother, and her would-be lover, Clennam, repeatedly demonstrate what is obvious even to her hypercritical sister Fanny: that "as a nurse, she is Perfection" (*LD,* 697).

Nonetheless, the quietly benign, nurturing power that Little Dorrit exerts is only one diminutive aspect of a much larger and more frightening female control over fate in the novel. Nowhere else in Dickens's works are women so much in command as in *Little Dorrit.* The fortunes of the major male characters—however rich and influential they may appear—are ultimately in the hands of women, two of whom wield such far-reaching and insidious authority that the novel virtually divides between them in order to establish and therefore anatomize the separate but always simultaneously existing dual realms of Fortune. The first of these women—and Dickens's most formidable incarnation of malevolent Fortune—is the horrible Mrs. Clennam, who sits paralyzed in a wheeled chair, "glowering" (appropriately) "like Fate in a go-cart," a woman "with no limbs and wheels instead," according to Arthur's ex-sweetheart, Flora Finching, née Casby (*LD,* 284, 624). The attribute of a "chair on wheels," which allows Mrs. Clennam "to attend to [her] business duties" (*LD,* 34; see plate 26), is the salient clue to her identity as Fortune, linking her with Mrs. Skewton in *Dombey and Son* and, later, Miss Havisham in *Great Expectations* as avatars of the goddess in her deathly aspect. Mrs. Clennam's paralysis does not prevent her from continuing to be, in Arthur's words, "the moving power of all this machinery," referring specifically to her command of the Clennam family's personal and commercial dealings, but also suggesting her larger symbolic role in the narrative (*LD,* 49). Indeed, Mrs. Clennam is the most repellent—and dangerous—of Dickens's decrepit death goddesses, as revealed through her response to her husband's affair with another woman, Arthur's mother. As we learn late in the novel, when Dickens reveals the central mystery of the plot, Mrs. Clennam, who identifies herself as "but a servant and a minister" of God, "appointed to be the instrument of their punishment," had driven Arthur's real mother to insanity and death by forcing her to relinquish all claims to her child; then suppressed a codicil to a will intended to make some reparation for the mother's sacrifice—a codicil bequeathing a fortune to the obviously needy Little Dorrit (*LD,* 775–76). The final desperate plea of the mother, the initial letters of "Do Not Forget" worked in beads on a silk watch paper for Arthur's father, aptly becomes the perverse motto of Mrs. Clennam's "vindictive pride and rage" (*LD,* 775). The motto's expression of the "Imperative Mood, Present Tense" (to use one of Dickens's favorite formulations), correlates with Mrs. Clennam's general mood and tenseness as she sits rigid and brooding over a past kept alive and palpable by her wrath, "beyond the reach of all changing emotions" and beyond even the changing seasons (*LD,* 34). Her vengeful nature demonstrates that Mrs. Clennam is not, as she claims, the instrument of a deity, but a woman who "reversed the order of Creation" by setting herself up as the malignant embodiment of a deity (*LD,* 775). Dickens suggests this reversal in the following passage: "Great need had the rigid woman of her mystical religion, veiled in gloom and darkness, with lightnings of cursing, vengeance, and destruction, flashing through the sable clouds. Forgive us our debts as we forgive our debtors, was a prayer too poor in spirit for her. Smite thou my debtors, Lord, wither them, crush them: do Thou as I would do, and Thou shalt have my worship: this was the impious tower of stone she built up to scale Heaven" (*LD*, 47).

Mrs. Clennam's debasing of Christian terms into purely economic ones and her insistence on retributive justice identify her as ruthless ill Fortune, the goddess whose malice toward "debtors" is made more awful by the fact that it is sanctioned—and paralleled—by the British government's similarly punitive attitude, manifested in its operation of the Marshalsea as a debtors' prison. This and other metaphorical and thematic associations established between Mrs. Clennam and the Marshalsea reveal that Arthur's stepmother is the incarnation of the grim, mercenary spirit that holds sway in London and wreaks havoc on its underworld of Poverty. Her "smoke-blackened," dilapidated house near the "Iron Bridge" over the Thames suggests both a tomb and an entrance to hell, realized in the prison on the other side of the river (*LD*, 31). Her widow's weeds, "stony head-dress," and her "worsted-muffled right hand" help to complete the picture of a deity who is one of the living dead, outfitted in her grave clothes (*LD*, 33–34). She is Dickens's most obvious representation of Fortune as Atropos, the death-dealing Fate, and in keeping with her fatal iconographic role, she sits enthroned (when out of her wheeled chair) "as mistress of all" on "her black bier-like sofa, propped up by her black angular bolster that was like the headsman's block" (*LD*, 763). Mrs. Clennam's exit from the novel reinforces her symbolic role as the nation of Poverty's fatal Fortune, the dark goddess who lords it over the down-and-out denizens inhabiting "the prison of this lower world." When, after years of sitting immobilized by her paralysis, Mrs. Clennam is quite literally moved to justify herself to Little Dorrit, in an act of superhuman will she runs to the prison, like a "spectral woman," and then returns home to collapse outside her collapsing house, thereby becoming once and for all a living statue: "There, Mrs. Clennam dropped upon the stones; and she never from that hour moved so much as a finger again, or had the power to speak one word. For upwards of three years she reclined in her wheeled chair, looking attentively at those about her, and appearing to understand what they said; but the rigid silence she had so long held was evermore enforced upon her, and except that she could move her eyes and faintly express a negative and affirmative with her head, she lived and died a statue" (*LD,* 794). This is Dickens's most outrageous example of the goddess Fortune as an iconographic Hell on Wheels, a grotesque and despotic woman who, by the sheer power of her own perverse will, has become a monument to misery by turning herself into an unholy rolling shrine.

As discussed in the previous chapters, Dickens's Fortunes typically come in mother-daughter pairs in his "women's" novels, and *Little Dorrit* is no exception—although, as usual, there is some variation in the pattern to be expected. Little Dorrit's unique position as the only female heir to a fortune held (or rather, withheld) by Mrs. Clennam would qualify her, by the logic of Dickens's previous novels, to play the surrogate daughter who represents the goddess's alternate aspect—in this case, the Fortune of desire. Amy does assume this role, as will be discussed later in this chapter; however, here it should be noted that, like Esther, Amy represents another effort on Dickens's part to domesticate Fortune by acknowledging but tempering both sides of the death/desire duality that the goddess always embodies. Amy's often shrouded figure and generally worn appearance function, like Esther's nicknames and scars, to call attention to her association with the goddess's dark side, even after she has come into her own as the heir and the child of Fortune. The fact that Dickens never even attempts to characterize Amy as a conventional "beauty" is a sign of the inherent threat that such attractiveness poses. Indeed, *Little Dorrit* is unique among Dickens's novels in its dearth of women who are described as both conventionally beautiful *and* good, with only the minor character Pet Meagles exhibiting both qualities (and even she, through her possession of youth and good looks, poses a potential threat to Clennam's masculine identity). In short, Dickens's female characters in *Little Dorrit* consistently bear out the novel's controlling vision concerning the inevitable ruin effected by the love of Fortune: the goddess has no unadulterated bright side.

In keeping with this negative view of Fortune is Dickens's characterization of Mrs. Merdle, the icy goddess whose reign in the heaven of "Riches" serves as the alternative and complement to Mrs. Clennam's rule over the inferno of "Poverty." Wittily described by Martin Meisel as "Dickens' exfoliating synecdochic fantasy the Bosom, all matter and no milk, a gorgeous marble presence and a jewel stand, the full physical antithesis to the childish and by all implications breastless figure of Little Dorrit,"[16] Mrs. Merdle is an amalgam of the qualities distinguishing Lady Dedlock and Edith Dombey; like them, Mrs. Merdle achieves her status as "Priestess of Society" by marriage. Thus Dickens transforms her epithetic bosom into a kind of trophy bust: "It was not a bosom to repose upon, but it was a capital bosom to hang jewels upon. Mr. Merdle wanted something to hang jewels upon, and he bought it for the purpose" (*LD,* 238, 394, 247). Clearly, Mrs. Merdle is the stunning but aloof embodiment of Mr. Merdle's miraculous Fortune, and we are continually reminded of her symbolic role: at a society dinner, the dignitaries (appropriately named only by professional status) identify her with archetypically desirable, but formidably powerful and patently dangerous, women: "Treasury said, Juno. Bishop said, Judith" (*LD,* 250). More interesting, however, is Dickens's method of suggesting that Mrs. Merdle and Mrs. Clennam are contrasting aspects of the same unfeeling goddess: while Mrs. Clennam is associated with gloom and darkness, Mrs. Merdle is all glitter and light. She is a "woman of snow" who wears, in contrast to Mrs. Clennam's "stony head-dress," a "rich white fillet tied over her head and chin"; her royal seat "in a nest of crimson and gold cushions on an ottomon" invites comparison with Mrs. Clennam's "black bier-like sofa" (*LD,* 240, 238). Most suggestive of all is the curious detail regarding Mrs. Merdle's hands. When Dickens tells us, "All her action was usually with her left hand because her hands were not a pair; the left being much the whiter and plumper of the two," we are reminded of Mrs. Clennam, who gestures toward her wheeled chair with her "worsted-muffled right hand" (*LD,* 238). This hint regarding the two women's complementarity urges us to consider that they are metaphorically the same being, the left/weal–right/woe orientation given here coinciding with the conventional split between Fortune's two sides. Even though we might imagine that, from Fortune's point of view, these sides would be reversed, we should recall that, according to Boethius, it is the goddess's "proud right hand" that turns the wheel and thus inflicts the damage on her subjects.[17]

It is, however, while residing in Rome—Fortune's birthplace—that Mrs. Merdle fully assumes her symbolic role as the other side of Fortune—as her letters to her husband demanding a position for her son Sparkler reveal: "In the grammar of Mrs. Merdle's verbs on this momentous subject, there was only one Mood, the Imperative; and that Mood had only one Tense, the Present. Mrs. Merdle's verbs were so pressingly presented to Mr. Merdle to conjugate, that his sluggish blood and his long coat-cuffs became quite agitated" (*LD,* 558). This is the Merdle family's variant of the "Do Not Forget" message; and Mr. Merdle's subservience to his wife's commands, which results in Sparkler's gaining a post at the Circumlocution Office and Henry Gowan's losing one, indicates that Mrs. Merdle, like Mrs. Clennam, wields the power in the marriage and thus over the business world her husband appears to control. Moreover, Dickens implies that the wives' power ultimately destroys the husbands—in Mr. Clennam's case by breaking his spirit, and in Merdle's case, by breaking his bank.

The Roman setting and the proliferation of Roman imagery not only substantiate Mrs. Merdle's identity as Fortune, but serve simultaneously to establish the parallel between Rome and Britain as empires dedicated to her worship—and thus fated for ruin when Fortune decides to withdraw her favor. It should be noted that *Little Dorrit* is the most global of Dickens's novels—book 1 begins in Marseilles, with Clennam returning from twenty years in the family business in China, and book 2, with Little Dorrit on the triumphal grand tour of the Continent. This effort to represent as fully as possible both Britain's command of the world of Fortune and Fortune's command of Britain is highlighted by the presentation of Rome as a mirror for a decaying Empire, a critique that is continued and parodied in *Our Mutual Friend* through Weggs's ceremonial readings of Gibbon's *Decline and Fall.*[18] Dickens makes the parallel clear by noting that the same corrupt and destructive values obtain whether on "the shore of the yellow Tiber or the shore of the black Thames," the colors of the rivers (one suggesting the choleric and the other, the melancholic) merely reinforcing their polluted condition (*LD,* 586). As Dickens explains in the unlucky chapter 13 of book 2, "The Progress of an Epidemic," the fatal disease that infects both shores is speculation in Merdle's enterprises, which begins "in the wickedness of men" but reaches epidemic proportions when "communicated to many sufferers who are neither ignorant nor wicked" (*LD,* 582). This disease, which spreads from Pancks (whose epithet, "fortune- teller," proves ironic in the process) to Clennam, lands the latter in Marshalsea prison when Merdle's investments collapse, but also spawns a "whirlwind" of ruin in England, thereby reminding the reader of Rome's imperial fate (*LD,* 711). That the necessary end to Mr. Dorrit's brief life as a man of fortune is to see Rome and die—being struck down, appropriately, in the company of Mrs. Merdle—corroborates the connection via Fortune between the two empires. Finally, the peculiarly Roman flavor of Mr. Merdle's suicide by bloodletting in the "warm-baths" is Dickens's last reminder that Mrs. Merdle's "magnificent spouse," "whom it was heresy to regard as anything less than all the British Merchants since the days of Whittington rolled into one," has sacrificed himself to Fortune, in this case incarnated as the fashionable deity who resides regally in the Eternal City, but who is just as deadly as her wrathful counterpart who rules gloomily by the Thames in London (*LD,* 705, 557–58).

The duality of Fortune, represented by Mrs. Merdle in her role as the desirable trophy wife and Mrs. Clennam's complementary position as Fortune's death-dealing dark side, is highlighted and brilliantly parodied in that inextricable pair, Flora Finching and "Mr. F's Aunt." The florid, garrulous, fleshy, bibulous Flora, who becomes, after numerous insistent proposals, Mr. F's "statue bride" (having "turned to stone," "all . . . marble inside," following the forced breakup with Clennam), is always accompanied by her late husband's "legacy," that incomparable and incomprehensible "original figure" known only (and significantly) by way of her relation to a dead man (*LD,* 285, 157). Dickens's magnificent characterization of "this amazing little old woman" suggests her role as a cartoon version of Mrs. Clennam and ill Fortune: "The major characteristics discoverable by the stranger in Mr F's Aunt, were extreme severity and grim taciturnity: sometimes interrupted by a propensity to offer remarks in a deep warning voice, which, being totally uncalled for by anything said by anybody, and traceable to no association of ideas, confounded and terrified the mind. Mr F's Aunt may have thrown in these observations on some system of her own, and it may have been ingenuous, or even subtle; but the key to it was wanted" (*LD,* 157). Mr. F's Aunt is unpredictable in everything but her wrathful nature and her penchant for inexplicable, ominous pronouncements; as Lionel Trilling says in his excellent introduction to the Oxford *Little Dorrit,* hers is "the voice of one of the Parcae" (*LD,* xiv).

Mrs. Merdle, like Mrs. Clennam, is obviously "the moving power behind all [the] machinery" of her husband's business; but she is a more peripheral character than Mrs. Clennam. She is also less important—and inherently far less attractive—than either Edith Dombey or her most recent predecessor, Lady Dedlock of *Bleak House,* in her comparable role as the trophy wife and gilded idol representing (sexually) desirable Fortune. Nevertheless, Mrs. Merdle's very place as the personification of book 2's title, "Riches," holding court at the fountainhead of Fortune-worship outside and beyond England, helps to underscore her symbolic deific position, while allowing Dickens to emphasize the devastatingly fatal effects of Fortune's power rather than the goddess's desirability. Most pervasive of these ruinous effects is the general mood of depression that has settled on England even more insistently than *Bleak House*'s fog; and this "dire despondency," this "melancholy" that is so palpable to Clennam on his return to London, is the malaise of "an overworked people," a society so habituated to a life of bondage to Fortune that it willingly submits to a spirit-dulling existence—as Pancks says, to a monotonous round of "fag and grind, fag and grind, turn the wheel, turn the wheel!" (*LD,* 28, 802).

Dickens's exquisite example of this malaise is Fanny Dorrit, Amy's proud and beautiful sister, self-styled as "the wretchedest girl in the world" who "wished she was dead" because of her humble social position as a dancer and daughter of an imprisoned debtor (*LD,* 244). High-spirited by nature, Fanny has tragically concluded that there is nothing to live for but fortune. She is therefore so driven by her envy of Mrs. Merdle's exalted position—even though the younger woman recognizes the older "to be as false and insolent as a woman can be" (*LD,* 243)—that she marries the tender-hearted but dunderheaded Sparkler just to get at his mother: as Fanny says, to "oppose her in everything, and compete with her" as "the business of [Fanny's] life." The "desolate tone" in which Fanny admits, "Whether by disposition, or whether by circumstances; I am better fitted for such a life than for almost any other," reveals the clear-sightedness of her bondage to Fortune: her obsession with money and rank, the extent of her need to dazzle "the Eye of the Great World"—defined by Fanny as the orb that peers down through the eyeglass of Mrs. Merdle (*LD*, 592, 597, 238). Like Petronius's Fortunata, as presented by Erich Auerbach in *Mimesis,* Fanny becomes the quintessential parvenu, "that bitch" with "a nasty tongue" who was nothing yesterday, but who now "sits on top of the world and is [her husband's] one and only."[19] Given the parallel that Dickens establishes between the Roman and British Empires, it is not surprising that Auerbach's entire discussion of Trimalchio's banquet has particular relevance to the satirical presentation of "Society" (always archly capitalized) in *Little Dorrit*—and to the later novels as well. In Petronius's satire of first-century Italian nouveau-riche vulgarity, we see what Auerbach calls an "intrahistorical" view of the "ups and downs of fortune"—a view from "within" a society of "southern Italian freedmen-parvenus" for whom "the world is in ceaseless motion, nothing is certain, and wealth and social position are highly unstable." What becomes clear from this inside view of a fortune-driven society—a view provided by the characters themselves—is the "similarity" of their narratives concerning fortune:

> we see in imagination a whole world of similar lives, and finally find ourselves contemplating an extremely animated historico-economic picture of the perpetual ups and downs of a mob of fortune-hunters scrambling after wealth and stupid pleasures. It is easy to understand that a society of businessmen of the humblest origins is particularly suitable material for a representation of this nature, for conveying this view of things. Such a society most clearly reflects the ups and downs of existence, because there is nothing to hold the balance for it; its members have neither inward tradition nor outer stability; they are nothing without money.[20]

This description of Petronius's arrivistes applies perfectly to the Veneerings and Podsnaps of *Our Mutual Friend,* but it fits Dickens's generalized view of the social world in *Little Dorrit* as well. Even though we are not led to believe that the Dorrit family's instantaneous rise to prosperity is typical, we are everywhere presented with "a mob of fortune-hunters scrambling after wealth and stupid pleasures." Mr. Merdle, of course, serves as the crucial metonym for "a society of businessmen of the humblest origins" who "are nothing without money"; and Dickens's portrayal of Merdle's influence makes his indictment more sweeping than Petronius's, for in England, even those evidently not "of humble origins" are now shown to be worshipping at the feet of such "upstarts" and longing to emulate Merdle's superficially opulent, but monotonous and meaningless—in fact bankrupt—existence (*LD,* 390). When "Society" in *Little Dorrit* comes together—whether in London, in Rome, or elsewhere—we are always made to realize how much the majority of its members' respectability is merely a surface effect or performance, a matter of varnish and powder. Indeed, most of those who pretend to breeding actually live in reduced circumstances—with William Dorrit, as head of the Collegians in the Marshalsea, of course setting the supreme standard for faded and faked magnificence. Other examples include Mr. Tite Barnacle, august head of the Circumlocution Office, who lives in a mews; the snooty Mrs. Gowan, as one of many shabby "gipsies of gentility" trying to keep up appearances at Hampton Court; and Mrs. General, chief matron of "surface and varnish, and show without substance," who is at least as impecunious as she is proper (*LD,* 109, 312, 504). We see, in short, the instability of this society from the perspective of characters intimately acquainted with its fallen side. The novel is full of "Self Tormentors," like Miss Wade, whose claim, "I have the misfortune of not being a fool"—translating what would normally be considered an advantage into a condition of deprivation—reveals an obsession with a sense of being excluded from a position that ought by rights to be hers (*LD,* 663). By showing us this constant jockeying for position on Fortune's wheel in the lives of his major characters, Dickens reminds us that poverty and riches, like Merdle's ruin and Fanny's rise, are simply the complementary aspects of the same, uniformly tragic, Fortune-driven world. From Marseilles to the Marshalsea, from the Circumlocution Office to Bleeding Heart Yard, from the Pyrenees to the dance-hall orchestra pit, from the yellow Tiber to the black Thames, no one in the novel can escape from the prison house of Fortune.

The top scene of *Little Dorrit*'s cover wrapper serves as a warning concerning Britain's dangerous national obsession with Fortune (plate 27). This political cartoon depicts a tired Britannia in a Bath chair,[21] a vehicle by this time so closely associated with Fortune in Dickens's textual iconography that it now serves to conflate the two goddesses, just as it suggests a conflation of Mrs. Merdle and Mrs. Clennam. This deity, who is being pushed by fools and led by the blind toward Fortune's conventionally ruinous right side, is Browne's adumbration of Ruskin's "'Goddess of Getting-on' or 'Britannia of the Market,'" who is eloquently described in "Traffic" (1864) and clearly a representation of Fortune: "But, look strictly into the nature of the power of your Goddess of Getting-on; and you will find she is the Goddess—not of everybody's getting on—but only of somebody's getting on. This is a vital, or rather deathful, distinction." Through the top scene, and the directionless crowd depicted at the bottom, the *Little Dorrit* cover raises Ruskin's question: "Getting on—but where to?"[22] The figures in the crowd scene are the fortune-hunters of the "roaring streets" among whom Little Dorrit and Clennam "went down" on the autumn morning of their marriage, at the novel's conclusion: "the noisy and the eager, and the arrogant and the froward and the vain, [who] fretted, and chafed, and made their usual uproar" (*LD,* 826). Interestingly, the cover for *Our Mutual Friend* answers Ruskin's question by implying the vicious circularity of Britannia's route: the same image of the goddess appears below the title, lower on the page and headed in the opposite direction (plate 28).

Clennam's Prison Eye, or the Pupil of the Marshalsea

The autumnal mood that pervades *Little Dorrit* is Dickens's own, but within the novel this melancholy, attributed to many characters, is most intimately and sympathetically examined with respect to the "disappointed mind" of Arthur Clennam, the novel's middle-aged, introspective hero, who best articulates the tragic vision that informs Dickens's mature works. Like his author, Clennam conceives of life as a pilgrimage in a circle, and considers himself to be embarked on "his downward journey" toward old age and the grave (*LD,* 165). As Clennam explains to Little Dorrit: "I counted up my years, and considered what I am, and looked back, and looked forward, and found that I should soon be grey. I found that I had climbed the hill, and passed the level ground upon the top, and was descending quickly" (*LD*, 381). Picking up where Mr. Conductor in the "Preliminary Word" to *Household Words* leaves off just five years earlier, Clennam's image not only registers Dickens's sense that both the trajectory of his personal life and the great linear projectile of English history were now sloping downward; it also replaces Dickens's former giddy expectation of imminent victory with Clennam's sense that the best of life has completely passed him by. Evidently, for Clennam, there never was any "glow," never any refreshing "air from yonder height," nor any "inspirating voices" to signal arrival at a summit in life's journey. Clennam blames his upbringing for his having reached middle age already "broken, not bent" from a life of "always grinding in a mill [he] always hated" (*LD*, 20). Nevertheless, Clennam is not completely devoid of hope that he can "begin the world anew"—a hope that he associates with righting some unknown wrong he suspects his family to have done to Little Dorrit. But his consideration of such an act in terms of the sacred serves to disguise the possibility that his motive might be romantic love rather than ascetic duty:

> As the fierce dark teaching of his childhood had never sunk into his heart, so the first article in his code of morals was, that he must begin in practical humility, with looking well to his feet on Earth, and that he could never mount on wings of words to Heaven. Duty on Earth, restitution on earth, action on earth; these first, as the first steep steps upward. Strait was the gate and narrow was the way; far straiter and narrower than the broad high road paved with vain professions and vain repetitions, motes from other men's eyes and liberal delivery of others to the judgment—all cheap materials costing absolutely nothing. (*LD*, 319)

Clennam sees a new beginning through service to Little Dorrit as a change of direction, but not one that would seem to promise earthly happiness: quoting Matthew 7:14, "Strait was the gate and narrow was the way," suggests that Clennam's is a rather somber spiritual pilgrimage whose "steep steps upward" imply a struggle toward heavenly, rather than earthly, redemption. But the mote in Clennam's eye is his inability to see the nature and extent of the value he places on Little Dorrit herself—to see how she can provide him with a more palpable, earthly happiness than he realizes or chooses to acknowledge. It is only when he is imprisoned for debt in the Marshalsea—only when this "marked stop in the whirling wheel of life brings the right perception with it" (*LD,* 720)—that Clennam fully understands Little Dorrit's necessary and central place in his life: "Looking back upon his own poor story, she was its vanishing-point. Every thing in its perspective led to her innocent figure. He had travelled thousands of miles towards it; previous unquiet hopes and doubts had worked themselves out before it; it was the centre of the interest of his life; it was the termination of everything that was good and pleasant in it; beyond there was nothing but mere waste and darkened sky" (*LD,* 733). This epiphany, this revolution in Clennam's perception of Little Dorrit, is the pivotal moment of the novel. For the first time Clennam sees Little Dorrit in his mind's eye not as the unobtrusive being who occupies a peripheral or insignificant place proportional to her size, but as the alpha and omega of his faith and repressed sexual desire. The curious play of the neuter pronoun in the passage underscores the re-vision that was necessary to bring Little Dorrit into psychic focus: referring to "his own poor story," "her innocent figure," and "his life" all as "it," Clennam in essence consolidates the three terms, for "her innocent figure" has become the signifier—the element that endows his story and his life with purpose and meaning. Here at last Little Dorrit is recognized as the stable center around which Clennam has been circling throughout the novel in his grim meditations and wanderings.

Quite significantly, this epiphanic passage and as the novel's important "whirling wheel of life" image occur in the chapter entitled "The Pupil of the Marshalsea," which originally opened the novel's final double number and which most obviously refers to the schooling in prison life and love given Clennam by John Chivery, the turnkey's son, who, despite his own unrequited love for Amy, nobly discloses Amy's love for, and to, Clennam. But the title also emphasizes the firsthand knowledge that Clennam gains of physiological—not simply psychological and metaphorical—imprisonment: he is now the "eye" of the Marshalsea, the character, replacing William Dorrit and his daughter, who has the first-person, insider's view of confinement within high blank walls and behind a locked iron gate. Applying an optical meaning to the "pupil" in Dickens's title therefore serves to highlight the insistently visual nature of Clennam's epiphany as well as to locate it within the Marshalsea: "nothing but mere waste and darkened sky" is the view from the prison window that Clennam returns to "[n]ight after night" when, instead of sleeping, he sits up "watching the sickly lamps in the yard, and looking upward for the first wan trace of day" (*LD,* 754). This alternative meaning of "pupil" also suggests a dramatic, conclusive reinterpretation of the novel's cover wrapper that appropriately coincides with Clennam's epiphany (plate 27). The focal point of the cover is Little Dorrit herself, standing in the doorway of the prison with her figure cast into relief by light streaming through the aperture. Presumably, the image is of Little Dorrit leaving the prison;[23] but as Michael Steig has noted, the redemptive light surrounding Amy "comes from *within* the prison," thereby suggesting "that in a sense Amy goes into a world much darker than the prison."[24] This interpretation, of course, makes sense thematically given the Marshalsea's status as a microcosm of "the prison of this lower world" (*LD,* 763). Nevertheless, it is possible that the title "The Pupil of the Marshalsea" signals an imaginative inversion or reorientation of the cover image corresponding to the view of Amy that enters Clennam's head for the first time in this chapter: that is, Little Dorrit now appears as the image held in Clennam's inner eye—an image seen as if inside the "pupil," in this case understood as the opening in the eye through which light passes. Amy is therefore the "little doll" (from which the term "pupil" derives, referring to the appearance of objects reflected in the eye) who at last fully occupies Clennam's psychic field of vision; and, as in the convention of Renaissance love poetry, the figure embraced by the eye quickly makes its way to the beholder's heart. When Clennam's eye finally and figuratively takes in Little Dorrit—finally sees her as in herself she really is (to use Matthew Arnold's terms for such a critical distinction)—she brings with her the light of love, which will roll away the stones and break the chains of the prison, represented in the cover image by the letters of the title. As her name suggests, Amy is Clennam's "little door": she is his access and guide to a new life of love, freedom, and redemption.

This re-visioning of the cover wrapper's central image parallels Dickens's preoccupation in *Little Dorrit* with point of view, which in book 2 becomes a litany that includes Clennam's earlier, contrasting perception of Little Dorrit: "He regarded her from a point of view which in its remoteness, tender as it was, he little thought would have been unspeakable agony to her" (*LD*, 519). The last of these references to point of view significantly occurs in the chapter following "The Pupil of the Marshalsea," when Ferdinand Barnacle attempts to revise Clennam's opinion of the Circumlocution Office: "You don't regard it from the right point of view. It is the point of view that is the essential thing" (*LD*, 736). Barnacle, the ideal spokesperson for "circumlocution," is appropriately both right and wrong—as Dickens brilliantly demonstrates throughout the novel. For example, the young monk serving as host in the convent of the Great Saint Bernard voices his author's opinion when he tells Mr. Dorrit that "almost all objects had their various points of view" (*LD*, 441). In *Little Dorrit* the ability to see something from a new perspective is the necessary condition for enlightened self-renewal, just as an enforced change in situation (as in Clennam's imprisonment) is often required to produce such a re-vision.

Over and over Dickens demonstrates how the eye—although certainly "the preeminent organ of truth" for the Victorians[25]—nevertheless sees partially; consequently, the eye capable of seeing relationships in a new way is open to new dimensions of understanding. A brief, tragicomic example of this theme occurs when Fanny's tears offer a revelatory vision of her father-in-law: "they had the effect of making the famous Mr. Merdle, in going down the street, appear to leap, and waltz, and gyrate, as if he were possessed by several Devils" (*LD*, 701). In keeping with this theme, Dickens tells us early in the novel that, although Clennam's is the controlling consciousness, the primary "eye" of the narrative, "This history must sometimes see with Little Dorrit's eyes." This comment prefaces the following description of Clennam from Amy's point of view: "At first in the chair before the gone-out fire, and then turned round wondering to see her, was the gentleman she sought. The brown, grave gentleman, who smiled so pleasantly, who was so frank and considerate in his manner, and yet in whose earnestness there was something of his mother, with the great difference that she was earnest in asperity and he in gentleness. Now he regarded her with that attentive and inquiring look before which Little Dorrit's eyes had always fallen, and before which they fell still" (*LD*, 167). This passage reveals a Clennam that Clennam cannot see: a "brown, grave gentleman" who has already won Little Dorrit's love with his "attentive and inquiring look" so that he is, in a much broader sense than the context at first suggests, "the gentleman she sought." But the fact that Little Dorrit's perceptive eyes always fall when observed by Clennam helps to explain why he cannot (at this early point in the novel) see the way she sees him: as the gentleman who has taken possession of her heart. In Dickens's words: "He never thought that she saw in him what no one else could see. He never thought that in the whole world there were no other eyes that looked upon him with the same light and strength as hers" (*LD*, 381).

Describing the novel as a "world in reverse," Richard Stang has argued that Dickens's image of Fanny and the other dancers backstage at the theater—"They seemed to have got on the wrong side of the pattern of the universe" (*LD*, 234)—applies to the entire novel, that indeed, "the whole world of *Little Dorrit* is on the wrong side of the pattern of the universe."[26] While this provocative claim may overstate the case a bit, it certainly calls attention to Dickens's preoccupation with shifting points of view in the novel, especially as these re-visions relate to reversals of fortune. As frequently happens in Dickens's works, the most graphic expression of this theme comes from one of the most comic (and supposedly least articulate) of characters. Visiting Clennam in the Marshalsea in the "Pupil" chapter, Mr. Plornish attempts to comfort him with the following observation:

> Mr. Plornish amiably growled, in his philosophical but not lucid manner, that there was ups you see and there was downs. It was in wain to ask why ups, why downs; there they was, you know. He had heerd it given as a truth that accordin' as the world went round, which round it did rewolve undoubted, even the best of gentlemen must take his turn of standing with his ed upside down and all his air a flying the wrong way into what you might call Space. Wery well then. What Mr. Plornish said was, wery well then. That gentleman's ed would come up'ards when his turn come, that gentleman's air would be a pleasure to look upon being all smooth again, and wery well then! (*LD*, 731)

Plornish's ridiculous portrayal of an upside-down and wild-haired Clennam captures the idea not only of being on the wrong side of a pattern, but also of being spun about on Fortune's wheel, which has momentarily stopped, leaving her victim in this most unfortunate position. It is only when Little Dorrit later walks into the prison, "[s]o faithful, tender, and unspoiled by Fortune," that Clennam is able to come round, for this inverted view of everything has at last enabled him to see Little Dorrit aright: "She looked something more womanly than when she had gone away, and the ripening touch of the Italian sun was visible upon her face. But otherwise she was quite unchanged. The same deep, timid earnestness that he had always seen in her, and never without emotion, he saw still. If it had a new meaning that smote him in the heart, the change was in his perception" (*LD*, 757). Little Dorrit returns to the Marshalsea as the embodiment of Clennam's diminished, but enduring, good Fortune, as both her womanliness and her new Italian bronzing indicate. The cover wrapper thus renders Clennam's enlightened point of view that now apprehends why "everything his memory turned upon should bring him round to Little Dorrit" (*LD*, 720), for he sees her as the woman located at the fixed point of Fortune's wheel, the only position safe from the imprisoning wheel's movement. Little Dorrit's refusal to be spoiled by Fortune therefore also identifies her with Lady Philosophy, who consoled Boethius when he, like Clennam, was imprisoned.

Fairy Fortune

Little Dorrit is the most apparently symbolic of all Dickens's heroines, and although what she symbolizes has been variously identified, most critics agree on its spiritual or religious nature. To Lionel Trilling, she is "the Beatrice of the Comedy, the Paraclete in female form" (*LD*, xvi); to Alexander Welsh, the "Spirit of Love and Truth" who "proves constant amid inconstant fortunes."[27] Most interestingly, Martin Meisel focuses on Little Dorrit as the novel's embodiment of "Roman Charity," referring not to her role as Good Fortune (although the title would be equally applicable), but to a familiar emblem in nineteenth-century literature and art representing Euphrasia, a legendary "classical daughter" who breast-fed her father when he was in prison. Dickens alludes to her in the following passage: "There was a classical daughter once—perhaps—who ministered to her father in his prison as her mother had ministered to her. Little Dorrit, though of the unheroic modern stock, and mere English, did much more, in comforting her father's wasted heart upon her innocent breast, and turning to it a fountain of love and fidelity that never ran dry or waned, through all his years of famine" (*LD,* 229). This discreet, but provocative, representation of "Roman Charity" calls attention to Amy's role (like that of Polly Toodle in *Dombey and Son*) as the bosom of the family, the "little mother" who, of course, does not breast-feed her father, but offers the metaphorical milk of human kindness in the form of nourishing and sacrificial affection. Nevertheless, as Meisel explains, Dickens's "sublimation" of the classical image's secular and disturbing eroticism "was an attempt to respiritualize" it while also asserting its association with "the darker regions of dependency and desire." By calling attention to this image of Little Dorrit nursing her father as "a generative source for the novel as a whole," Meisel offers a corrective to the more typical assessment of Amy's symbolic status.[28] Unlike Dickens's previous saintly heroines, Amy is explicitly linked to the sensual, an attribute that had been either understated (in the case of Agnes and Florence) or represented as somehow dangerous (in the case of Esther and Louisa). In his characterization of Amy Dorrit we see Dickens struggling to offer a reconfigured image of a virtuous woman who is the object of male desire: a woman who demonstrably partakes of both the sacred and the sensual, the spiritual and the erotic.

To accomplish the sensual side of this reconfiguration, Dickens draws on the same symbolic code that he had used to convey Dora Spenlow's sex appeal. David's halting attempt to categorize Dora's fascination for him—"She was a Fairy, a Sylph, I don't know what she was" (*DC,* 390)—anticipates Clennam's more mature acknowledgment "that to make a kind of domesticated fairy of [Little Dorrit] . . . would be but a weakness of his own fancy" (*LD,* 259). Yet, even before Clennam can identify the feeling that Amy arouses in him with romantic or sexual love, he can neither dismiss the fairy classification nor resist the intrinsic attractiveness of her fairy nature, apparent in "her youthful and ethereal appearance, her timid manner, the charm of her sensitive voice and eyes, the very many respects in which she had interested him out of her own individuality, and the strong difference between herself and those about her" (*LD,* 259). Little Dorrit therefore possesses those qualities most essential both to female sexual charm, in Dickens's view, and to fairyhood: diminutive size, a perennially childlike appearance, and an ineffable uniqueness or otherness suggestive of a superior—a refined—sensibility.[29]

The erotic nature of Little Dorrit's appeal is first made apparent to the reader (if not to Clennam) in the chapter titled "Little Dorrit's Party," referring to the pretence she uses to stay out all night attending to various family concerns. When she visits Clennam's lodgings with Maggy—arriving on his doorstep at the magical hour of midnight—he is clearly enchanted by her physical appearance: "But what was really in his mind, was the weak figure with its strong purpose, the thin worn shoes, the insufficient dress, and the pretence of recreation and enjoyment. He asked where the supposititious party was? At a place where she worked, answered Little Dorrit, blushing. She had said very little about it; only a few words to make her father easy. Her father did not believe it to be a grand party—indeed he might suppose that. And she glanced for an instant at the shawl she wore" (*LD,* 169). The hour, the idea of a make-believe party, the pitiful and presumably scanty dress, and the sensitive intelligence emanating from Little Dorrit's words, skin, and eyes combine to suggest that she could be an evanescent creature from fairyland, one who might disappear as mysteriously as she has materialized; and this ephemeral quality is to Dickens the quintessence of feminine sexuality. Little Dorrit's gamine appearance is reminiscent of the pantomime actress whom Dickens had recently described in a *Household Words* article titled "Gaslight Fairies," a young woman from the lower orders whose makeup and profession suggest her sensuality.[30] This connection and the latent eroticism of Amy's appearance are corroborated not only by her encounter with a prostitute later that night, but also by Clennam's thoughts about her as she and Maggy disappear down the street: "So diminutive she looked, so fragile and defenceless against the bleak damp weather, flitting along in the shuffling shadow of her charge, that he felt, in his compassion, and in his habit of considering her a child apart from the rest of the rough world, as if he would have been glad to take her up in his arms and carry her to her journey's end" (*LD,* 173). Clennam understands that he desires to take possession of Little Dorrit's body, but fails to acknowledge the full significance of this desire. It is clear, though, that the essence of her sensual appeal to Clennam is not despite, but *because* of her childlike, "diminutive," "fragile and defenceless" being, her fairy presence. For Dickens, the image of this frail, gentle creature "flitting along" the night streets of London is as erotically charged as Shakespeare's fairies and Fuseli's paintings of them. Even Clennam's final recognition of Amy as the "vanishing point" of "his own poor story" is another way of asserting Amy's fairyhood.

But Amy as symbolic fairy is also "domesticated," that household word in Dickens's vocabulary indicating less a fairy princess like Dora and more a "diviner" like Esther, who brings order to the home and tells home truths. Amy is a spiritual creature whose capacity for sacrifice serves, like Esther's scars, to disguise her sensuality. This is the side of Little Dorrit seen by David Holbrook, in *Charles Dickens and the Image of Woman,* as "Little Doormat,"[31] and it is this more somber image of herself that she recognizes, as she reveals in the fairy tale she tells Maggy. In the chapter suggestively titled "Fortune-telling"—which most obviously refers to the role Pancks assumes in tracking down the Dorrit fortune, but which also refers to "female storytelling" by Flora and, finally, by Little Dorrit herself[32]—Amy improvises a tale about two women in which she engages in some fortune-telling of her own. These women, a princess who spends her time riding about in a carriage and a "poor tiny woman" who "lived all alone by herself spinning at her wheel," represent two extremes—and thus two aspects—of Fortune, as is suggested by the princess's status, wealth, and carriage, and by the tiny woman's poverty and spinning. As the story goes, the "wonderful Princess [who] had the power of knowing secrets" stops one day to ask the tiny woman about hers and learns that she keeps in "a very secret place" her only "treasure": "the shadow of Some one who had gone by long before; of Some one who had gone on far away quite out of reach, never, never to come back." The Princess passes the tiny woman's cottage daily, always finding her spinning, until "At last one day the wheel was still, and the tiny woman was not to be seen." The Princess learns that the tiny woman is dead, mourns briefly, then visits the cottage to search for the shadow, which, as the tiny woman had predicted, is nowhere to be found. "Then [the Princess] knew that the tiny woman had told her the truth, and that it would never give anybody any trouble, and that it had sunk quietly into her own grave, and that she and it were at rest together" (*LD,* 293–95).

As Nancy Aycock Metz has shown, this "Tale of the Princess" has fascinated feminist critics with its "striking metaphors," but it lacks the magic and (quoting Harry Stone) the "dazzling transformations" that are the usual stuff of Dickens's fairy tales. Instead, Amy's story is a kind of "anti-narrative" that "articulates her profound wish to be *understood* and that in some non-verbal, *a priori* way."[33] It is clear, of course, that the model for the "poor tiny woman" is Amy herself, and the shadow is Clennam's, but except for the (inevitable) death of the tiny woman, nothing really happens—there is no "story" here. Yet the tale is important in helping to identify Little Dorrit symbolically not only as another good housewife Fortune, but also with all those fairy spinners and lovelorn spinsters of ballad and legend who are linked, through their dual tasks of spinning and fortune-telling, with the working out of time and fate. In other words, what is telling about this tale is the way it confirms Amy's role as the novel's Fairy Fortune.

As Marina Warner explains in *From the Beast to the Blonde: On Fairy Tales and Their Tellers,* there are significant connections among the terms "fairy," "fate," and "spinning" that inform their relation to tale-telling, women, and time. First, the word "fairy" derives from "a Latin feminine word, *fata,* a rare variant of *fatum* (fate) which refers to a goddess of destiny" and means "literally, that which is spoken." Hence, "fairies share with Sibyls knowledge of the future and the past, and in the stories which feature them, both types of figure foretell events to come, and give warnings." Second, Warner quotes Isidore of Seville's seventh-century *Etymologies* to explain that the classical interpretation of the Fates as three women spinners derives from the association of the "threefold nature of time"—past, present, and future—with the three-part task of spinning wool: "the past, which is already spun and wound onto the spindle; the present, which is drawn through the spinner's fingers; and the future, which lies in the wool on the distaff, and which must still be drawn out by the fingers of the spinner onto the spindle, as the present is drawn to the past." Because the very act of spinning so vividly imitates (or perhaps even originally inspired) an ancient conception of the passage of time, spinners have been traditionally associated with fortune-telling powers—a tradition handed down in folklore and fairy tales. Moreover, Warner argues, the gender link between fairy stories and females is not only etymological, but historical: the traditional tellers of these tales were the "Old Wives" and "Gossips" whose stories and task of spinning are bound together actually and metaphorically.[34]

It is no wonder, then, that spinning figures prominently in many traditional folktales, like those of Perrault and the Grimm Brothers, where it is often associated with fairy powers, such as the curse on the spindle in "Sleeping Beauty" and the magical spinning of Rumpelstiltskin. Indeed, the connection between fairies and spinning seems to be as deeply embedded in folklore as the connection between women and spinning. Quoting I. F. Grant's *Highland Folkways,* Patricia Baines notes the popular belief that "it was considered inadvisable to leave the band on the wheel when the household retired for the night for fear that the fairies might then use the wheel."[35] This connection between night spinning and the fairies recurs in Wordsworth's "Song for a Spinning Wheel," which records the folk belief that spinning is easier when the sheep are resting: "Night has brought the welcome hour, / When the weary fingers feel / Help, as if from faery power."[36] An old Irish spinning song even credits the fairies with the spinning wheel's invention or origin:

They say a fairy has no heart,
    but sorrow now they feel.
For mortal souls that grieve apart,
    they've sent a spinning wheel.

Spin the warmth of wool, little wheel.
    Forget your fairy days.
Spin for men so brave and leal
    who guard the ocean ways.[37]

Here, as a gift from the fairies to assuage human (and especially women's) grief, the spinning wheel is endowed with enormous symbolic significance; as in numerous examples from folklore and legend, it becomes an instrument that works like a sedative in its capacity to soothe and equalize the emotions. This is the point of Wordsworth's sonnet "Grief, Thou Hast Lost an Ever-Ready Friend," which laments the disappearance of the "cottage Spinning-wheel" as a result of the Industrial Revolution, much in the same way the rural mill was elegized in Romantic painting. Wordsworth's poem, composed in 1819, celebrates not only the spinning wheel's ability to mollify "Grief" and "Care," but also its power to temper the more desirable, if sometimes too-excessive, emotions of "Love" and "Joy."[38]

Similarly, as R. Rupert Roopnaraine asserts, the spinning wheel in Little Dorrit's story "becomes the symbol of life's activity, a source of consolation, the circumscribed symmetry of habit."[39] Both Wordsworth's and Little Dorrit's spinning wheels provide the "Consolation" of Boethius's Philosophy, because minding this preindustrial wheel seems to work like sympathetic magic against Fortune's less predictable, yet inevitable, turnings: the extremes of Fortune—its highs and lows—achieve harmony and balance so long as the wheel continues to spin. Thus in "The Tale of the Princess," as in Hogarth's *The Lottery* (plate 11), the tiny woman and her spinning wheel together function as an emblem for female industry, one that reveals Little Dorrit's understanding of the redemptive capacity of labor (Flora's referring to Amy as "You industrious little fairy" is relevant here [*LD,* 284]). In the larger context of the novel, however, the tiny woman at her wheel serves as a miniature of the already diminutive Amy, to reiterate her role as Fairy Fortune, the humble, benevolent, diminutive, and domesticated version of the goddess whose love of order and sense of justice quite literally put a different spin on things. Little Dorrit's fairy power is the power of reversal that allows Arthur to reclaim his life; as Meisel says, "From the womb or grave of the Marshalsea he is resurrected, and his infancy and childhood are given him, by the child-woman who reverses time and Nature to redeem them."[40]

The nexus of association that links fairies, fortune, women, and spinning, therefore, has special relevance to Little Dorrit's tale, because it calls attention to the spinning wheel as the story's central symbol while suggesting its symbolic function. As in Elizabeth Barrett's "A Year's Spinning," the wheel represents female labor, the endless round of work that actually and metaphorically characterizes the tiny woman's very existence. By the same token, the motionless wheel signals that the "spinning is all done" and remains as the only vestige of the woman, her work, and her disappointed love. It is the "marked stop in [her] whirling wheel of life," and as such it becomes the symbol for her tragic story, with its matter-of-fact acceptance of life's round of labor and suffering. Both associations identify it with Fortune's wheel and indicate that, in T. E. Hulme's words, this wheel symbolizes the "closing of all roads," the "realisation of the *tragic* significance of life" and "the futility of existence." Hulme continues: "Such a realisation has formed the basis of all great religions, and is most conveniently remembered by the symbol of the *wheel*."[41] In Amy's story, even the all-knowing Princess has something to learn that is symbolized by the wheel: it is the "truth" at the heart of the tiny woman's secret—and it is the same "truth" that Dickens wishes to convey in his own story, in the novel that bears the tiny woman's name (*LD*, 295).

The conclusion of the "Fortune-telling" chapter reiterates the idea that Little Dorrit, and not Pancks, is the more reliable "fortune-teller," because only she—certainly at this point of the novel—fully understands and accepts the inevitability and the necessity of the wheel's movement. Dickens suggests Amy's superior understanding through her answers to Maggy's questions about Pancks when he appears in the prison courtyard below Amy's window:

> "I have heard him called a fortune-teller," said Little Dorrit. "But I doubt if he could tell many people, even their past or present fortunes."
>
> "Couldn't have told the Princess hers?" said Maggy.
>
> Little Dorrit, looking musingly down into the dark valley of the prison, shook her head.
>
> "Nor the tiny woman hers?" said Maggy.
>
> "No," said Little Dorrit, with the sunset very bright upon her. "But let us come away from the window." (*LD*, 295)

Appropriately, the chapter ends with Little Dorrit's desire to recede from view—to return to the world of her imagination, where the tiny woman never ceases to spin; in so doing, she maintains the philosophical equipoise that is necessary to deal with the inevitable sorrows and vicissitudes of life. Like the "little pocket-housewife" she carries to hold her needlework supplies, Amy is the small repository for the essentials of Dickens's ideal woman (*LD*, 284). She is a woman of infinite resourcefulness, and even the rather drab, miniature version of herself that she projects as the cottage spinster in her tale is a creature of magical potency; for this tiny woman, like Amy herself, understands the uses of enchantment. Secretly but successfully stealing a treasured shadow from the man she loves is another way of expressing the power of the mind to overcome loss by creating and nurturing images, so that the work of life and the life of work can go on. Thus Amy's fairy nature does not suggest a state of perpetual childhood, like Dora's, but a superior ability to use her mental powers to transcend the world's weeping, which she does indeed understand.

Dickens's habitual practice of presenting Little Dorrit through receding or increasingly miniaturizing images therefore reasserts her identity as Fairy Fortune: a tiny goddess whose very ephemerality is a sign of her monumental powers. This distancing or minimalizing technique allows the reader to see "around" Little Dorrit in a way that Esther can never be seen; thus the constant focus on her slight form has the effect of magnifying her physical presence. It is this method of characterizing Amy that primarily accounts for the fact that, as Michael Slater says, "for once" Dickens "manages to breathe life into his feminine ideal."[42] When Clennam is himself finally reduced to his lowest state, he is able to see Amy for what she is: the "vanishing point" in his life, the domesticated fairy who, besides keeping his shadow, has also stolen his heart. She not only becomes his "pocket-housewife," the necessary woman he will happily carry to their journey's end; she is also a "pocket Venus," like the woman Dickens imagined his first love to be: a tiny goddess whose very diminutiveness is the key to her sensual charm.[43]

Little Dorrit is the most tender of all Dickens's love stories, and the painstaking care with which he records the trials of Arthur and Amy's romance is surely indicative of his preoccupation with the joys and sorrows of wedded love. Just as the idea of "vanishing" casts Little Dorrit in a new light, so Dickens's dawning realization of his own marriage's disintegration seems to have renewed his faith in the primacy of love; and the poignancy of this understanding is everywhere apparent in the novel. This preoccupation with wedded love is not simply a personal, but a larger, contemporary, concern, as evidenced by Tennyson's exploration of the marital and courtly affairs of that more famous Arthur in *Idylls of the King,* which he began writing at the same time that *Little Dorrit* was being serially published. In what would eventually become "The Marriage of Geraint," Tennyson introduces Enid, the ideal wife, who bears a close resemblance to Little Dorrit. When Geraint first meets her, her family has fallen on poverty; yet Enid, in her "faded silk" dress, maintains her equanimity by dutifully carrying out her "lowly handmaid-work" (lines 366, 400). Geraint falls in love with Enid, however, even before he sees her—when he hears her "sweet voice" singing "[o]f Fortune and her wheel" in a way that is reminiscent of Amy (lines 336, 346):

> Turn, Fortune, turn thy wheel and lower the proud;
> Turn thy wild wheel thro' sunshine, storm, and cloud;
> Thy wheel and thee we neither love nor hate.
>
> Turn, Fortune, turn thy wheel with smile or frown;
> With that wild wheel we go not up or down;
> Our hoard is little, but our hearts are great. (lines 347–52)[44]

As in Dickens, so in Tennyson: women who are "unspoiled by Fortune" have a peculiar power over men because of their refusal to be swept away by the goddess's "wild wheel." Instead, by minding their round of domestic duties and, indeed, sacrificing themselves to men, they simultaneously nullify and appropriate fickle Fortune's powers to gain sovereignty over their husbands and lovers—that is, they become, as it were, pocket Fortunes in their own right. Although Enid's song goes on to claim that "man is man and master of his fate" (line 355), Tennyson's idyll seems to suggest otherwise: Enid is the mistress of Geraint's fate, who eventually saves his life (and their marriage) through her enduring love, superior insight, wise deeds, and gentle nature. The gender lesson of their story is expressed by her cousin and would-be lover Edyrn, who eventually learns to curb his wild nature at the queen's court, where he observes "that gentleness, / Which, when it weds with manhood, makes a man."[45] Although Edyrn is referring to the wedding of gentleness and manhood in his own person, the lesson equally applies to the marriage of Geraint, for Geraint has to learn twice over that he is lost without Enid. The idyll therefore suggests that, whether man chooses the "wild wheel" of Fortune or the soothing song of his wife, woman is mistress of man's fate. The other, positively fatal women of Tennyson's *Idylls of the King*—Vivien, Guinevere, and the three queens who carry Arthur away at the conclusion—corroborate this point.

Similarly, the world of Little Dorrit is controlled by cold, unfeeling women, like Mrs. Clennam and Mrs. Merdle, whose power destroys men—who, in turn, can be saved only by loving women like Amy. *Little Dorrit* therefore records Dickens's complete rejection of his earlier grounding faith in masculine authority, previously rendered through images celebrating the linear progress of history, such as "the wheel of Time [that] is rolling for an end" at the conclusion of *Pictures from Italy.* Like his contemporary, the French historian Michelet, Dickens finally comes around to a belief that, as man's destroyer and savior, "Woman" is "Religion."[46] As Roland Barthes explains with regard to Michelet, such a conjunction is a "*necessary tyranny, for it alone saves man from History by replacing him within circular time, at once in movement and fixed.*" Like Michelet, Dickens in *Little Dorrit "hands himself over to Woman,"* for she is the "*ultimate medication*": "*she halts time and, better still, makes it begin again.*"[47] Dickens's next novel, *A Tale of Two Cities,* records this revolution in his thinking about man's fate not only through its historical circumstancing, but through the image of Doctor Manette, "recalled to life" from prison, whose daughter is "the golden thread that united him to a Past beyond his misery, and to a present beyond his misery" (*TTC,* 74). Lucy Manette, another of Time's threads "spun into a woman," is the foil for that most celebrated of knitters, Madame Defarge, but Dickens's imagery suggests that both women wield the Fates' formidable power. Moreover, this new perception of woman's ascendancy is reflected in Dickens's obsession with cyclical time, apparent in several of the titles considered for *A Tale of Two Cities,* such as "The Great Wheel," "Round and Round," "Rolling Years," and "Rolling Stones"; it is also evident in the title of Dickens's new magazine, which began publication in 1859 and in which the novel was serialized—*All The Year Round.*[48] Dickens's new interest in revolution and women's time registers the revolution in his own life that had recently taken place: his official separation from his wife in 1858, and his affair with Ellen Ternan, probably begun the year before.

WINTER 1860

The World Turned Upside Down

Wipe your hands across your mouth, and laugh;
The worlds revolve like ancient women
Gathering fuel in vacant lots.

—T. S. ELIOT, *"Preludes"*

The Language of Fortune

By the time Dickens wrote the opening scene of *Great Expectations* for *All the Year Round* in 1860, his use of inversion had become so familiar that it could have been considered his trademark.[1] Delight in disorder, the sheer pleasure of turning things topsy-turvy, had been a staple of Dickens's comedy from the start, but in his more recent works—notably in *Little Dorrit*—inversion, representing the relentless cyclicality of fate and the inevitability of its turnings, had taken on a solemn aspect, charged with a somber moral and metaphysical meaning.[2] Dickens's most astute readers now knew the serious attention he gave to a first number or installment, particularly to the opening words; and Dickens could trust them to ponder these words with an equally serious attention. It is not surprising, then, that in the short paragraph recalling Pip's first encounter in the church graveyard with Magwitch, Pip's description of the convict's gesture of inversion is fraught with symbolic significance: "The man, after looking at me for a moment, turned me upside down, and emptied my pockets. There was nothing in them but a piece of bread. When the church came to itself—for he was so sudden and strong that he made it go head over heels before me, and I saw the steeple under my feet—when the church came to itself, I say, I was seated on a high tombstone, trembling, while he ate the bread ravenously" (*GE,* 2). Both the gesture and Pip's description of it comically visualize for the reader that most Dickensian of themes: the reversal of fortune. From Pickwick on, as the central gesture of plot and the surest test of character, Dickens had been turning his protagonists upside down and emptying their pockets. Such a reversal has the effect of reordering one's priorities and changing one's view of things, as Pip realizes immediately, but then must learn several times over during the course of the novel. In other words, the reversal not only inverts Pip, but changes the world and revolutionizes Pip's understanding of it.

The gesture is emblematic. It is the kind of detail, reminiscent of Hogarth, for which Dickens had become famous, proof of an imagination that had its source in the visual, that created a narrative by linking a series of highly graphic scenes or essentially symbolic pictures.[3] Here, the ultimate seriousness of the comic gesture is captured, first, by reference to the upside-down and then upright church, suggesting a complete revolution of belief, a radical upheaval of all that is sacred in the institution at the very heart of the social organism. Second, reference to the child on the tombstone deftly reinforces the fact that Pip, like David Copperfield before him, is a "posthumous child," now reborn to a new consciousness and a new parental order. And finally, the high seriousness is conveyed by the stark image of the hungry man, taking communion, as it were, in a graveyard and from the pocket of a trembling boy—rather than in the church and by the grace of a heavenly father. In this upside-down, godforsaken world, Dickens seems to be saying, the old patriarchal order born of the church and sanctified by society has been overturned, indeed buried. Father figures are either outlaws, like Magwitch, or good, but ineffectual, illiterates, like Joe; and boys, with neither god nor man to look to as a model, are "naterally wicious" until they can carve out a new morality appropriate to this new, inverted social order in which women have gained ascendancy.

Magwitch's gesture, more particularly, evokes an image of "The World

Turned Upside Down," a motif traditionally associated with fools' days—carnival or Shrove Tuesday, for example.[4] But since the English Civil Wars in the seventeenth century, WUD (as the motif is called by anthropologists) had also been associated with political and religious revolution—as historian Christopher Hill documents.[5] By the early nineteenth century—the time of Dickens's childhood—this motif was still in currency among the poor, the semiliterate, and their children by way of a popular chapbook. *The World Turned Upside Down or The Folly of Man Exemplified in Twelve Comical Relations upon Uncommon Subjects,* "Illustrated with Twelve curious Cuts Truly adapted to each Story," was a cheap publication of the sort produced by James Catnach and John Pitts in the Seven Dials section of London and described by Dickens with a tone of nostalgic affection in *Sketches by Boz.*[6] The woodcuts, clearly the most salesworthy part of the chapbook, depict "Things quite form'd out of nature's rules," as the accompanying poem tells us (plate 29). These aberrations include such reversals as an "ox turned butcher," a "roasted cook," and "fishes lords of creation," flying like birds and angling for men. In one cut with a Dickensian theme, children are nursing and punishing adults; and in another—the one with primary relevance to the upside-down world of *Great Expectations*—the reversal "out of nature's rules," is of gender. In this cut, labeled "The Old Soldier Turned Nurse," the male sits holding a distaff and a baby, while the woman paces the room wearing a helmet and sword and toting a rifle. Two other cuts, however, seem directly pertinent to Magwith's gesture, as if Dickens is recalling these quaint and memorable pictures and perhaps expecting that his description will trigger his readers' memories as well. The lead cut shows two jesters holding a ball or globe, from which a man's head and legs protrude upside down; and another shows a village skyline on top and the sun, moon, and stars below. Taken together, these two cuts illustrate inversion moving from the personal to the cosmic in a grotesque reversal of the natural. Part of the power of the novel's opening scene derives from its implied connection to this motif of a reversible world and therefore to a folk and a radical tradition that was largely ignored by official taste in the early nineteenth century, but was kept alive through cheap street literature like this chapbook. Dickens's particular genius was to tap into this richly illustrative, semiliterate world and recycle its defining images and themes as part of the official aesthetic of Victorian bourgeois tradition. Perhaps the most explicit and magnificent example of Dickens's use of this topos occurs in *Little Dorrit* as Mr. Plornish's philosophy of life: "even the best of gentlemen must take his turn of standing with his ed upside down and all his air a flying the wrong way into what you might call Space" (*LD*, 731). Plornish's philosophy, like's Magwitch's gesture, seems to find its source in the lead cut from the WUD chapbook.[7] Both images underscore Dickens's mature vision of a world in the hands of Fortune.

In *Great Expectations,* through the language of fortune that Dickens appropriated from the folk tradition and from the chapbooks and other street literature popular in his childhood, Dickens creates an autobiographical fantasy that is roughly based on the stories of all those heroes who are the minions of Fortune. His writing—here and elsewhere—is saturated not only with references to, but with imaginative recreations of, these heroes, as Harry Stone's *Dickens and the Invisible World* so convincingly demonstrates.[8] Typical street literature stories include the adventures of folk heroes like Dick Whittington, who rises from humble circumstances to become thrice Lord Mayor of London, and whose fortunate turn in fate is comically recalled in *The Old Curiosity Shop* in the character of Dick Swiveller (and alluded to via both his names) and more ironically remembered in the character of Richard Carstone in *Bleak House.* Other stories feature notorious reprobates like George Barnwell (whose tragical history becomes a motif in *Great Expectations*), who falls, simultaneously, in love and into a life of crime, ultimately getting himself hanged. But the fate of Fortunatus in particular bears such an uncanny resemblance to Dickens's own life that he could serve as the prototype for Pip. As discussed in chapter 1, *The History of Fortunatus* begins, like Dickens's own story, with the birth of a son to an improvident father who has lost not only his own wealth but his wife's as well. Fortunatus must therefore seek his own fortune, which he miraculously finds in the form of the goddess Fortune herself. When she offers to bestow one of six gifts on our hero, and Fortunatus chooses riches, Fortune gives him the magically refillable purse that is the chief interest of the narrative. Although the moral of the story is that Fortunatus should have chosen wisdom, the goddess's gift of a purse is more appropriate, considering Fortune's identity; it also suggests (as Machiavelli indicated in *The Prince*) that Fortune's favors are sexual favors. The goddess as donor thus figuratively stands in relation to the male recipient of her gift as mother or lover. Because her choice has nothing to do with merit—with the sterling character of a beneficiary selected through reason, virtue, or wisdom—it must have to do simply with chance or emotion, with the often cryptic logic of love.

This fantasy of becoming the darling of Fortune understandably captured the imagination of the poor and downtrodden just as it certainly made a permanent impression on Dickens, who refers to it in his fiction throughout his career. After all, Dickens was, in one sense, a Victorian Fortunatus: his own purse was constantly being filled by his writing but depleted by his enormous family, restless habits, and extravagant housekeeping. Pip's status as a gentleman is defined by just such a continually renewable purse. But, unlike Dickens, more like Fortunatus, and most of all like those fortunate Victorian gentlemen born into wealth and leisure, Pip does not have to *earn* his living: he simply takes it out of his purse, which has been magically filled by some secret, external power. Such wealth, derived without the exercise of reason or personal effort, is itself an aberration of nature, according to the self-help-loving Dickens. Pip's rise to gentility through such means must therefore be depicted as a monstrous parody, or as a parable about the dangers of Victorian middle-class affluence not properly grounded in an ethic that holds work as a sacred value; and it is telling to compare Pip's rise to David Copperfield's, which results from "habits of punctuality, order, and diligence" (here manifested in learning shorthand), habits that reflect Dickens's own (*DC*, 606).[9]

Thus discovering the identity of Pip's benefactor and, concomitantly, the source of his wealth, becomes the chief mystery around which the narrative pivots, because it presumably will reveal something about Pip's own intrinsic worth. And when Magwitch, the convicted thief, proves to be this benefactor, generously repaying the boy many times over for the bread taken from his pocket in the novel's opening scene, Dickens's plot demonstrates that Pip's wealth in fact derives from the boy's own merit. But this reward is hardly providential: Pip's ignorance about the source of his riches and, by extension, his blindness to his own and others' real value reveal themselves to be as destructive as unmerited fortune. Pip's long-held conviction that

Miss Havisham has made his fortune while disregarding her own relations—imperiously ignoring a whole family of impecunious Pockets in order to fill his—not only reinforces the connection between *Great Expectations* and the story of Fortunatus; it also reveals how willing Pip is to profit at the expense of others. Certainly, Mr. Pumblechook's toast to Pip and Fortune underscores this connection: "Let us drink, Thanks to Fortune, and may she ever pick out her favourites with equal judgment!" (*GE,* 145). Judgment, of course, has nothing to do with Pip's rise; and Fortune—rather perversely like Justice, but with more insidious implications—is of course a blind goddess.

Miss Havisham is certainly Dickens's strangest and most symbolically suggestive Fortune, a masterful creation fraught with enormous psychological significance. Like Mrs. Skewton and Mrs. Clennam (with whom she is specifically linked by her attribute of a "light chair on wheels" that Pip pushes her in "round her own room"), Miss Havisham is a deathly Fortune who is more interested in wreaking revenge on men than in bestowing favors on them (*GE,* 88). Thus the "Fortune" she has to bequeath is the beautiful Estella, the surrogate daughter who represents her desirable aspect, but whose identity, in all its dangerousness, is apparent from the beginning. Appropriately, then, the early scenes of Pip's visits to Satis House are patently emblematic, revealing that this is the palace/prison of the two-faced goddess; and Estella's explanation of the house's name connects it with both of Fortune's aspects. She tells Pip on his first visit that "Satis" means "enough": "but it meant more than it said. It meant, when it was given, that whoever had this house, could want nothing else." Speaking as the desire she embodies, Estella adds, "They must have been easily satisfied in those days, I should think" (*GE,* 51). But the name also suggests the other side of Fortune by way of its closest English equivalent "sated," which describes the deathlike state that Miss Havisham has achieved by glutting herself on her own thwarted desire. Miss Havisham in her yellowed wedding dress is Dickens's most explicit representation of Fortune's desire/death duality, as Pip sees with his very own eyes: "I saw that everything within my view that ought to be white, had been white long ago, and had lost its lustre, and was faded and yellow. I saw that the bride within the bridal dress had withered like the dress, and like the flowers, and had no brightness left but the brightness of her sunken eyes. I saw that the dress had been put upon the rounded figure of a young woman, and the figure upon which it now hung loose, had shrunk to skin and bone" (*GE,* 53). Miss Havisham is "waxwork" and a "skeleton"; and her outfit—the "withered bridal dress" that "looked so like grave-clothes," and "the long veil so like a shroud"—is a grisly parody of Fortune's other, sexual aspect (*GE,* 55). Her injunction to Pip simply to "play, play, play!" underscores her role as Fortune incarnate, the goddess who enforces leisure and pleasure; and the card game he plays with Estella to entertain her (appropriately a game of "beggar my neighbor") is a graphic emblematic representation of Pip's being made a fool of by Fortune (*GE,* 54–55). Nevertheless, Miss Havisham's gentility—her fortune—is so attractive to Pip that he falls under her spell, and she transmogrifies in his imagination from witch to fairy godmother with very little effort on her part. As her name suggests, however, she is not a donor, but a sham: it is an illusion that anything of real value comes from her hand.

By contrast and in an interesting gender reversal, the real author of Pip's fortune proves to be a male Mag*witch*—a magician/witch given also to disguise, but neither a female goddess nor a godmother. Magwitch makes his money (clearly like Dickens) through the prosaic but ultimately more valuable means of hard work and self-sacrifice. As he tells Pip, "I lived rough, that you should live smooth; I worked hard that you should be above work" (*GE,* 304). Unfortunately, work does not make Magwitch genteel, which is the other quality, besides fortune, that Pip wants in a benefactor. That the source of Pip's fortune is not a woman and goddess is bad enough; that he turns out instead to be a "warmint," and a man of the lowest social caste, is even worse. Magwitch's pivotal role demonstrates that, although no goddess presides over the distribution of wealth in the novel, Fortune's wheel represents a frightening economic truth: for Pip to be "high," Magwitch (and legions like him) must be "low." And Magwitch's assurance to Pip, "I ain't a going to be low," is a reminder of his own painfully acute sense of this class distinction (*GE,* 314, 333). The "low," common criminal working for his gentleman in the land down under elevates Pip to high noon on Fortune's wheel, just as the mid-Victorian leisured class balanced itself on the backs and with the hands of the working class. Fortune is everything, and how one gets it evidently means nothing—as the apparently genteel and presumably charming Compeyson demonstrates. Even the kindly, domestic Wemmick shares this mercenary spirit, which he reveals through his regular advice to Pip, "Get hold of personal property"—an appropriate first principle for this Fortunatus-inspired novel (*GE,* 190). Indeed, through his personal experience of "The World Turned Upside Down" and his reenactment of the "The History of Fortunatus," Pip finally comes to understand that in the fully industrialized nineteenth-century world, "manly" and "gentlemanly" have ceased to be synonymous. The wheel of Fortune, now operating with accelerated motion, misplaces value, rewarding and punishing without regard to justice or merit. In so doing, Fortune emasculates all her minions, because the high and the low are equally subject to her power. Thus, in his snobbishness, Pip becomes an effeminate fop; Joe is emasculated in Pip's eyes by his lowly occupation as blacksmith and in Dickens's eyes by a termagant wife; and Pip's self-proclaimed "second father" so violates Pip's equation of the manly with the gentlemanly that Magwitch seems not only like an asexual being, but like one of another species.

On the other hand, even though women prove not to be the producers of fortune in a material sense, they in fact exercise total control over Pip's fortune in the novel. As Michael Cottsell says, *Great Expectations* can be defined as "a man's story of restless female characters."[10] Mrs. Joe has taken over household discipline, bringing Pip "up by jerks" and playing soldier to her husband's role as nurse in true WUD fashion (*GE,* 58). Like Goneril in *King Lear,* Mrs. Joe represents the woman who "must change arms at home, and give the distaff / Into my husband's hands," thereby perverting the presumably natural order of gender and domestic relationships.[11] Her ill temper and her violence terrorize both brother and husband; but Joe considers her "a master-mind" and is reluctant to educate himself on her account, for, as he tells Pip, she "would not be over partial to my being a scholar, for fear I might rise. Like a sort of rebel, don't you see?" (*GE,* 44). And we have seen how Miss Havisham exercises control by demanding and exploiting the servile attentions of Pip as well as the Pocket family, a situation parodied by Herbert's "highly ornamental, but perfectly helpless and useless" mother, who nevertheless controls the

Pocket household through her haughty disregard for order—a comic representation of Fortune in reduced circumstances (*GE,* 178).

But it is Estella who reigns as Pip's Fortune in *Great Expectations,* and Dickens's emphasis on her supreme attractiveness amounts to a frightening and poignant confession regarding his own desire for Fortune, even after learning the sordid truth about the deadly goddess. From the first Pip realizes that she is "very proud," "very pretty," and "very insulting," but this mixture of qualities inflames rather than repels him (*GE,* 56). Like Machiavelli's Fortune, her insolence and her combativeness are part of her charm. This is no Esther or Little Dorrit, but a young Mrs. Merdle, a Juno or Judith in the making. And just as Miss Havisham in her wedding clothes is immediately recognizable to Pip as a two-faced Fortune, so is Estella. In one of the novel's most compelling early scenes, when Pip retires to the yard at the end of his first visit to Satis House, Dickens brilliantly depicts her as a young witch who fascinates Pip by moving in and around the old (and appropriately designated) "brewery," walking on the casks and across the "rank garden." Like Miss Havisham she is a shape-shifter, here evidenced by her ability to appear and disappear, apparently, at will: "Estella was walking away from me even then. But she seemed to be everywhere. For when I yielded to the temptation presented by the casks, and began to walk on them, I saw *her* walking on them at the end of the yard of casks. She had her back towards me, and held her pretty brown hair spread out in her two hands, and never looked round, and passed out of my view directly." Dickens demonstrated in *Little Dorrit* how appealing this receding female figure could be; but here the hair as an emblematic detail is also a reminder of Occasion, and certainly of goddesshood. When Estella reappears in "the large paved lofty place" that was "the brewery itself," Pip tells us, "I saw her pass among the extinguished fires, and ascend some light iron stairs, and go out by a gallery high overhead, as if she were going out into the sky." This beautiful vision registers Estella's transcendence as the "star" of Pip's desiring but may also be reminiscent of the Dedlock ghost, for the next vision that Pip has is a frightening, hallucinatory one of a "figure hanging . . . by the neck" whose "face was Miss Havisham's, with a movement going over the whole countenance as if she were trying to call to me" (*GE,* 58–59). This conclusion to Pip's visions is a horrific reminder that Estella is, if not in body, at least in spirit, Miss Havisham; and the fact that it is Pip who puts these images together—calling up the "fancy" as a response to the reality—indicates that he already intuits the danger that Estella poses. Dickens's way of bringing together Pip's two points of view about the "brewery" females symbolizes more dramatically than anywhere else in his fiction the duplicity of Fortune and her ability to spellbind her subjects.

Thus Estella—whose real mother is a murderess and whose surrogate mother is a man-hater—becomes the sexy woman operating the cosmic emotional wheel that subjugates Pip in the present and around whom he spins a dreamy future, even though, as she acknowledges and he realizes, she has "no heart" (*GE,* 224). On two occasions Pip points out that she takes "delight" in other people's pain, inviting Pip to kiss her as a reward, presumably, after he bloodies the pale young gentleman. And Pip's way of describing this kiss further associates Estella with Fortune: "I think I would have gone through a great deal to kiss her cheek. But I felt that the kiss was given to the coarse common boy as a piece of money might have been, and that it was worth nothing" (*GE,* 86). Moreover, the attention Dickens gives to her hands as she knits, which suggests her connection to Madame Defarge, indicates that Estella is surely the most fatal of all Dickens's femmes fatales; yet Pip, even though he realizes that his passion for her is "against reason, against promise, against peace, against hope, against happiness, against all discouragement that could be," nevertheless finds her "irresistible" (*GE,* 219). This tyrannical control over Pip's imagination and emotions is proof that Estella is the victor in their battle of the sexes, for, like Machiavelli's Fortune, she is a ruthless goddess who must be cuffed and mauled to be won by a lover. In a sinister inversion of the chapbook fantasy, Estella is not to be won (or, if won, belatedly) by Pip as Fortunatus, but by Bentley Drummle, born gentleman and Machiavellian prince, who knows how to manhandle Pip's goddess. Drummle maintains his position of ascendancy by subjugating Fortune herself.

Reluctantly, both Dickens and Pip demonstrate that the *gentle* man of *Great Expectations* is Joe Gargery, who always defers to women and remains at the bottom of Fortune's wheel, working away. Like Boethius, Joe accepts with philosophy a position that Pip (and, perforce, even Dickens) can evaluate only in terms of fortune. This valuation reflects the not quite tacit belief of the industrialized Victorian world that male power derives most clearly from capital, rather than physical strength—that masculinity is indeed a function of control over one's fortune. Joe's gentle nature, humility, poverty, and innocence temper his masculinity and render his massive strength of character and body unmanly; and this most unsettling inversion of gender and value relations is the tragic reality underlying the topsy-turvy comedy of *Great Expectations.* In Havelock Ellis's terms describing what has happened in Pip's and Dickens's time, industrial civilization has made the world more "womanly," while men have become less "manly."[12]

Joe is the novel's embodiment of virtue—in its dual meaning of strength and goodness; but he is clearly not the role model for the nineteenth-century hero, as the novel has generically defined him. Joe's indifference to Fortune renders him uninteresting as the focus for readers more worldly than he: he is as foolish as he is wise, in Dickens's terms, and he is humiliating to Pip. In the gender reversal of the novel, Joe ultimately stands for the goodness and artlessness at the center of hearth and home that Dickens had habitually assigned (after Pickwick and Sam) to female characters like Florence Dombey, Agnes Wickfield, Esther Summerson, Sissy Jupe, and Little Dorrit. This central, eternally *female* virtue that Joe represents had always been at the heart of Dickens's novels; but in *Great Expectations,* virtue—rather emphatically—undergoes a change of sex. There is no attempt to domesticate Fortune here, as there had been in *Bleak House* and *Little Dorrit:* Dickens's sweet, innocent Fortune appears only in the peripheral, down-at-heel Biddy, who has almost none of Esther's or even Little Dorrit's physical attractiveness. With Estella, we are back to an image of sexy Fortune more like Edith Dombey or, marginally, Lady Dedlock. Thus the theme, seriously explored in *Little Dorrit,* of a world governed by women is parodied rather bitterly as the dream of a Little Dorrit vanishes for good. The era of men's time is over and women have gained full control in both the public and private spheres.

Perhaps not coincidentally, when, at the urging of Bulwer-Lytton, Dickens decided to rewrite the conclusion of *Great Expectations* to suggest a happy ending for Pip and Estella, he referred to this re-visioning as his "hav[ing] resumed the wheel and taken another turn at it"—a sign of his own acknowledged imprisonment to Fortune and resignation to the fact that the goddess's wheel had come full circle.[13]

Feminine Endings

My purpose in this book has been to show how the image of Fortune's wheel accrues tragic significance over the course of Dickens's career until it becomes the controlling vision of his mature novels. Dickens had no illusions about the fact that Fortune was a fickle, dangerous, two-faced deity, but it was impossible for him to resist her power—as his last years demonstrated. Giving himself over to mistress worship on the one hand and public performances for financial gain on the other, Dickens proved that he had become, to use Silas Wegg's favorite phrase, "the minion of fortune and worm of the hour"; but, unlike Mr. Boffin, to whom Wegg refers (and unlike Little Dorrit, earlier), Dickens was not "unspoiled by Fortune" (*OMF,* 96). Nevertheless, his personal receptivity to the icon's rich implications served his art well. Dickens's Fortune is as multiform as Machiavelli's, but in all her incarnations—whether feral or domesticated, great or small, old or young, beautiful or horrific—she embodies the grandeur and the terror of a female deity who reigns supreme in the eyes of her worshipper.

It is yet another sign of Dickens's sensitivity to cultural currents that his use of Fortune's wheel both partakes of and anticipates the preoccupation with fatal women in the guise of classical subjects that marks the latter third of the nineteenth century. This interest surfaces everywhere, but certainly the Pre-Raphaelites were leaders in the visual representation of formidable females drawn from the classical tradition to serve as prototypes for the assertive New Woman of the period; the Pre-Raphaelite influence is especially apparent in the work of artists and illustrators who designed for William Morris's Kelmscott Press. For example, Walter Crane, whose illustrations appeared everywhere during the last two decades of the century, designed a bold Fortuna framed by spindles, suggesting the goddess's association with the Fates, as a tailpiece for "The Three Spinsters," among his illustrations for *Grimm's Fairy Tales.*[14] But particularly relevant to Dickens's motif is Edward Burne-Jones's *Wheel of Fortune* (plate 30), since the painting communicates Dickens's final vision regarding gender relations, fate, and time. Conceived in 1871, begun in 1877, and completed in 1883, this painting, of which there are several versions, became an obsession with the artist, who commented in a letter of 1893, "my Fortune's Wheel is a true image, and we take our turn at it, and are broken upon it." Like Estella, Burne-Jones's Fortune is a young, beautiful, apparently "indifferent" goddess;[15] she wears a shroudlike gown that calls attention to her breasts and shapely figure while turning what looks like a huge industrial wheel. She has no blindfold, but her eyes are cast down, qualifying her as one of many "sightless seers" so prevalent in art of the Decadence; her trancelike state suggests femme-fatale status, an erotic nature, and overdetermination as sensual and treacherous Eternal Woman.[16] The three athletic, nude young men in head-to-foot contact on the wheel's waning side are gorgeous physical specimens, but they are half Fortune's size, eerily calling attention to the goddess's "monumental" quality, to use Joseph Kestner's and Julia Kristeva's term.[17] The three, in descending order a slave in fetters, a king with crown and scepter, and a poet wearing a laurel wreath, represent the range of male power relations as ultimately subsumed by the categorically different but unquestionably greater and explicitly deific power of the female. A. P. de Mirimonde's description of the men communicates their desperate condition and its meaning: "They have ceased struggling and, conquered by Destiny, they have resigned themselves to their ultimate defeat. . . . Such are the reflections of a great artist at the end of the nineteenth century in the face of a world and of values whose decline is approaching."[18] It is no doubt coincidental, but nevertheless striking, that Burne-Jones's painting is fearfully symmetrical to the Rochester wheel of Fortune: it portrays the same number of figures and employs the same scale, with Fortune twice as large as the men, but differs most saliently in its orientation toward Fortune's tragic right side. Taken together the two images offer a complete narrative of the rise and fall of Victorian fortunes from the 1840s to the 1880s—a trajectory that is mirrored in Dickens's own career and novelistic vision.

A less sublime image of Fortune—but one equally relevant to Dickens's vision—is that of the queen at her spinning wheel, which, according to Adrienne Munich, became "Victoria's particular Scottish attribute." Victoria (who, as Munich says, "came into the world as already an allegory"), learned to spin at Balmoral as part of the royal effort to embrace Highland culture—"royal tartanitis," as it was called by Ivor Brown. She was evidently pleased to be pictured spinning flax, a pleasure attested to by several reproductions, including one woodcut of a domestic scene with Victoria spinning while listening to her chaplain, Norman MacLeod, read Robert Burns's poetry. In this scene Victoria holds the thread like the reins of state; and, seated with her head down and flanked by men, she is an emblem of virtuous domesticity minding the wheel of humble household industry—"a kind of guardian angel."[19] Late in the century there was a spinning wheel named the "Lady Victoria" marketed by the Scottish firm of Hugh McMaster; and in the 1870s, a photograph of the queen spinning appears as an advertisement for the Belfast-based manufacturer James McCreery and Son (plate 31).[20] The trancelike expression on the elderly queen's face in the McCreery's trade-card photograph helps to convey an impression less of virtue and industry and more of a formidable Fate who twists the thread of empire, the widowed sovereign with a deadly power over all within her sway. The flax on the distaff (or "mother-of-all," as it is provocatively called) is like an effigy of the queen herself, suggesting that this late imperial spinning necessitates the unraveling of her former virtuously maternal and humbly domestic image. Munich's assessment of the iconographic implications of Victoria spinning certainly applies to this photograph, for the activity of spinning communicates a mixed and ultimately threatening message. As Munich says, "Such an image complicates Victoria's self-representation. As a simple spinner of yarn, the fundamental stuff of human bodily covering, she could be seen as the faithful Penelope (the subject of a statue she bought for Albert), but she could also be seen as the spider, who, when Albert died, she was said to resemble. Like the spider, her appetites killed her mate, and when he was dead, so the story went, she turned to a more authentic and hardy Highlander, John Brown."[21] Victoria as royal cloth maker is the Wife of Bath's dream come true: the woman with sovereignty not just over a husband and (alleged) lover, but over the body politic as represented by this latter, powerfully masculine figure.

The Brown affair also precipitated another, frankly derisive association of Victoria with wheels that is reminiscent of Dickens's characterizations of

Mrs. Skewton, Mrs. Clennam, and Miss Havisham, as well as Phiz's Bath-chaired Britannias on the cover wrappers of *Little Dorrit* and *Our Mutual Friend.* Munich discusses Daniel Joseph Kirwan's satirical *Palace and Hovel* (1870), which includes a cartoon entitled "John Brown Exercising the Queen," featuring the vigorous Highlander pushing a dozing (and perhaps drunk) Victoria in a perambulator (plate 32).[22] This image of Victoria indulging herself in a second infancy while Brown mans her wheel has larger gender implications than simply suggesting the couple's erotic relations: like Dickens's imagery surrounding Mrs. Skewton and her manservant, Withers, it illustrates woman's power to cast a spell over a presumably masculine time to create and control its revolutions—a power coincident with (and represented by) her manipulation of masculine desire. Brown's propelling the queen diagonally toward the lower-left corner of the illustration in a buggy that looks like a coffin creates an image of "a 'turning backward' or returning of time," to quote Philippa Berry in *Shakespeare's Feminine Endings,* "inflected as feminine."[23] As in several of Shakespeare's tragedies and Dickens's mature novels, the tragic hero here is feminized; Brown not only is emasculated in his role as nanny, but is "exercising" himself toward his own end, not the queen's. Thus Victoria becomes horrific Fortune, the eternal female capable of endless recurrence, whose survival of husband, lover, ministers, and advisors "ignited fantasies about the fatal woman's destructive power."[24] Victoria would even survive her own century, making this cartoon an appropriate final commentary on the image of Fortune's wheel in Victorian England, one that acknowledges the replacement of a linear-progressive, historical, and masculine model of time with a cyclical and feminine one. Behind the humor of the illustration lies the "tragic discovery" of circularity revealed to Edmund at the conclusion of *King Lear* and to Cassius at the conclusion of *Julius Caesar:* that "the linear and lineal time of the king or *pater familias*" has been overturned by "the spectre of a perpetual mutability in nature as well as in history."[25] Victoria is Fortune once again habited as a queen whose pleasures—however capricious or ridiculous—dictate the turns and returns of time's whirling wheel.

In "Acting, Reading, Fortune's Wheel: *Sister Carrie* and the Life History of Objects," Philip Fisher brilliantly demonstrates how Theodore Dreiser adapts the image of Fortune's wheel to the novel's "Naturalist plot of decline," which, he argues, focuses on "the realm of energy rather than value." Fisher explains that, because writers like Dreiser, Hardy, and Zola subscribe to the Darwinian narrative "of struggle, survival, extinction," the rise and fall graphed by the Naturalist plot is biological rather than social: it is really a tragic "history of the body and not that of social position." In other words, the inevitable fall of the protagonist from fortune to ruin has little to do with morality or even with class: it is the tragic cycle of human life as it moves through a world of suffering toward its own decay and death, which is written into the existence of every living being. In *Sister Carrie,* for example, we "see and comprehend the rise of Carrie by means of the fall of Hurstwood," but just as they are connected really as a matter of chance, so their position on the wheel with reference to each other is determined not by their relative worth as defined by some larger ethical code, but by age, or "energy"—as Fisher says, by Carrie's "not-yet" pitted against Hurstwood's "has-been."[26]

This assessment of the Naturalist plot articulates the reordering of tragedy that takes place from Elizabethan times to the late nineteenth century; and it does so in a way that helps to locate Dickens's pivotal role in effecting this change. If, as Northrup Frye argues in *Fools of Time,* Shakespearean tragedy reveals "the impact of heroic energy on the human condition, the wheel of fortune creaking against the greater wheel of nature,"[27] then Naturalist tragedy intensifies this struggle by conflating the two wheels, thereby completing the movement toward convergence that is recorded in Dickens's novels over his career. At the outset, the reversals of the over-the-hill, but ageless, Pickwick are wholly those of Fortune, rather than Nature, because Pickwick lives in what might be called the providential present, a comic realm in which Fortune will ultimately be as "kind" as Nature is benevolent and generous. David Copperfield is born to this realm, but, because his story is Dickens's own, his rise begins the trajectory of the Naturalist narrative, which is completed by Clennam's "plot of decline" in *Little Dorrit.* When Clennam is temporarily able to reverse the wheel through the magically rejuvenating power of love, the Elizabethan and Naturalist Wheels—the wheels of Fortune and Nature—achieve a moment of harmonic synchronization, but the equipoise that Arthur and Amy find together does not erase the fact that they are headed "down" at the novel's conclusion. Dickens's vision therefore enlarges the wheel of Fortune to its full tragic potential as the "greater wheel of nature": as the monumental wheel of cyclical time, the single "whirling wheel of life." George Eliot's celebrated web, which serves as the controlling image of *Middlemarch,* seems to propose a less tragic novelistic vision by focusing on a network of entangled human lives at a single historical moment; but the web shares the wheel's associations with fatality, destiny, and spinning, thereby suggesting a particularized, inside view rather than a negation of Dickens's—and Naturalism's—larger vision.

The Naturalists' shock at the truth represented by Fortune's wheel, at recognizing themselves in a world whirling with technology and commerce—but not in any individually realizable sense "moving forward," except to the grave—finds its most dramatic objective correlative in the Ferris wheel, which amuses by translating, according to Fisher, "the pleasure of rising and the fear of falling into one repeatable smooth motion." Invented for the Chicago World's Fair of 1893, the Ferris wheel quickly became "the central identifying symbol—like a cathedral spire seen at a distance marking a medieval town—of the presence of a carnival or fair." In contrast to the spire—or the Eiffel Tower, which had performed a similar symbolic function at the Paris World's Fair just four years earlier, in 1889—the Ferris wheel replaces linearity with the "economical circle" that so aptly symbolizes a modern apprehension of death and desire, fortune and time.[28] And so, with the Naturalists, Fortune's wheel returns once again to a prominent place in the landscape of the twentieth century. The latest and most spectacular incarnation is British Airway's London Eye, towering 450 feet above the Thames as the world's "highest observation wheel," which "represents the turning of time," according to the ads on British Airways' Web site. Neither Hogarth nor Dickens would have been surprised.

NOTES

Introduction

1. R. A. Buchanan, *The Power of the Machine* (London: Penguin, 1992), 46–47; Donald Cardwell, *The Norton History of Technology* (New York: W. W. Norton, 1995), 49, 212.

2. Thomas Carlyle, *Past and Present,* ed. A. M. D. Hughes (Oxford: Clarendon, 1918), 169–76.

3. For excellent discussions of Watt's specific contributions to steam technology see R. A. Buchanan, *The Power of the Machine,* 53–59; and Ian McNeil, ed., *An Encyclopaedia of the History of Technology* (London: Routledge, 1990), 275–77.

4. William Blake, *Complete Writings* (London: Oxford Paperbacks, 1969), 337.

5. McNeil, *Encyclopaedia,* 558–65.

6. Gustave Doré and Blanchard Jerrold, *London: A Pilgrimage* (London: Grant, 1872), 118.

7. John Francis, *The History of the English Railway: Its Social Relations and Revelations 1820–1845,* 2 vols. (1851; reprint, New York: Augustus M. Kelley, 1968), 2:139, 147.

8. C. H. Gibbs-Smith, *The Great Exhibition of 1851: A Commemorative Album* (London: Her Majesty's Stationery Office, 1950), 26.

9. Numerous examples of the wheeled conveyances displayed at the exhibition are pictured in *The Crystal Palace Exhibition Illustrated Catalogue* originally published by the Art-Journal (1851; reprint, New York: Dover, 1970); in Eric de Maré, *London 1851: The Year of the Great Exhibition* (London: Folio Society, 1972), figs. 33–34, 44–49, and 92; and Gibbs-Smith, *The Great Exhibition of 1851,* 78–83, figs. 58–64, 70–74.

10. Adam Smith, *An Inquiry into the Nature and Causes of the Wealth of Nations,* ed. Edwin Cannan (New York: Modern Library, 1937), 273–74; Friedrich Engels, *The Condition of the Working Class in England,* trans. and ed. W. O. Henderson and W. H. Chaloner (Oxford: Basil Blackwell, 1958), 97, 96, 102, 97.

11. E. P. Thompson, *The Making of the English Working Class* (New York: Penguin, 1968), 487.

12. The Folger Shakespeare Library Exhibition held in 2000 celebrated the importance of Fortune in the Renaissance. The accompanying volume, *Fortune: "All Is But Fortune,"* edited by Leslie Thomson (Washington, D.C.: Folger Shakespeare Library, 2000), provides a wealth of information and images on the subject, including excellent essays by Renaissance scholars. My thanks to Heidi Brayman Hackel for alerting me to this volume.

13. This is Keith Thomas's argument about the Puritans' denigration of Fortune in *Religion and the Decline of Magic* (New York: Oxford University Press, 1971), 78–89.

14. Stephen Wall, "Dickens's Plot of Fortune," *Review of English Literature* 6 (1965): 56.

15. John Ashton, *Chap-Books of the Eighteenth Century* (London: Chatto & Windus, 1882), 124–37.

16. Jerome Buckley, *The Triumph of Time* (Cambridge: Harvard University Press, Belknap Press, 1966), 34–42.

17. R. Rupert Roopnaraine, "Time and the Circle in *Little Dorrit,*" *Dickens Studies Annual* 3 (1974): 55.

18. In addition to Buckley's groundbreaking *The Triumph of Time,* which discusses the Victorians' temporal obsession at length, a host of studies on Dickens and time have been published. Three that consider sacred or metaphysical time in ways that are germane to this study are Robert L. Patten, "Dickens Time and Again," *Dickens Studies Annual* 2 (1972): 163–96; Stephen L. Franklin, "Dickens and Time: The Clock without Hands," *Dickens Studies Annual* 4 (1975): 1–35; and Patrick J. Creevy, "In Time and Out: The Tempo of Life in *Bleak House,*" *Dickens Studies Annual* 12 (1983): 63–80.

19. Julia Kristeva, "Women's Time," trans. Alice Jardine and Harry Blake, in *The Kristeva Reader,* ed. Toril Moi (New York: Columbia University Press, 1986), 190–93.

20. G. R. Owst, *Literature and Pulpit in Medieval England* (Oxford: Basil Blackwood, 1966), 238–39.

21. Kristeva, "Women's Time," 193.

Chapter 1

1. Michael Steig, *Dickens and Phiz* (Bloomington: Indiana University Press, 1978), 40.

2. Ibid.

3. Howard R. Patch, *The Goddess Fortuna in Mediaeval Literature* (New York: Octagon, 1974), 3.

4. Stephen Wall, "Dickens's Plot of Fortune," *Review of English Literature* 6 (1965): 56–67.

5. W. J. T. Mitchell, *Iconology: Image, Text, Ideology* (Chicago: University of Chicago Press, 1986), 2.

6. Erwin Panofsky, *Studies in Iconology: Humanistic Themes in the Art of the Renaissance* (1939; reprint, New York: Harper & Row, 1967), 70–71, 81.

7. Samuel C. Chew explicitly comments on and implies this conflation of Fortune and Time throughout his magnificent study of Renaissance iconography, *The Pilgrimage of Life* (New Haven: Yale University Press, 1962), 26.

8. Kristeva, "Women's Time," 193.

9. Havelock Ellis, *Man and Woman* (1894; reprint, Boston: Houghton Mifflin, 1929), 476–77.

10. How this female authority comes into its own in the novel is brilliantly developed in Nancy Armstrong's *Desire and Domestic Fiction: A Political History of the Novel* (New York: Oxford University Press, 1987).

11. Jerome H. Buckley, ed., *The Worlds of Victorian Fiction* (Cambridge: Harvard University Press, 1975), vi.

12. J. Hillis Miller, *Charles Dickens: The World of His Novels* (Cambridge: Harvard University Press, 1959), xv.

13. The daunting task faced by Dickens of representing the city, especially as it appears in

Nicholas Nickleby, has been the focus of two provocative discussions. See David Trotter, *Circulation: Defoe, Dickens, and the Economies of the Novel* (London: Macmillan, 1988), 85–89; and Richard L. Stein, "Street Figures: Victorian Urban Iconography," in *Victorian Literature and the Victorian Visual Imagination,* ed. Carol T. Christ and John O. Jordan (Berkeley and Los Angeles: University of California Press, 1995), 236–40.

14. Joseph Kestner, *Mythology and Misogyny: The Social Discourse of Nineteenth-Century British Classical-Subject Painting* (Madison: University of Wisconsin Press, 1989), 106, 133.

15. Alexander Welsh, *The City of Dickens* (1971; reprint, Cambridge: Harvard University Press, 1986), v.

16. J. Hillis Miller, *Illustration* (Cambridge: Harvard University Press, 1992), 104.

17. Steven Marcus, *Dickens from Pickwick to Dombey* (New York: Norton, 1965), 39.

18. Steig records that the odd creatures themselves represent "will-o'-the-wisps" or (using George Cruikshank's term) "Jack-o'-Lanterns," which "had for him the specific meaning of the temptation of riches leading one astray into a swamp of materialism" (*Dickens and Phiz,* 41).

19. Chew, *The Pilgrimage of Life,* xxiii.

20. Ronald Paulson describes Hogarth's "progresses" (such as the Harlot's and the Rake's) as "not simply linear but layered"—and as "spiritual allegories *manqué.*" *Popular and Polite Art in the Age of Hogarth and Fielding* (Notre Dame: University of Notre Dame Press, 1977), 118.

21. Chew discusses several examples of this familiar Renaissance topos that indicate the path by way of a raised bridge or staircase (*The Pilgrimage of Life,* 147–48 and figs. 101–4).

22. Rosemary Woolf, *The English Religious Lyric in the Middle Ages* (Oxford: Clarendon, 1968), 334; and Panofsky, "Father Time," in *Studies in Iconology,* 69–93.

23. E. H. Gombrich, *Symbolic Images* (London: Phaidon, 1972), 183.

24. It is not surprising that Thackeray would be the other major Victorian novelist to participate in the continuation of the iconographical tradition of Fortune, since, as Steig notes, Dickens and Thackeray "shared certain artistic traditions" (*Dickens and Phiz,* 4). They were not only familiar with the emblematic tradition, but used similar methods of representation that drew heavily on this method of visualization.

25. For a discussion of the providential elements in Victorian literature, see Catherine Gallagher, *The Industrial Revolution of English Fiction, 1832–1867* (Chicago: University of Chicago Press, 1985), 36–61; Thomas Vargish, *The Providential Aesthetic in Victorian Fiction* (Charlottesville: University of Virginia Press, 1985); and Buckley, *The Triumph of Time,* 34–52. Welsh, in *The City of Dickens,* describes Dickens's fiction as having a "quasi-providential design" (213).

26. For example, Vargish notes the intrinsic connection of providence with linear time (*Providential Aesthetic,* 31).

27. Buckley, *The Triumph of Time,* 36 and 162 n.

28. Loren Eiseley, *Darwin's Century* (Garden City, N.Y.: Doubleday Anchor, 1961), 332.

29. Eiseley, *Darwin's Century,* 332; Mircea Eliade, *Cosmos and History: The Myth of the Eternal Return* (New York: Harper Torchbooks, 1959), 144.

30. Kristeva, "Women's Time," 191–93.

31. Quoted in C. H. Gibbs-Smith, *The Great Exhibition of 1851,* 26.

32. V. S. Pritchett, *The Living Novel and Later Appreciations* (New York: Random House, 1964), 142.

33. Henry Mayhew, *London Labour and the London Poor,* 4 vols. (1861–62; reprint, New York: Dover, 1968), 1:213–323. More recent accounts of Victorian cheap street literature include Ashton, *Chap-Books;* Percy Muir, *Victorian Illustrated Books* (New York: Praeger, 1971), 1–24; Robert Collison, *The Story of Street Literature: Forerunner of the Popular Press* (Santa Barbara,

Calif.: American Bibliographical Center, Clio Press, 1973); and Leslie Shepard, *The History of Street Literature* (Detroit: Singing Tree, 1973).

34. See Christopher Hill, *The World Turned Upside Down: Radical Ideas during the English Revolution* (Harmondsworth, England: Penguin, 1972); Ashton, *Chap-Books,* 265.

35. Thomas Hardy, *Tess of the d'Urbervilles* (Harmondsworth, England: Penguin, 1978), chap. 3, 60–61.

36. Cf. Fredric Jameson, *The Political Unconscious* (Ithaca, N.Y.: Cornell University Press, 1981), 84–86.

37. Charles Dickens, "A Preliminary Word," *Household Words* 1 (30 March 1850): 2.

38. Quotations from Dickens's novels, cited with title abbreviations and page numbers, as given here, refer to the Oxford Illustrated Dickens series.

39. V. Propp, in *Morphology of the Folktale,* discusses the pivotal role in folktales of the "donor," who tests the hero and finally provides some magical agent or helper that is instrumental in the hero's ability to overcome misfortune (trans. Lawrence Scott [Austin: University of Texas Press, 1968], 39–40). In Dickens's formulation here, the donor and the gift are one and the same.

40. Many critics have commented on Agnes's providential role in the novel, notably Welsh, *The City of Dickens,* 180–82; and Miller, *Charles Dickens,* 156–59.

41. Jean Seznec, *The Survival of the Pagan Gods: The Mythological Tradition and Its Place in Renaissance Humanism and Art,* trans. Barbara F. Sessions (Princeton, N.J.: Princeton University Press, 1981), 4, 86.

42. St. Augustine, *City of God,* trans. and ed. Marcus Dods (New York: Hafner, 1948), 1:155–56.

43. Patch, *Goddess Fortuna,* 3–4, 12.

44. Boethius, *The Consolation of Philosophy,* bk. 2:24.

45. Ibid., bk. 2:40; bk. 4:91–92, 97–98, 99; bk. 2:22.

46. My argument in this section is informed by Richard Green's introduction to Boethius, *The Consolation of Philosophy;* and Frederick Kiefer, *Fortune and Elizabethan Tragedy* (Huntington Library, 1983), 1–9.

47. Patch, *Goddess Fortuna,* 60, 164.

48. Chew, *The Pilgrimage of Life,* xxiii.

49. Dante, *The Divine Comedy,* trans. Henry F. Cary (New York: Thomas Crowell, 1897), canto 7, lines 73–87.

50. Ibid., canto 7, lines 87–90, 97–99.

51. Patch, *Goddess Fortuna,* 148–50, 176–77.

52. Dante, *The Divine Comedy,* canto 15, line 96.

53. The earliest tarot cards still extant date from 1392 and were made in Italy. Conservative theorists argue that the cards were invented by combining a deck of Spanish playing cards with images taken from a pictorial encyclopedia used for teaching children. The Wheel of Fortune is one of the twenty-two additional picture cards called the "Major Arcana." Hans Biedermann, *Dictionary of Symbolism: Cultural Icons and the Meanings behind Them,* trans. William Hulbert (New York: Meridian, 1994), 337, s.v. "tarot." See also David Fontana, *The Secret Language of Symbols* (New York: Chronicle, 1994), 168–79; and J. E. Cirlot, *A Dictionary of Symbols,* trans. Jack Sage (New York: Barnes & Noble, 1993), 328–30, s.v. "tarot."

54. This summary draws from the discussions of Fortune's history in Patch, *Goddess Fortuna,* 16–24; and Kiefer's *Fortune and Elizabethan Tragedy,* chap. 1, "Pagan Fortune in a Christian World."

55. Matthew Arnold, *Culture and Anarchy* (New York: Macmillan, 1911), sec. 4, "Hebraism and Hellenism."

56. Ernst Cassirer, *The Myth of the State* (New Haven and London: Yale University Press, 1967), 156–57.

57. Machiavelli, *The Prince,* in *The Chief Works and Others,* trans. Allan Gilbert (Durham, N.C.: Duke University Press, 1965), 1:89–90.

58. Cassirer, *The Myth of the State,* 160. Tyche, goddess of chance, was the Greek equivalent of Fortune.

59. Machiavelli, *The Prince,* 1:91, 92.

60. Machiavelli, *Tercets on Fortune,* in *The Chief Works and Others,* 2:745–46.

61. Ibid., 2:746–48.

62. Ibid., 2:746.

63. Hanna F. Pitkin, *Fortune Is a Woman* (Berkeley and Los Angeles: University of California Press, 1984), 110, 120, 147. Machiavelli, *Tercets on Fortune,* lines 78–79.

64. Machiavelli, *Tercets on Fortune,* 109–10.

65. Francis Bacon, *The Essayes or Counsels, Civill and Morall, 1625,* in *A Selection of His Works,* ed. Sidney Warhaft (New York: Odyssey, 1965), 149–50.

66. Kiefer, *Fortune and Elizabethan Tragedy,* 335, 339 n.

67. Ibid., 193–231.

68. Barbara Bartholomew, *Fortuna and Natura: A Reading of Three Chaucer Narratives* (London: Mouton, 1966), 12.

69. *As You Like It,* in *The Complete Pelican Shakespeare* (New York: Viking, 1969), 1.2.39–40. Northrup Frye argues that this opposition of nature and fortune defines the structure of Elizabethan tragedy: "The organizing conceptions of Elizabethan tragedy are the order of nature and the wheel of fortune. . . . The order of nature provides the *data* of the human situation, the conditions man accepts by getting born. The wheel of fortune supplies the *facta,* what he contributes by his own energy and will." *Fools of Time: Studies in Shakespearian Tragedy* (Toronto: University of Toronto Press, 1967), 13.

70. *Hamlet,* in *The Complete Pelican Shakespeare,* 2.5.10–11.

71. Kiefer, *Fortune and Elizabethan Tragedy,* 261.

72. *Hamlet,* 2.2.226–33.

73. Henry Green, *Shakespeare and the Emblem Writers* (1870; reprint, New York: Burt Franklin, n.d.), vii. Mario Praz, in the pioneer work on emblem literature, *Studies in Seventeenth-Century Imagery* (1939; reprint, Rome: Edizioni di Storia e Letteratura, 1964), claims that Green's ignorance of the extent to which the emblem books were merely repositories of (essentially) literary images turned into pictures "invalidates all his conclusions" (207).

74. Rosemary Freeman, *English Emblem Books* (1948; reprint, New York: Octagon, 1966), 9.

75. Charles Moseley, *A Century of Emblems* (Hants, England: Scolar, 1989).

76. Freeman, in *English Emblem Books,* differentiates between the emblematic image, which works by a series of arbitrary equations, and the truly poetic image, which works by identification of an intrinsic or essential connection between the image and its significance (27). Praz, in *Studies in Seventeenth-Century Imagery,* considers this distinction to be Freeman's major contribution to emblem studies (157 n).

77. *Henry the Fifth,* in *The Complete Pelican Shakespeare,* 3.6.29–37. Henry Green notes the similarity between Fluellen's description and the image of Fortune in Corrozet's *Hecatomgraphie,* published in 1540 (*Shakespeare and the Emblem Writers,* 262–63).

78. Freeman, *English Emblem Books,* 1, 207.

79. Steig notes that the success of the Dickens/Browne collaboration results in part from the fact that both were strongly influenced by the emblematic tradition: "Dickens' use of imagery is often analogous to Browne's use of emblematic details, whereby perceptions of the sometimes daunting and sometimes comical circumstances of human existence may be expressed in condensed allusions—not reduced to them, but signposted, as it were, in a form reminiscent of the poem-plus-picture of the emblem book" (*Dickens and Phiz,* 4).

80. Erwin Panofsky, *Meaning in the Visual Arts* (Garden City, N.Y.: Doubleday Anchor, 1955), 159. Panofsky contrasts the Renaissance emblem books' desire to obfuscate with the opposite impulse in works of the Middle Ages: "mediaeval pictorialization had tried to simplify the complex and to clarify the difficult" (159).

81. Moseley, *A Century of Emblems,* 2.

82. Geffrey Whitney, *A Choice of Emblems* (1586; reprint, ed. Henry Green, 1866; reissued with an introduction by Frank B. Fieler, New York: Benjamin Blom, 1967), 181.

83. See J. E. Matzke, "Source of 'To Take Time by the Forelock,'" Modern Language Association, *Publications* 8, 303ff; referred to by Patch, *Goddess Fortuna,* 116, n. 1. Panofsky also discusses the fusion of the Greek "kairos" (meaning "opportunity") with Fortune and Occasion, and the change of gender from the masculine "kairos" to the Latin feminine forms "occasio" and "fortuna" (*Studies in Iconology,* 72, n. 5).

84. See Moseley, *A Century of Emblems,* for a reproduction of Alciati's "Occasion" (46, no. 2). Alciati's Occasion is also nude, with a razor (or perhaps a cornucopia) in her hand, a scarf, and the forward locks. The accompanying verse uses the same question-and-answer format, and the opening query suggests, like Whitney's verse, that this particular image originates with Lysippus: [in Latin] "is this a work of Lysippus, whose home was Sicyon?" Moseley explains that Lysippus was a "prolific sculptor" who was thought by Pliny to be a contemporary of Alexander the Great. Although there is no wheel in the illustration, the verse's imagery does admit the possibility of one. Moseley translates the fourth line of the verse from the Latin as "I am constantly whirled about like a wheel" (42).

85. Gilbert notes that Machiavelli himself conflates Fortune with Occasion in his poem "On Occasion" (*Machiavelli, The Chief Works,* n. 747).

86. Ronald Paulson, *Emblem and Expression* (Cambridge: Harvard University Press, 1975), 14–15.

87. Edward A. Maser, ed., *Cesare Ripa's Baroque and Rococo Pictorial Imagery* (New York: Dover, 1971), xx–xi, xix.

88. Ibid. (excerpted from 1603 edition of Ripa's *Iconologia,* 169), 152.

89. Ibid.

90. My discussion is informed by Panofsky's explanation of the conflation of the Greek Chronos (Time) with the Roman Kronos (Saturn), which resulted in the aged figure of Father Time with his sickle or hourglass (*Studies in Iconology,* 72–82).

91. Barry V. Qualls, *The Secular Pilgrims of Victorian Fiction* (Cambridge: Cambridge University Press, 1982), 85–138.

92. Freeman, *English Emblem Books,* 118–21; Moseley, *A Century of Emblems,* 19.

93. Selected plates from Quarles's *Emblems* and excellent discussions of his work appear in Moseley, *A Century of Emblems,* 254–93; and Freeman, *English Emblem Books,* 114–47. Ironically, Quarles's devout Protestantism did not stop him from drawing from Roman Catholic sources. Gordon Haight identified "The Sources of Quarles's 'Emblems'" (*The Library* 16 [1936]: 188–209) as the Jesuit devotionals *Pia Desiderata,* of Herman Hugo (Antwerp, 1624), and the *Typus Mundi* (Antwerp, 1627). According to Freeman (117 n), Praz identified these sources independently of Haight, in *Studies in Seventeenth-Century Imagery.*

94. Cf. Praz, *Studies in Seventeenth-Century Imagery,* 135. Praz provides a penetrating analysis of Quarles and his Catholic models (83–203), and ends his chapter on "Profane and Sacred Love" with a discussion of a Victorian imitation of Quarles, Johann Abricht's *Divine Emblems embellished on copper, after the fashion of Master Francis Quarles,* which was illustrated by Robert Cruikshank and published in 1838. The already cartoonlike style of Quarles's *Emblems* becomes even more "jocular" in Cruikshank's drawings: for example, Praz notes, the human soul, Anima, has now become a "pompous and bumptious little woman, like Queen Victoria as a child in the portrait in the Dulwich Galleries." Praz concludes: "In this way, in a humorous middle class Dickensian world, ends the pilgrimage of Amor and Anima, dolls of the spirit and distant descendants of Eros" (168).

95. Francis Quarles, *Emblems, Divine and Moral* (1635; reprint, New York: Robert Carter & Brothers, 1854), bk. 1, emblem 6, 38; bk. 1, emblem 9, 51–52.

96. Emblem 9 in *Typus Mundi* pictures a peacock on top of the globe to symbolize the world's vanity. Pictured and discussed in Moseley, *A Century of Emblems,* 183–84, 188–90.

97. The corresponding *Typus Mundi* emblem pictures a holy and an unholy Cupid playing at bowls with no other figures involved. Ibid., 185–86, 194–98.

98. Quarles, *Emblems, Divine and Moral,* bk. 1, emblem 10, 53–55; Freeman, *English Emblem Books,* 120, pl. 18.

99. Praz, 163.

100. Quarles, *Emblems, Divine and Moral,* bk. 1, emblem 2, 22; and bk. 1, emblem 4, 31.

101. Ibid., bk. 1, emblem 11, 57–58.

102. Ibid., bk. 1, emblem 4, 30, 32; bk. 1, emblem 6, 38; and bk. 2, emblem 10, 114–15.

103. The emblem appears in Moseley, *A Century of Emblems* (264, no. 89). Moseley describes the wheel as "both the wheel of fortune and the instability of the world" and provides the translations for the motto, which he describes as "deliberately ambiguous" (256).

104. Freeman, *English Emblem Books,* 204.

105. John Bunyan, *The Pilgrim's Progress,* ed. James B. Wharey (Oxford: Clarendon, 1960), vii–ix.

106. Freeman, *English Emblem Books,* 206.

107. Qualls, *Secular Pilgrims,* 89.

108. R. Chambers, ed., *Chambers's Book of Days* (Philadelphia: J. B. Lippincott, n.d.), 2:325.

109. Frederick Antal, *Hogarth and His Place in European Art* (London: Routledge & Kegan Paul, 1962), 8.

110. Paulson, *Emblem and Expression,* 35.

111. *Hogarth's Graphic Works,* comp. Ronald Paulson (New Haven: Yale University Press, 1965), 1:10.

112. Paulson, *Hogarth's Graphic Works,* 1:14. Henry Fielding, preface to *Joseph Andrews* (1742; reprint, New York: Oxford University Press, 1970).

113. Paulson, *Hogarth's Graphic Works,* 1:14.

114. Ibid., 1:91; 2, pl. 3.

115. Ibid., 1:95.

116. Antal notes the similarity of *The South Sea Scheme* to the widely influential anonymous Dutch engraving *The Actions and Designs of the World go round as if in a Mill,* and explains that Dutch cartoonists, like Hogarth himself, were much influenced by the seventeenth-century French artist Jacques Callot, in this case particularly by his *La Roue* and *La Pendaison* from the cycle *Misères de la Guerre* (*Hogarth and His Place,* 81, 84).

117. Paulson, *Hogarth's Graphic Works,* 1:94.

118. Ibid., 1:96; 2, pl. 13.

119. Ripa specifies that Diligence (*Industria*) have a beehive (Maser, *Cesare Ripa's Baroque,* 147).

120. The windmill appears in the advertisement for a pantomime *Dr. Faustus* on a signboard in Hogarth's *Masquerades and Operas.* Paulson explains that John Rich, the impresario of the Lincoln's Inn Fields Theater, used the windmill to refer to an episode in the pantomime when "a miller is caught and revolved on the blades of his own windmill while Faustus below makes love to his wife" (*Hogarth's Graphic Works,* 1:104; 2, pl. 37).

121. Ibid., 1:197; 2, pl. 4.

122. "*The World,* as *Milton* phrases it, *lay all before him;* and *Jones,* no more than *Adam,* had any Man to whom he might resort for Comfort or Assistance" (Fielding's italics). Henry Fielding, *Tom Jones,* ed. Sheridan Baker (1749; reprint, New York: Norton Critical Edition, 1973), 251. Future quotations from *Tom Jones* cited in the text refer to this edition.

123. Christine van Boheemen, *The Novel as Family Romance: Language, Gender, and Authority from Fielding to Joyce* (Ithaca, N.Y., & London: Cornell University Press, 1987), 83–84.

124. My argument here is in general agreement with Martin Battestin's: his chapter on "Fielding: The Argument of Design" and especially the section on "Fortune and Providence" in *The Providence of Wit* (Oxford: Clarendon, 1974) offer important historical sources for Fielding's view of Fortune as the agent of Providence.

125. Book 13 opens with an invocation to two worldly muses, "Love of Fame" and an unnamed "much plumper Dame" described as the offspring of "Ufrow Gelt, impregnated by a jolly Merchant of Amsterdam." This description and Fielding's appeal for the plumper dame to "hold forth thy tempting Rewards; thy shining, chinking Heap; thy quickly-convertible Bank-bill, big with unseen Riches; thy often-varying Stock" certainly suggests that she is another avatar of Fortune (524–25).

126. The terms are taken from Hogarth's description of the pleasure afforded the observer by "intricacy in form" in his treatise on aesthetics, *The Analysis of Beauty,* published in 1753 (reprint, Pittsfield, Mass.: Silver Lotus Shop, 1909), 50. Although Hogarth is referring to what he calls the serpentine "line of beauty" in graphic art, the aesthetic effect applies equally well for the reader of the picaresque novel. Hogarth himself suggests the analogy: "It is a pleasing labor of the mind to solve the most difficult problems; allegories and riddles, trifling as they are, afford the mind amusement: and with what delight does it follow the well-connected thread of a play, or novel, which ever increases as the plot thickens, and ends most pleased, when that is most distinctly unravelled!" (49–50).

127. *The Delightful History of Fortunatus* (London: printed by J. Davenport for C. Sheppard, n.d.), 23, 24. In Nursery Chapbooks, Bodleian Library, Oxford (Douce Adds. 5 [10]).

128. Ibid., 22, 26.

129. Gombrich, *Symbolic Images,* 183.

130. *The Delightful History of Fortunatus,* 31.

131. *The History of Fortunatus* (London: Dicey, n.d.), frontispiece, in Ashton, *Chap-Books,* 125.

132. Ibid., 131, 133.

133. Cf. Richard D. Altick, *The English Common Reader: A Social History of the Mass Reading Public, 1800–1900* (Chicago: University of Chicago Press, 1957), 287–88. Dickens memorializes Seven Dials, Pitts, and Catnach in *Sketches by Boz* (*SB,* 69–73).

134. Pepys's collection of street literature is housed at Cambridge. A representative sampling is contained in Roger Thompson, ed., *Samuel Pepys' Penny Merriments* (New York: Columbia University Press, 1977). Shepard provides an excellent discussion of the origins, printers, peddlers, and influence of street literature from the seventeenth to the nineteenth centuries in *The History of Street Literature.*

135. Harry Stone, *Dickens and the Invisible World: Fairy Tales, Fantasy, and Novel-Making* (Bloomington: Indiana University Press, 1979), 20–23.

136. The E. O. Table appears in two cartoons of 1782: "The W—st—r Just-Asses A Braying; or The Downfall of the E.O. Table," which attacks the government's attempt to outlaw gambling in the private sector while tolerating the stock exchange's version of the same thing; and "Gloria Mundi; or The Devil Addressing the Sun," which pictures the politician Charles Fox (who was notorious for his gambling) standing on an E. O. Table. See Thomas Wright and R. H. Evans, *Historical and Descriptive Account of the Caricatures of James Gillray* (New York: Benjamin Blom, 1968), vol. 1:10, 13; and vol. 2, pls. 9, 11.

Chapter 2

1. "Fresco Paintings Discovered in Rochester Cathedral," *Gentleman's Magazine*, n.s., 14 (August 1840): 137.

2. Later discussions of Rochester Cathedral's Wheel of Fortune and other examples of the icon in English medieval religious art appear in Tancred Borenius and E. W. Tristram, *English Medieval Painting* (Paris: Pegasus, 1926), 17, pls. 38 and 39; Frank Kendon, *Mural Paintings in English Churches during the Middle Ages* (London: John Lane, Bodley Head, 1923), 191, pl. 15; Chew, *The Pilgrimage of Life*, 38–39; and Kiefer, *Fortune and Elizabethan Tragedy*, 11.

3. "Fresco Paintings Discovered," 137.

4. Such a regard for the goddess's power over patriarchy could certainly have been born of experience, since Henry, son of the hated King John, never outlived his father's evil memory or his own incompetence, to be remembered by Dickens in *A Child's History of England* as "shabby and ridiculous . . . the mere pale shadow of a king at all times" (*CHE*, 249, 254).

5. Kendon notes that English church paintings of St. Katherine and her wheel were quite popular in medieval times, ranking just after representations of St. Christopher and St. George in number. Most of these representations are later than the Rochester Wheel of Fortune, however, since their major source was *The Golden Legend*, a collection of the lives of the saints compiled in 1270 (*Mural Paintings*, 137, 181–83, 230).

6. Owst, *Literature and Pulpit*, 238–39.

7. Buckley, *The Triumph of Time*, 13.

8. Alfred, Lord Tennyson, "Locksley Hall," in *The Poetic and Dramatic Works of Alfred Lord Tennyson*, ed. W. J. Rolfe (Boston: Houghton Mifflin, 1898), 94.

9. John W. Dodds, *The Age of Paradox: A Biography of England, 1841–1851* (London: Victor Gollancz, 1953), 7.

10. The formative effect of Rochester Cathedral on Dickens's imagination is suggested by Edgar Johnson in his definitive biography, *Charles Dickens: His Tragedy and Triumph* (New York: Simon and Schuster, 1952), 1:18–19; and more explicitly urged by Fred Kaplan in *Dickens: A Biography* (New York: William Morrow, 1988), 22–24.

11. See *David Copperfield*, 56; Chew, *The Pilgrimage of Life*, xxiii.

12. *The Letters of Charles Dickens*, Pilgrim Edition, vol. 2 (1840–41), ed. Madeline House and Graham Storey (London: Oxford University Press, 1969), 24. See also John Forster, *The Life of Charles Dickens* (London: Chapman & Hall, 1876), 97; and Johnson, *Charles Dickens*, 1:292.

13. Michael Slater, *Dickens and Women* (London: J. M. Dent, 1983), 221, 223.

14. Dickens, *The Old Curiosity Shop*, ed. Angus Easson (London: Penguin, 1972), 33.

15. Miller, *Charles Dickens*, 95.

16. Welsh, *The City of Dickens*, 184.

17. Dickens, *Letters,* 2:48–49.

18. Thomas Hood, review of *Master Humphrey's Clock* in the *Athenaeum* (7 November 1840): 887–88; quoted in John Harvey, *Victorian Novelists and Their Illustrators* (New York: New York University Press, 1971), 122–23. See also Jane Cohen, *Charles Dickens and His Original Illustrators* (Columbus: Ohio State University Press, 1980), 136–37.

19. Cohen, *Dickens and His Original Illustrators,* 129.

20. Dickens, *Letters,* 2:171–72.

21. See "hourglass" in Biedermann, *Dictionary of Symbolism,* 178–79; and J. C. Cooper, *An Illustrated Encyclopedia of Traditional Symbols* (London: Thames & Hudson, 1978), 86.

22. Dickens, *Letters,* 2:7–8; see also Joan Stevens, "Woodcuts Dropped into the Text," *Studies in Bibliography* 20 (1967): 113–33. I am grateful to Michael Steig for pointing out that the illustrations in *The Old Curiosity Shop* were not, in fact, woodcuts, but wood engravings, etched on polished wood with engraving tools rather than carved on a plank surface.

23. Forster, *The Life of Charles Dickens,* 94. Harvey, in *Victorian Novelists and Their Illustrators,* notes that Forster's comment refers to these two illustrations (122); as does Cohen, in *Dickens and His Original Illustrators* (137).

24. Welsh, *The City of Dickens,* 58–59.

25. Chew, *The Pilgrimage of Life,* xxiii.

26. Carl Jung, *Aion: Phenomenology of Self,* in *The Portable Jung,* ed. Joseph Campbell, trans. R. F. C. Hull (New York and London: Penguin, 1971), 151.

27. Quarles, *Emblems, Divine and Moral,* bk. 3, emblem 3, 149; bk. 4, emblem 7, 225–26.

28. Jung, *Aion,* 150.

29. Sigmund Freud, "The Theme of the Three Caskets," in *On Creativity and the Unconscious,* ed. Benjamin Nelson (New York: Harper Colophon, 1978), 75.

30. Patrick Brantlinger, *The Spirit of Reform* (Cambridge: Harvard University Press, 1977), 28. A version of this section appeared as "Minding the Wheel: Representations of Women's Time in Victorian Literature," *Rocky Mountain Review of Language and Literature* 48 (1994): 45–60.

31. Quoted in Gardner Taplin, *The Life of Elizabeth Barrett Browning* (New Haven: Yale University Press, 1957), 114–15.

32. Elizabeth Barrett Browning, "The Cry of the Children," in *Cambridge Edition of the Complete Poetical Works,* ed. Harriet W. Preston (Boston: Houghton Mifflin, 1900), 156–58.

33. Plato, *The Republic,* bk. 10, 616c, 617c.

34. Barrett Browning, "A Year's Spinning," in *Cambridge Edition of the Complete Poetical Works,* 209.

35. See Shepard, *The History of Street Literature,* 174, 208.

36. Geoffrey Chaucer, "The Wife of Bath's Prologue," line 401, in *The Canterbury Tales,* in *The Works of Geoffrey Chaucer,* ed. F. N. Robinson (Boston: Houghton Mifflin, 1957), 80.

37. Kathleen Tillotson, *Novels of the Eighteen-Forties* (Oxford: Oxford University Press, 1956), 13.

38. Raymond Williams, *The English Novel from Dickens to Lawrence* (New York: Oxford University Press, 1970), 9.

39. *Fraser's,* January 1851, 75; quoted in Tillotson, *Novels of the Eighteen-Forties,* 39. For specific information about the patterns, advantages, and disadvantages of serialization for sixteen of the best-known artists of the period, see J. Don Vann, *Victorian Novels in Serial* (New York: Modern Language Association of America, 1985).

40. D. A. Miller, "Discipline in Different Voices: Bureaucracy, Police, Family, and *Bleak House,*" *Representations* 1 (1983): 72–73; republished in D. A. Miller, *The Novel and the Police* (Berkeley and Los Angeles: University of California Press, 1988), 58–106.

41. In a discussion of "The Politics of Domestic Fiction: 1848," Armstrong argues that externally produced violence and dangerous desire in *Vanity Fair, Wuthering Heights, Jane Eyre, Mary Barton,* and *Oliver Twist* are ultimately controlled by an appeal to gender and domestication. "Novels incorporated new political material and sexualized it in such a manner that only one resolution would do: a partitioned and hierarchical space under a woman's surveillance." This assimilation of self- and home discipline coincides with the rise of female authorship and authority in the Victorian novel (*Desire and Domestic Fiction,* 185).

42. Marcus, *Dickens from Pickwick to Dombey*, 297.

43. I am counting the births of Florence's brother Paul and her two children Paul and Florence; the deaths of Fanny, Paul, and Mrs. Skewton; the Dombey/Edith and Florence/Walter weddings; and the flights of Florence and Edith.

44. See Dickens's calculations regarding Florence's age and events in the novel in Harry Stone, ed., *Dickens' Working Notes for His Novels* (Chicago: University of Chicago Press, 1987), 70–73.

45. *Economist,* 10 October 1846, 1324–25; quoted in *Dickens: The Critical Heritage,* ed. Philip Collins (New York: Barnes & Noble, 1971), 214–15.

46. Carlyle, *Past and Present* (1837), bk. 3, chap. 12, and bk. 4, chap. 4. Hill locates in the seventeenth century the assimilation by the English middle class of the Protestant work ethic—"the Puritan horror of waste of time" and the undisciplined life (*World Turned Upside Down,* 327). But, as E. P. Thompson explains, it was not until after the Industrial Revolution that the lower classes, in response to the new factory system that institutionalized timed labor, came to share a similar consciousness of the economic valuation of time, as something not "passed but spent." "Time, Work-Discipline and Industrial Capitalism," in *Essays in Social History,* ed. M. W. Flinn and T. C. Smout (Oxford: Clarendon, 1974), 39–77; quoted in N. N. Feltes, "To Saunter, To Hurry: Dickens, Time, and Industrial Captialism," *Victorian Studies* 20 (spring 1977): 248.

47. It is interesting to note that the name "Dombey," besides sounding like the Latin for "God," rhymes with "Zombi," an African word meaning "Deity," according to Robert Southey, who first brought the term into currency in English via his 1822 *History of Brazil* (*OED*). The occasion for Southey's definition is his recounting of the late-seventeenth-century "short but memorable history" of the "Negroes of the Palmares," who had been brought to Brazil as slaves, but had escaped into the palm forests and there set up a fugitive community engaged in trafficking stolen goods. Southey's description of the Africans' reverence for their Zombi—as well as their opportunistic blending of Christianity, traditional beliefs, and superstitions with an entrepreneurial spirit—finds a parallel in the House of Dombey (and English mercantilism in general), with its love of profit and its allegiance to the Protestant work ethic. Southey tells us that the Africans' elected leader "was obeyed with perfect loyalty," and that "[p]erhaps a feeling of religion contributed to this obedience; for Zombi, the title whereby he was called, is the name for Deity, in the Angolan tongue. They retained the use of the cross, some half-remembered prayers, and a few ceremonies which they had mingled with superstitions of their own, either what they preserved of African idolatry, or had invented in their present state of freedom." *History of Brazil* (1822; reprint, New York: Burt Franklin, 1970), 24–25.

48. These are Julian Moynahan's terms from his hilarious and insightful essay, "Dealings with the Firm of Dombey and Son: Firmness *versus* Wetness," in *Dickens and the Twentieth Century,* ed. John Gross and Gabriel Pearson (London: Routledge & Kegan Paul, 1962), 130.

49. Cf. Janet Larson, *Dickens and the Broken Scripture* (Athens: University of Georgia Press, 1985), 85.

50. Stone, *Dickens' Working Notes,* 57.

51. Lindley Murray, *English Grammar* (Menston, England: Scolar, 1968), 25.

52. Barrett Browning, "The Cry of the Children," stanza 4. Steven Marcus makes a similar point, but attributes the image to the parliamentary bluebooks rather than to Barrett Browning's poem (*Dickens from Pickwick to Dombey,* 323).

53. Gerda Lerner, *The Creation of Patriarchy* (New York: Oxford University Press, 1986), 239–40.

54. Dorothy Van Ghent, "On *Great Expectations,*" in *The English Novel: Form and Function* (New York: Harper & Row, 1953), 34.

55. Dickens, *Dombey and Son,* ed. Peter Fairclough (Harmondsworth, England: Penguin, 1970), 240.

56. Juliet McMaster, "Biological Clocks: Time, Gentlemen, Please," in *Time, Literature, and the Arts: Essays in Honor of Samuel L. Macey,* ed. Thomas R. Cleary (University of Victoria: English Literary Studies, 1994): 57.

57. Sir James Frazer notes a belief common in coastal communities that "people are born when the tide comes in, and die when it goes out," and he cites Mr. Peggotty's comment to this effect in *David Copperfield. The Golden Bough* (abridgment, Ware, England: Wordsworth Editions, 1993), 35. Dickens's first use of this motif, however, is in *Dombey and Son.*

58. Marina Warner, in *Alone of All Her Sex* (New York: Knopf, 1976), offers an excellent discussion of Mary's various roles in Christian iconography, which include this most exalted position after her Assumption.

59. Compare Janice Carlisle's point that the movement of *Dombey and Son* is from temporality to transcendence. *The Sense of an Audience: Dickens, Thackeray, and George Eliot at Mid-Century* (Athens: University of Georgia Press, 1981), 71.

60. Deirdre David, *Rule Britannia: Women, Empire, and Victorian Writing* (Ithaca, N.Y.: Cornell University Press, 1995), 67–68.

61. Steig, *Dickens and Phiz,* 108.

62. Van Ghent, "On *Great Expectations,*" 156.

63. David Copperfield's being "born with a caul" makes a similar point, I think, about the burden of patriarchy as a sacred vocation or "call," which, in David's case, weighs down on the male infant's head (*DC,* 1).

64. Compare Nina Auerbach's comments that "never afterwards does [Dickens] explore so thoroughly the schism between masculinity and femininity as his age defined them," and that "his treatment of sexuality" in the later novels "is infused with a troubled, tragic awareness of the gulf between the sexes." "Dickens and Dombey: A Daughter After All," *Dickens Studies Annual* 5 (1976): 113.

65. In a paragraph restored in the Penguin edition, Dickens derogatorily refers to these women as "the domestic militia" and questions Miss Tox's motives for joining its ranks. The cut passage perhaps explains her name by suggesting that she is "toxic" to Polly: "Miss Tox's constancy and zeal were a heavy discouragement to Richards, who lost flesh hourly under her patronage, and was in some danger of being superintended to death" (*DS,* 100).

66. Charles Parish hypothesizes that this celebrated phrase from *Great Expectations* probably signifies bottle-feeding. "A Boy Brought Up 'By Hand,'" *Nineteenth-Century Fiction* 17 (1962): 286–88. Citing evidence from Patricia Branca's *Silent Sisterhood: Middle Class Women in the Victorian Home* (Pittsburgh: Carnegie-Mellon, 1975), 100, 103, Patricia Marks explains the phrase as "a common euphemism for spoon feeding before glass bottles and rubber nipples became readily available." "Paul Dombey and the Milk of Human Kindness," *Dickens Quarterly* 11 (March 1994): 19.

67. Phiz's later illustration in *David Copperfield,* "Changes at Home," together with the passage to which it refers, suggests just how overladen with sensual and sacred meaning this

image is for Dickens. The plate (which precedes the related textual passage) shows Clara Copperfield "sitting by the fire, suckling an infant" as young David stands in the doorway peeping into the room. Dickens, via David, describes what then happens in the following terms:

> I spoke to her, and she started and cried out. But seeing me, she called me her dear Davy, her own boy! and coming half across the room to meet me, kneeled down upon the ground and kissed me, and laid my head down on her bosom near the little creature that was nestling there, and put its hand to my lips.
>
> I wish I had died. I wish I had died then, with that feeling in my heart! I should have been more fit for Heaven than I ever have been since. (DC, 109)

68. Compare Dickens's letter to Forster of 7 August 1846 regarding the illustrations for the first number: "What should you say, for a notion of the illustrations, to 'Miss Tox introduces the Party'? and 'Mr. Dombey and family'? meaning Polly Toodle, the baby, Mr. Dombey, and little Florence." *The Letters of Charles Dickens,* vol. 4 (1844–46), ed. Kathleen Tillotson, (Oxford: Clarendon, 1977), 599.

69. Warner, *Alone of All Her Sex,* 193.

70. Moynahan, "Dealings with the Firm," 126.

71. Dickens to Forster, 18 July 1846, *Letters,* 4:586.

72. Slater, *Dickens and Women,* 306.

73. Merryn Williams, *Women in the English Novel, 1800–1950* (New York: St. Martin's, 1984), 73, 81.

74. These are the terms Dickens used to describe the episode in his working notes. Stone, *Dickens' Working Notes,* 85.

75. For example, as a contrast to Polly, Dickens pointedly tells us that Mrs. Pipchin (visualized in Phiz's illustration "Paul and Mrs. Pipchin" as lean and flat chested) is a woman whose "waters of gladness and milk of human kindness, had been pumped out dry" (*DS,* 99). Compare Marks's argument in "Paul Dombey," which considers the novel as a celebration of motherhood largely defined by the function of providing nourishment: "Motherhood is the optimal position in domestic and public life: it is communal and egalitarian, distributing the food supply where needed" (23). Moreover, we learn some time after the climactic scene, when Dombey strikes Florence, that the blow has left "a darkening mark on her bosom [which] made her afraid of herself, as if she bore about her something wicked" (*DS,* 688).

76. Thompson, *English Working Class,* 487.

77. Much of the best criticism of *Dombey and Son* has focused on the topicality of the railroad as metaphor for technological speed and change in the novel. Excellent examples include Jonathan Arac's *Commissioned Spirits: The Shaping of Social Motion in Dickens, Carlyle, Melville, and Hawthorne* (New Brunswick, N.J.: Rutgers University Press, 1979), especially chapter 5, "The House and the Railroad," which compares Hawthorne's and Dickens's use of these major tropes in *Dombey* and *The House of Seven Gables.* Arac asserts that the "problematic ambivalence in Dickens's sense of the railroad emerges in the relation that the book establishes, but never quite avows, between the railroad and Dombey" (106), further identifying this connection by claiming, "Dombey and the railroad both represent a society . . . that cares more for the future, for getting ahead, than for the present or the past" (109). In his essay "The Crisis of Representation in *Dombey and Son,*" Roger B. Henkle draws on observations made by Wolfgang Shivelbusch in *The Railway Journey* (Berkeley and Los Angeles: University of California Press, 1986) to corroborate this connection: "the steam engine train . . . [is] the creator of a new sense of time and space, and even of human stimulus. The train symbolizes something more: the projective mentality that we associate with the middle class in a capitalist growth

phase. The class is characterized by its disposition to think ahead, to plan for the future, to save and to invest—Dombey's way of thinking" (in *Critical Reconstructions: The Relationship of Fiction and Life,* ed. Robert M. Polhemus and Roger B. Henkle [Stanford: Stanford University Press, 1994], 98). Murray Baumgarten also cites Shivelbusch in his fine article "Railway/Reading/Time: *Dombey and Son* and the Industrial World," *Dickens Studies Annual* 19 (1990): 65–89. Baumgarten compares Dombey's inability caused by his "self-absorption" to experience the new "concept of panorama" provided by railway travel (Shivelbusch 61, Baumgarten 75). Unlike Arac and Henkle, however, Baumgarten sees Dombey as a type of the "Static Man" who resists the relentless motion represented by the train (76).

78. Dickens to Browne, 10 March 1847, *Letters,* 5:34.

79. Ibid. In his chapter on *Dombey and Son* (appropriately subtitled "Iconography of Social and Sexual Satire") in *Dickens and Phiz,* Steig notes that Dickens's instructions to Phiz for "Major Bagstock is delighted to have that Opportunity" serve as a "kind of ur-text" since they precede Dickens's actual composition of the chapter (93).

80. Engels, *Condition of the Working Class.*

81. Marcus, *Dickens from Pickwick to Dombey,* 329, 332.

Chapter 3

1. Thomas Carlyle, *Heroes, Hero-Worship and the Heroic in History* (New York: Clark, n.d.), 148; Carl Dawson, *Victorian Noon: English Literature in 1850* (Baltimore: Johns Hopkins Press, 1979), 5, 9.

2. Stone, *Dickens and the Invisible World,* 198.

3. See V. Propp, *Morphology of the Folktale,* trans. Laurence Scott (Austin: University of Texas Press, 1968), 39–40.

4. Johnson, *Charles Dickens,* 2:670–71; Altick, *The English Common Reader,* 384.

5. *Fraser's Magazine,* December 1850, xlii, 698–710; Philip Collins, ed. *Dickens: The Critical Heritage* (New York: Barnes & Noble, 1971), 243.

6. Dawson, *Victorian Noon,* 4.

7. Dickens, "A Preliminary Word," *Household Words* 1 (30 March 1850): 1.

8. Anne Lohrli, comp. *Household Words: A Weekly Journal, 1850–59, Conducted by Charles Dickens* (Toronto: University of Toronto Press, 1973), 72, 462.

9. Extracts from the queen's journal, quoted in Gibbs-Smith, *Great Exhibition of 1851,* 16.

10. Dickens to W. H. Wills, 27 July 1851, *The Letters of Charles Dickens,* vol. 6 (1850–52), ed. Graham Storey, Kathleen Tillotson, and Nina Burgis (Oxford: Clarendon, 1988), xii, 447.

11. *The Works of John Ruskin,* ed. E. T. Cook and A. Wedderburn (London: George Allen, 1902–12), 37:7; quoted in Robert Newsom, *Dickens on the Romantic Side of Familiar Things* (New York: Columbia University Press, 1977), 4.

12. Dickens, "A Preliminary Word," 2.

13. Forster, *The Life of Charles Dickens,* 396.

14. Dickens, "A Preliminary Word," 1.

15. Newsom, *Dickens on the Romantic Side,* 2–3; 6, 7; 116.

16. Johnson, *Charles Dickens,* 2:765. See also Miller, *Charles Dickens,* 187–90; and W. J. Harvey, "Chance and Design in *Bleak House,*" in *Dickens and the Twentieth Century,* ed. John Gross and Gabriel Pearson (London: Routledge & Kegan Paul, 1962), 152.

17. Newsom, *Dickens on the Romantic Side,* chap 2, esp. 40.

18. H. M. Daleski "*Bleak House,*" in *Critical Essays on Charles Dickens's 'Bleak House,'* ed. Elliot Gilbert (Boston: G. K. Hall, 1989), 14–15.

19. Martin Meisel, *Realizations: Narrative, Pictorial, and Theatrical Arts in Nineteenth-Century England* (Princeton, N.J.: Princeton University Press, 1983), 29–30.

20. James M. Brown, *Dickens: Novelist in the Market-Place* (Totowa, N.J.: Barnes & Noble, 1982), 60.

21. The connection between the two primary meanings of "suitor" has been explored provocatively by Barbara Gottfried in "Fathers and Suitors: Narratives of Desire in *Bleak House,*" *Dickens Studies Annual* 19 (1990): 169–203. In discussing the novel's sexual politics, Gottfried asserts that (especially in the case of Richard) "[a] suitor may choose to sue or woo, but once he has begun the action, there is always the danger he will 'never get out of Chancery': in initiating a suit, he relinquishes control, ceding power to the arbiter of that suit, whether legal, or marital" (179–80).

22. The choice of verbs here may be an echo of Bassanio's plea in *The Merchant of Venice* to "[w]rest once the law to your authority" (*The Complete Pelican Shakespeare,* 4.1.213), since Jarndyce is probably and Dickens is surely thinking in legal terms.

23. Robert Burton, *The Anatomy of Melancholy* (1621; reprint, London: Dent, Everyman's Library, 1932), 9. My claim that Burton popularized this fable is based on the more frequent appearance of "Hercules and carter" illustrations in seventeenth-century England after 1621. See Edward Hodnett, *Aesop in England: The Transmission of Motifs in Seventeenth-Century Illustrations of Aesop's Fables* (Charlottesville: University Press of Virginia, 1979), 96.

24. See especially part 3 of Welsh's *The City of Dickens,* "The Bride From Heaven"; and part 2 of Slater's *Dickens and Women,* "The Women of the Novels."

25. Marcia Renee Goodman, "'I'll Follow the Other': Tracing the (M)Other in *Bleak House,*" *Dickens Studies Annual* 19 (1990): 155.

26. The expression "Fortunatus's Purse" takes on added significance in *Bleak House.* Esther uses it as the measure of financial inexhaustibility needed by Richard, since "he made so light of money," and the unnamed narrator uses it to describe the gossip around Lincoln's Inn court following Krook's demise and the subsequent invasion of his rag-and-bottle shop by the Smallweeds (*BH,* 242, 557).

27. It is interesting to note that "Nemo" is not only, as Tulkinghorn explains, "Latin for no one," (*BH,* 133), but also, as Henry Mayhew records, costermonger slang for "woman" (*London Labour,* 1:23). Given Hawdon's poverty and his association with street people, like Jo, this name that annihilates the self and the masculine sex is doubly appropriate.

28. Steig, *Dickens and Phiz,* 154.

29. Dickens's wheel imagery here may also be an echo of the Fool's remark in *King Lear* that continues the drama's Fortune and wheel motifs: "Let go thy hold when a great wheel runs down a hill, lest it break thy neck in following it; but the great one that goes up the hill, let him draw after thee" (*The Complete Pelican Shakespeare,* 2.4.65–67).

30. Important studies that discuss Esther's divided sense of self and evaluate her effectiveness as narrator include William Axton, "The Trouble with Esther," *Modern Language Quarterly* 26 (1965): 543–57; Alex Zwerdling, "Esther Summerson Rehabilitated," *PMLA* 88 (1973): 429–39; and Suzanne Graver, "Writing in a 'Womanly' Way and the Double Vision of *Bleak House,*" *Dickens Quarterly* 4 (1987): 3–15.

31. Monica Feinberg notes Esther's use of the subjunctive, but links it to her idealization of Bleak House in "Family Plot: The Bleak House of Victorian Romance," *Victorian Newsletter* 76 (1989): 5–17.

32. William Axton, "Esther's Nicknames: A Study in Relevance," *The Dickensian* 62 (September 1966): 159–60.

33. Ibid., 161–63.

34. Axton explains that Charles Hindley's 1863 republication of S. Baker's 1797 edition of

Mother Shipton and Nixon's Prophecies included this prediction. Even though Hindley was discovered to be a fraud ten years later, Axton says, the prophecy's "hold on the popular imagination was such that thousands of rural families took to churches and open fields on the eve of the expected millennium." See Axton's note on page 161 of "Esther's Nicknames," which cites "Mother Shipton Investigated," *Journal of the British Archeological Association* 19 (1881), 308ff., as its source.

35. *Household Words,* 30 August 1856; author identified in Lohrli's *Household Words: A Weekly Journal,* 157.

36. Thomas, *Religion and the Decline,* 392–93, 410,

37. Ashton, *Chap-Books,* 88–91. The "Aldermary Church Yard, London," site of publication indicates that this chapbook was probably the work of printer William Dicey—according to publication information in an article on Dicey Chapbooks in the British Library, 1865. c. 3. (24).

38. Bodleian, Douce FF 72 (15). The Bodleian has a copy of another "history" of Mother Shipton, printed by J[ohn]. Pitts, Seven Dials, circa 1810. Like Ashton's history, it has an abbreviated description of her appearance, and a third rendering of her head and shoulders—quite different from the other two—in a woodcut illustration.

39. British Library, 8630.a.55.(b.) dated [1861]; Bodleian 9390 E 8 (19).

40. Slater, *Dickens and Women,* 255, 320–21; Graver, "Writing in a 'Womanly' Way," 12, 14 n; Dickens to Mrs. Richard Watson, 22 November 1852; Dickens to Miss Mary Boyle, 25 December 1852; Dickens to Mrs. Cowden Clarke, 28 December 1852; *Letters,* 6:807, 835–36, 839–40.

41. This is Thomas's phrase for describing the essential feature of Puritan diarists concerned with communicating their belief in providence (*Religion and the Decline,* 93).

42. Sarah Stickney Ellis, *The Daughters of England* (London, 1845), 73; quoted in Martha Vicinus, ed., *Suffer and Be Still: Women in the Victorian Age* (Bloomington and London: Indiana University Press, 1972), x, 207 n.

43. Slater, *Dickens and Women,* 306.

44. As *Brewer's Dictionary of Phrase and Fable* points out, "Dame Durden" is a "generic name for a good old-fashioned housewife" (ed. Ivor H. Evans [New York: Harper & Row, 1989], s.v. "Durden, Dame").

45. Newsom, *Dickens on the Romantic Side,* 112. Newsom notes that Dickens began writing *Bleak House* after the deaths of his father, John Dickens, and his infant daughter, Dora.

46. Graver, "Writing in a 'Womanly' Way," 13.

Chapter 4

1. In *The Old Curiosity Shop,* for example, Nell's great-uncle eulogizes this phenomenon as a familiar form of genetic reincarnation: "If you have seen the picture-gallery of any old family, you will remember how the same face and figure—often the fairest and slightest of them all—come upon you in different generations; and how you trace the same sweet girl through a long line of portraits—never growing old or changing—the Good Angel of the race—abiding by them in all reverses—redeeming all their sins" (*OCS,* 524).

2. Buchanan, *The Power of the Machine,* 104.

3. Creevy, "In Time and Out," 64–65.

4. Feltes, "To Saunter, To Hurry," 245–67.

5. Kristeva, "Women's Time," 191–92.

6. George Eliot, *The Mill on the Floss* (London: Penguin, 1979), 506, 54.

7. Citing F. G. Kitton, *Dickens and His Illustrators* (London: Redway, 1899), 107, as his

source, Steig suggests that the mill in "The Lonely Figure" is a "device for crushing lime" (*Dickens and Phiz,* 154, 334 n).

8. Cf. Feltes, "To Saunter, To Hurry," 259.

9. Brown, *Dickens,* 17.

10. K. Theodore Hoppen, *The Mid-Victorian Generation: 1846–1886* (Oxford and New York: Oxford University Press, 1998), 390–91.

11. Roopnaraine, "Time and the Circle," 54–56.

12. Dickens, *Letters,* 7:608–9.

13. Johnson, *Charles Dickens,* 2:885.

14. Slater, *Dickens and Women,* 331.

15. *Household Narrative,* April 1855, 88. (The *Narrative* was the monthly installment published as part of *Household Words.*)

16. Meisel, *Realizations,* 313.

17. Boethius, *The Consolation of Philosophy,* bk. 2., poem 1, p. 23. In keeping with Boethius's direction, the Rochester Fortune also has her right hand on the wheel.

18. Compare Deirdre David's excellent discussion regarding the role of gender in the representation of empire in nineteenth-century literature, *Rule Britannia.* David discusses *The Old Curiosity Shop* and *Dombey and Son* as Dickens's two novels that "represent particularly well the complex embrace and interrogation of imperial glory," but does not deal with Dickens's interesting critique of imperialist values in *Little Dorrit* (44).

19. Erich Auerbach, *Mimesis: The Representation of Reality in Western Literature,* trans. Williard R. Trask (Princeton, N.J.: Princeton, University Press, 1953), 25.

20. Auerbach, *Mimesis,* 29–30.

21. John Butt and Kathleen Tillotson, *Dickens at Work* (London: Methuen, 1957), 225; quoted in Steig, *Dickens and Phiz,* 159.

22. Ruskin, "Traffic," in *The Works of John Ruskin,* 18:452–53, 451.

23. A similar illustration, titled "Little Dorrit Leaving the Marshalsea," which appears in book 2, chapter 30 of the Oxford edition (*LD,* 764), was used for the title page of the first edition, published in 1857 (a facsimile appears in the Penguin *Little Dorrit,* ed. John Holloway [New York, 1985], 33).

24. Steig, *Dickens and Phiz,* 159.

25. Christ and Jordan, *Victorian Literature and the Victorian Visual Imagination,* xx.

26. Richard Stang, "*Little Dorrit:* A World in Reverse," in *Dickens the Craftsman: Strategies of Presentation,* ed. Robert B. Partlow Jr., (Carbondale: Southern Illinois University Press, 1970), 141.

27. Welsh, *The City of Dickens,* 165–66.

28. Meisel, *Realizations,* 303–5, 319.

29. The troublesome but clear link between fairies and female sexuality—as well as the trait of superiority, a recurring attribute of the "fairy bride" in folkloric tradition—is discussed by Carole G. Silver in *Strange and Secret Peoples: Fairies and Victorian Consciousness* (Oxford: Oxford University Press, 1999), 98–102.

30. "Gaslight Fairies," *Household Words* 11 (10 February 1855): 25–28.

31. David Holbrook, *Charles Dickens and the Image of Woman* (New York: New York University Press, 1993), 70.

32. Cf. Nancy Aycock Metz, "The Blighted Tree and the Book of Fate: Female Models of Storytelling in *Little Dorrit,*" *Dickens Studies Annual* 18 (1989): 222–23.

33. Metz, "Blighted Tree," 234–36; Stone, *Dickens and the Invisible World,* 39.

34. Marina Warner, *From the Beast to the Blonde: On Fairy Tales and Their Tellers* (New York: Farrar, Straus & Giroux, 1994), 14–16, 23.

35. Patricia Baines, *Spinning Wheels, Spinners and Spinning* (McMinnville, Oreg.: Robin and Russ Handweavers, n.d.), 175.

36. William Wordsworth, *The Complete Poetical Works,* Cambridge Edition, ed. Andrew J. George (Boston and New York: Houghton Mifflin, 1904), 401. Baines notes that this belief is probably "based on fact, since the warmth of the fire eases the natural grease of the wool and facilitates teasing and spinning" (*Spinning Wheels,* 175).

37. Bette Hochberg, *Spin Span Spun: Fact and Folklore for Spinners and Weavers* (Santa Cruz, Calif.: Bette Hochberg, 1979), 13.

38. Wordsworth, *The Complete Poetical Works,* 570.

39. Roopnaraine, "Time and the Circle," 59.

40. Meisel, *Realizations,* 315.

41. T. E. Hulme, *Speculations* (London: Routledge & Kegan Paul, 1924), 34.

42. Slater, *Dickens and Women,* 258.

43. "Pocket Venus" was the nickname given to Dickens's first real love, Maria Beadnell, whose youthful person is the model for Dora Spenlow and whose middle-aged person is the model for Flora Finching. C. G. L. Du Cann, *The Love-Lives of Charles Dickens* (Westport, Conn.: Greenwood, 1972), 34.

44. Alfred, Lord Tennyson, "The Marriage of Geraint," *Idylls of the King,* ed. J. M. Gray (New York: Penguin, 1983), 84–86.

45. Tennyson, "Geraint and Enid," lines 866–67, 122.

46. Jules Michelet, *Woman,* trans. J. W. Palmer (New York: Rudd & Carleton, 1860), 76, 80.

47. Roland Barthes, *Michelet,* trans. Richard Howard (New York: Hill & Wang, 1987), 155.

48. Forster, *The Life of Charles Dickens,* 578.

Chapter 5

A version of this chapter appeared as "*Great Expectations:* Dickens and the Language of Fortune," in *Dickens Studies Annual* 24 (1996): 153–65.

1. Dickens's use of inversion—under a variety of names—has been frequently (and eloquently) discussed by critics analyzing the play of his imaginative genius. See, for example, Taylor Stoehr, *Dickens: The Dreamer's Stance* (Ithaca, N.Y.: Cornell University Press, 1965), 139; John Carey, *The Violent Effigy: A Study of Dickens's Imagination* (London: Faber & Faber, 1973), 174–75; Stone, *Dickens and the Invisible World,* 298–339. An excellent earlier examination of Dickens's use of this device in *Great Expectations* appears in E. Pearlman's "Inversion in *Great Expectations,*" *Dickens Studies Annual* 7 (1978): 190–202.

2. Cf. Stang, *"Little Dorrit,"* 140–64.

3. Cf. Harry P. Marten, "The Visual Imagination of Dickens and Hogarth: Structure and Scene," *Studies in the Novel* 6 (1974): 150; and Harvey, *Victorian Novelists and Their Illustrators,* 155.

4. In literature, this motif is traceable to the Middle Ages, according to Ernst R. Curtius, *European Literature and the Latin Middle Ages,* trans. Willard Trask (New York: Pantheon, 1953), 94–98. Excellent book-length discussions of the history and the comic uses of this motif can be found in Barbara A. Babcock, ed., *The Reversible World: Symbolic Inversion in Art and Society* (Ithaca, N.Y.: Cornell University Press, 1978); and Ian Donaldson, *The World Turned Upside Down: Comedy from Jonson to Fielding* (Oxford: Clarendon, 1970).

5. Babcock, *Reversible World,* 39–94; Hill, *World Turned Upside Down.*

6. See Ashton, *Chap-Books,* 265–72; and Collison, *Story of Street Literature,* 112–14; Stone, *Dickens and the Invisible World,* 22–24.

7. Tom Scott, the acrobatic boy who haunts Quilp's countinghouse in *The Old Curiosity Shop* and spends most of his time in the novel walking on his hands or standing on his head, may serve to represent, by Dickensian shorthand, Quilp's perversely inverted world.

8. Stone, *Dickens and the Invisible World,* chap. 3, "Dickens' Fabling Mind."

9. Welsh compares David's and Dickens's work ethic and offers an outstanding discussion of the way this ethic is grounded in Calvinism in *The City of Dickens,* chap. 5, "Work."

10. Michael Cottsell, ed. *Critical Essays on Charles Dickens's 'Great Expectations'* (Boston: G. K. Hall, 1990), 13.

11. *King Lear,* in *The Complete Pelican Shakespeare,* 4.2.18–19.

12. Ellis, *Man and Woman,* 475–82.

13. Dickens to Wilkie Collins, 23 June 1861, *Letters,* 9:428; quoted in Kaplan, *Dickens: A Biography,* 437.

14. Untitled tailpiece from *Household Stories by the Brothers Grimm,* trans. Lucy Crane and illustrated by Walter Crane (New York: MacMillan, 1886; reprint, New York: Dover, 1963), 84. Walter Crane uses this same illustration as the tailpiece for his *The Decorative Illustration of Books* (London: G. Bell & Sons; reprint, London: Bracken, 1984), 233.

15. Malcolm Bell, *Sir Edward Burne-Jones: A Record and Review* (London: George Bell & Sons, 1898; reprint, New York: AMS, 1972), 15; Penelope Fitzgerald, *Edward Burne-Jones* (London: Michael Joseph, 1975), 245, 293 n, 140.

16. See Kimberley Reynolds and Nicola Humble's excellent discussion of "Sightless Seers" in the chapter by that name in *Victorian Heroines: Representations of Femininity in Nineteenth-Century Literature and Art* (New York: New York University Press, 1993), 62–97.

17. Kestner, *Mythology and Misogyny,* 106, 133; Kristeva, "Women's Time," 192.

18. A. P. de Mirimonde, "Les Allégories de la Destinée Humaine et 'La Roue de Fortune' d'Edward Burne-Jones," *Gazette des Beaux-Arts* 99 (1982): 84 (my translation).

19. Adrienne Munich, *Queen Victoria's Secrets* (New York: Columbia University Press, 1996), 47, 221, 46. The woodcut appears on page 47.

20. Baines, *Spinning Wheels,* 171–74. The photograph appears on page 174.

21. Munich, *Queen Victoria's Secrets,* 48.

22. Ibid., 161; Daniel Joseph Kirwin, *Palace and Hovel; or, Phases of London Life* (Hartford, Conn.: Belknap & Bliss, 1870), 53.

23. Philippa Berry, *Shakespeare's Feminine Endings: Disfiguring Death in the Tragedies* (London and New York: Routledge, 1999), 113.

24. Munich, *Queen Victoria's Secrets,* 158.

25. Berry, *Shakespeare's Feminine Endings,* 104–5.

26. Philip Fisher, "Acting, Reading, Fortune's Wheel: *Sister Carrie* and the Life History of Objects," in *American Realism: New Essays,* ed. Eric J. Sundquist (Baltimore: Johns Hopkins Press, 1982), 271–72, 270, 274.

27. Frye, *Fools of Time,* 17.

28. Fisher, "Acting, Reading," 259–60.

WORKS CITED

Altick, Richard D. *The English Common Reader: A Social History of the Mass Reading Public, 1800–1900.* Chicago: University of Chicago Press, 1957.

Antal, Frederick. *Hogarth and His Place in European Art.* London: Routledge & Kegan Paul, 1962.

Arac, Jonathan. *Commissioned Spirits: The Shaping of Social Motion in Dickens, Caryle, Melville, and Hawthorne.* New Brunswick, N.J.: Rutgers University Press, 1979.

Armstrong, Nancy. *Desire and Domestic Fiction: A Political History of the Novel.* New York: Oxford University Press, 1987.

Arnold, Matthew. *Culture and Anarchy.* New York: MacMillan, 1911.

Ashton, John. *Chap-Books of the Eighteenth Century.* London: Chatto & Windus, 1882.

Auerbach, Eric. *Mimesis: The Representation of Reality in Western Literature.* Trans. Willard Trask. Princeton, N.J.: Princeton University Press, 1953.

Auerbach, Nina. "Dickens and Dombey: A Daughter After All." *Dickens Studies Annual* 5 (1976): 95–114.

Augustine, St. *City of God.* Trans. and ed. Marcus Dods. New York: Hafner, 1948.

Axton, William. "Esther's Nicknames: A Study in Relevance." *The Dickensian* 62 (September 1966): 158–74.

———. "The Trouble with Esther." *Modern Language Quarterly* 26 (1965): 543–57.

Babcock, Barbara, ed. *The Reversible World: Symbolic Inversion in Art and Society.* Ithaca, N.Y.: Cornell University Press, 1978.

Bacon, Francis. *The Essayes or Counsels, Civill and Morall, 1625. Francis Bacon: A Selection of His Works.* Ed. Sidney Warhaft. New York: Odyssey, 1965.

Baines, Patricia. *Spinning Wheels, Spinners and Spinning.* McMinnville, Oreg.: Robin and Russ Handweavers, n.d.

Barthes, Roland. *Michelet.* Trans. Richard Howard. New York: Hill and Wang, 1987.

Bartholomew, Barbara. *Fortune and Natura: A Reading of Three Chaucer Narratives.* London: Mouton, 1966.

Battestin, Martin. *The Providence of Wit.* Oxford: Clarendon, 1974.

Baumgarten, Murray. "Railway/Reading/Time: *Dombey and Son* and the Industrial World." *Dickens Studies Annual* 19 (1990): 65–89.

Bell, Malcolm. *Sir Edward Burne-Jones: A Record and Review.* London: George Bell & Sons, 1898. Reprint, New York: AMS, 1972.

Berry, Philippa. *Shakespeare's Feminine Endings: Disfiguring Death in the Tragedies.* London and New York: Routledge, 1999.

Biedermann, Hans. *Dictionary of Symbolism: Cultural Icons and the Meanings behind Them.* Trans. William Hulbert. New York: Meridian, 1994.

Blake, William. *Complete Writings.* Ed. Geoffrey Keynes. London: Oxford University Press, 1969.

Boethius. *The Consolation of Philosophy.* Trans. Richard Green. Indianapolis: Bobbs-Merrill, 1962.

Boheemen, Christine van. *The Novel as Family Romance: Language, Gender, and Authority from Fielding to Joyce.* Ithaca, N.Y.: Cornell University Press, 1987.

Borenius, Tancred, and E. W. Tristram. *English Medieval Painting.* Paris: Pegasus, 1926.

Brantlinger, Patrick. *The Spirit of Reform.* Cambridge: Harvard University Press, 1977.

Brewer's Dictionary of Phrase and Fable. Ed. Ivor H. Evans. New York: Harper & Row, 1989.

Brown, Carleton, ed. *Religious Lyrics of the Fourteenth Century.* 1924. 2nd ed. revised by G. V. Smithers. London: Oxford University Press, 1965.

Brown, James M. *Dickens: Novelist in the Market-Place.* Totowa, N.J.: Barnes & Noble, 1982.

Browning, Elizabeth Barrett. *Cambridge Edition of the Complete Poetical Works.* Ed. Harriet W. Preston. Boston: Houghton Mifflin, 1900.

Buchanan, R. A. *The Power of the Machine: The Impact of Technology from 1700 to the Present.* London: Penguin, 1994.

Buckley, Jerome. *The Triumph of Time.* Cambridge: Harvard University Press, Belknap Press, 1966.

———, ed. *The Worlds of Victorian Fiction.* Cambridge: Harvard University Press, 1959.

Bunyan, John. *The Pilgrim's Progress.* Ed. John B. Wharey. Oxford: Clarendon, 1960.

Burton, Robert. *The Anatomy of Melancholy.* 3 vols. London: Dent, Everyman's Library, 1932.

Butt, John, and Kathleen Tillotson. *Dickens at Work.* London: Methuen, 1957.

Campbell, Elizabeth. "Great Expectations: Dickens and the Language of Fortune." *Dickens Studies Annual* 24 (1996): 153–65.

———. "Minding the Wheel: Representations of Women's Time in Victorian Narrative." *Rocky Mountain Review of Language and Literature* 48 (1994): 45–60.

Cardwell, Donald. *The Norton History of Technology.* New York: W. W. Norton, 1995.

Carey, John. *The Violent Effigy: A Study of Dickens's Imagination.* London: Faber and Faber, 1973.

Carlisle, Janice. *The Sense of an Audience: Dickens, Thackeray, and George Eliot at Mid-Century.* Athens: University of Georgia Press, 1981.

Carlyle, Thomas. *Heroes, Hero-Worship and the Heroic in History.* New York: Clark, n.d.

———. *Past and Present.* Ed. A. M. D. Hughes. Oxford: Clarendon, 1918.

Cassirer, Ernst. *The Myth of the State.* New Haven and London: Yale University Press, 1967.

Chambers, R., ed. *Chambers's Book of Days.* Philadelphia: J. B. Lippincott, n.d.

Chaucer, Geoffrey. *The Works of Geoffrey Chaucer.* Ed. F. N. Robinson. Boston: Houghton Mifflin, 1957.

Chew, Samuel C. *The Pilgrimage of Life.* New Haven and London: Yale University Press, 1962.

Christ, Carol T., and John O. Jordan, eds. *Victorian Literature and the Victorian Visual Imagination.* Berkeley and Los Angeles: University of California Press, 1995.

Cirlot, J. E. *A Dictionary of Symbols.* Trans. Jack Sage. New York: Barnes & Noble, 1993.

Cohen, Jane. *Charles Dickens and His Original Illustrators.* Columbus: Ohio State University Press, 1980.

Collins, Philip, ed. *Dickens: The Critical Heritage.* New York: Barnes & Noble, 1971.

Collison, Robert. *The Story of Street Literature: Forerunner of the Popular Press.* Santa Barbara, Calif.: American Bibliographical Center, Clio Press, 1973.

Cooper, J. C. *An Illustrated Encyclopedia of Traditional Symbols.* London: Thames & Hudson, 1978.

Cottsell, Michael, ed. *Critical Essays on Charles Dickens's 'Great Expectations.'* Boston: G. K. Hall, 1990.

Crane, Lucy, trans. *Household Stories by the Brothers Grimm.* Illustrations by Walter Crane. New York: MacMillan, 1886. Reprint, New York: Dover, 1963.

Crane, Walter. *The Decorative Illustration of Books.* London: G. Bell & Sons, 1986. Reprint, London: Bracken, 1984.

Creevy, Patrick J. "In Time and Out: The Tempo of Life in *Bleak House.*" *Dickens Studies Annual* 12 (1983): 63–80.

Crystal Palace Exhibition Illustrated Catalogue, The. New York: Dover, 1970.

Curtius, Ernst. *European Literature and the Latin Middle Ages.* Trans. Willard Trask. New York: Pantheon, 1953.

Daleski, H. M. "*Bleak House.*" In *Critical Essays on Charles Dickens's 'Bleak House,'* ed. Elliot Gilbert. Boston: G. K. Hall, 1989.

Dante. *The Divine Comedy.* Trans. Henry F. Cary. New York: Thomas Crowell, 1897.

David, Deirdre. *Rule Britannia: Women, Empire, and Victorian Writing.* Ithaca, N.Y.: Cornell University Press, 1995.

Dawson, Carl. *Victorian Noon: English Literature in 1850.* Baltimore: Johns Hopkins Press, 1979.

Delightful History of Fortunatus, The. London: printed by J. Davenport for C. Sheppard, n.d. Nursery Chapbooks, Bodleian Library, Oxford (Douce Adds. 5 [10]).

Dickens, Charles. *Dombey and Son.* Ed. Peter Fairclough. Harmondsworth, England: Penguin, 1970.

———. *Household Words.* London: Bradbury & Evans, 1850–59.

———. *The Letters of Charles Dickens.* Pilgrim Edition. 12 vols. Ed. Madeline House, Graham Storey, Kathleen Tillotson, et al. Oxford: Clarendon, 1965–2002.

———. *The Old Curiosity Shop.* Ed. Angus Easson. London: Penguin, 1983.

———. *The Oxford Illustrated Dickens.* 21 vols. Oxford and New York: Oxford University Press.

Dodds, John W. *The Age of Paradox: A Biography of England, 1841–1851.* London: Victor Gollancz, 1953.

Donaldson, Ian. *The World Turned Upside Down: Comedy from Jonson to Fielding.* Oxford: Clarendon, 1970.

Doré, Gustave, and Blanchard Jerrold. *London: A Pilgrimage.* London: Grant, 1872.

Du Cann, C. G. L. *The Love-Lives of Charles Dickens.* Westport, Conn.: Greenwood, 1972.

Eiseley, Loren. *Darwin's Century.* Garden City, N.Y.: Doubleday Anchor, 1961.

Eliade, Mircea. *Cosmos and History: The Myth of the Eternal Return.* New York: Harper Torchbooks, 1959.

Eliot, George. *The Mill on the Floss.* 1860. Reprint, London and New York: Penguin Classics, 1985.

Eliot, T. S. *Four Quartets.* New York: Harcourt Brace Jovanovich, 1943.

———. *The Wasteland and Other Poems.* New York: Harvest/HBJ, 1979.

Ellis, Havelock. *Man and Woman.* Boston: Houghton Mifflin, 1929.

Engels. Friedrich. *The Condition of the Working Class in England.* Trans. W. O. Henderson and W. H. Chaloner. Oxford: Basil Blackwell, 1958.

Feinberg, Monica. "Family Plot: The Bleak House of Victorian Romance." *Victorian Newsletter* 76 (1989): 5–17.

Feltes, N. N. "To Saunter, To Hurry: Dickens, Time, and Industrial Capitalism." *Victorian Studies* 20 (spring 1977): 245–67.

Fielding, Henry. *Joseph Andrews.* Ed. Douglas Brooks-Davies. New York: Oxford University Press, 1970.

———. *Tom Jones.* Ed. Sheridan Baker. New York: Norton Critical Edition, 1973.

Fisher, Philip. "Acting, Reading, Fortune's Wheel: *Sister Carrie* and the Life History of Objects." In *American Realism: New Essays,* ed. Eric Sundquist, 259–77. Baltimore: Johns Hopkins University Press, 1982.

Fitzgerald, Penelope. *Edward Burne-Jones.* London: Michael Joseph, 1975.

Fontana, David. *The Secret Language of Symbols.* New York: Chronicle, 1994.

Forster, John. *The Life of Charles Dickens.* London: Chapman & Hall, n.d.

Francis, John. *The History of the English Railway: Its Social Relations and Revelations, 1820–1845.* 1851. Reprint, New York: Augustus M. Kelley, 1968.

Franklin, Stephen. "Dickens and Time: The Clock without Hands." *Dickens Studies Annual* 4 (1975): 1–35.

Franz, Marie-Louise von. *Time: Rhythm and Repose.* 1978. Reprint, London: Thames & Hudson, 1992.

Frazer, James. *The Golden Bough.* Ware, England: Wordsworth Editions, 1993.

Freeman, Rosemary. *English Emblem Books.* New York: Octagon, 1966.

"Fresco Paintings Discovered in Rochester Cathedral." *Gentleman's Magazine.* New series, 14 (August 1840): 137.

Freud, Sigmund. "The Theme of the Three Caskets." In *Creativity and the Unconscious,* ed. Benjamin Nelson, 63–75. New York: Harper Colophon, 1978.

Frye, Northrup. *Fools of Time: Studies in Shakespearian Tragedy.* Toronto: University of Toronto Press, 1967.

Gallagher, Catherine. *The Industrial Revolution of English Fiction, 1832–1867.* Chicago: University of Chicago Press, 1985.

Gibbs-Smith, C. H. *The Great Exhibition of 1851: A Commemorative Album.* London: Victoria and Albert Museum, Her Majesty's Stationery Office, 1964.

Gombrich, E. H. *Symbolic Images.* London: Phaidon, 1972.

Goodman, Marcia Renee. "'I'll Follow the Other': Tracing the (M)Other in *Bleak House.*" *Dickens Studies Annual* 19 (1990): 155.

Gottfried, Barbara. "Fathers and Suitors: Narratives of Desire in *Bleak House.*" *Dickens Studies Annual* 19 (1990): 169–203.

Graver, Suzanne. "Writing in a 'Womanly' Way and the Double Vision of *Bleak House.*" *Dickens Quarterly* 4 (1987): 3–15.

Green, Henry. *Shakespeare and the Emblem Writers.* 1870. Reprint, New York: Burt Franklin, n.d.

Haight, Gordon. "The Sources of Quarles's 'Emblems.'" *The Library* 16 (1936): 188–209.

Hardy, Thomas. *Tess of the d'Urbervilles.* Harmondsworth, England: Penguin, 1978.

Harvey, John. *Victorian Novelists and Their Illustrators.* New York: New York University Press, 1971.

Harvey, W. J. "Chance and Design in *Bleak House.*" In *Dickens and the Twentieth Century,* ed. John Gross and Gabriel Pearson. London: Routledge & Kegan Paul, 1962.

Henkle, Roger B. "The Crisis of Representation in *Dombey and Son.*" In *Critical Reconstructions: The Relationship of Fiction and Life,* ed. Robert M. Polhemus and Roger B. Henkle, 90–110. Stanford: Stanford University Press, 1994.

Hill, Christopher. *The World Turned Upside Down: Radical Ideas during the English Revolution.* Harmondsworth, England: Penguin, 1972.

History of Mother Shipton, The. London: John Pitts, Seven Dials, n.d.

Hochberg, Bette. *Spin Span Spun: Fact and Folklore for Spinners and Weavers.* Santa Cruz, Calif.: Bette Hochberg, 1979.

Hodnett, Edward. *Aesop in England: The Transmission of Motifs in Seventeenth-Century Illustrations of Aesop's Fables.* Charlottesville: University of Virginia Press, 1979.

Hogarth, William. *The Analysis of Beauty.* 1753. Reprint, Pittsfield, Mass.: The Silver Lotus Shop, 1909.

———. *Graphic Works.* 2 vols. Comp. Ronald Paulson. New Haven: Yale University Press, 1965.

Holbrook, David. *Charles Dickens and the Image of Woman.* New York: New York University Press, 1993.

Hoppen, K. Theodore. *The Mid-Victorian Generation: 1846–1886.* Oxford: Oxford University Press, 1998.

Hulme, T. E. *Speculations.* London: Routledge & Kegan Paul, 1924.

Jameson, Fredric. *The Political Unconscious.* Ithaca, N.Y.: Cornell University Press, 1981.

Johnson, Edgar. *Charles Dickens: His Tragedy and Triumph.* 2 vols. New York: Simon & Schuster, 1952.

Jung, Carl. *Aion: Phenomenology of Self.* The Portable Jung. Ed. Joseph Campbell. Trans. R. F. C. Hull. New York: Penguin, 1971.

Kaplan, Fred. *Dickens: A Biography.* New York: William Morrow, 1988.

Kendon, Frank. *Mural Paintings in English Churches during the Middle Ages.* London: John Lane, Bodley Head, 1923.

Kestner, Joseph. *Mythology and Misogyny: The Social Discourse of Nineteenth-Century British Classical-Subject Painting.* Madison: University of Wisconsin Press, 1989.

Kiefer, Frederick. *Fortune and Elizabethan Tragedy.* Los Angeles: Huntington Library, 1983.

Kirwin, Daniel Joseph. *Palace and Hovel; or, Phases of London Life.* Hartford, Conn.: Belknap & Bliss, 1870.

Kitton, F. G. *Dickens and His Illustrators.* London: Redway, 1899.

Kristeva, Julia. "Women's Time," trans. Alice Jardine and Harry Blake. In *Feminist Theory: A Critique of Ideology,* ed. Nannerl O. Keohane, Michelle Rosaldo, and Barbara Gelpi. Chicago: University of Chicago Press, 1982. Reprinted in *The Kristeva Reader,* ed. Toril Moi. New York: Columbia University Press, 1986.

Larson, Janet. *Dickens and the Broken Scripture.* Athens: University of Georgia Press, 1985.

Lerner, Gerda. *The Creation of Patriarchy.* New York: Oxford University Press, 1986.

Lohrli, Anne, comp. *Household Words: A Weekly Journal, 1850–59, Conducted by Charles Dickens.* Toronto: University of Toronto Press, 1973.

Machiavelli. *The Chief Works and Others.* 2 vols. Trans. Allan Gilbert. Durham: Duke University Press, 1965.

Marcus, Steven. *Dickens from Pickwick to Dombey.* New York: Norton, 1965.

Maré, Eric de. *London 1851: The Year of the Great Exhibition.* London: Folio Society, 1972.

Marks, Patricia. "Paul Dombey and the Milk of Human Kindness." *Dickens Quarterly* 11 (March 1994): 14–25.

Marten, Harry P. "The Visual Imagination of Dickens and Hogarth: Structure and Scene." *Studies in the Novel* 6 (1974): 145–64.

Maser, Edward A., ed. *Cesare Ripa's Baroque and Rococo Pictorial Imagery.* New York: Dover, 1971.

Mayhew, Henry. *London Labour and the London Poor.* 3 vols. 1861–62. Reprint, New York: Dover, 1968.

McMaster, Juliet. "Biological Clocks: Time, Gentleman, Please." In *Time, Literature, and the Arts: Essays in Honor of Samuel L. Macey,* ed. Thomas R. Cleary. Victoria, B.C.: University of Victoria English Literary Studies, 1994.

McNeil, Ian, ed. *An Encyclopaedia of the History of Technology.* London: Routledge, 1990.

Meisel, Martin. *Realizations: Narrative, Pictorial, and Theatrical Arts in Nineteenth-Century England.* Princeton, N.J.: Princeton University Press, 1983.

Metz, Nancy Aycock. "The Blighted Tree and the Book of Fate: Female Models of Storytelling in *Little Dorrit.*" *Dickens Studies Annual* 18 (1989): 221–41.

Michelet, Jules. *Woman.* Trans. J. W. Palmer. New York: Rudd & Carleton, 1860.

Miller, D. A. *The Novel and the Police.* Berkeley and Los Angeles: University of California Press, 1988.

Miller, J. Hillis. *Charles Dickens: The World of His Novels.* Cambridge: Harvard University Press, 1959.

———. *Illustration.* Cambridge: Harvard University Press, 1992.

Mirimonde, A. P. de. "Les Allégories de la Destinée Humaine et 'La Roue de Fortune' d'Edward Burne-Jones." *Gazette des Beaux-Arts* 99 (1982): 79–86.

Mitchell, W. J. T. *Iconology: Image, Text, Ideology.* Chicago: University of Chicago Press, 1986.

Moseley, Charles. *A Century of Emblems.* Hants, England: Scolar, 1989.

Moynahan, Julian. "Dealings with the Firm of Dombey and Son: Firmness versus Wetness." In *Dickens and the Twentieth Century,* ed. John Gross and Gabriel Pearson, 121–31. London: Routledge & Kegan Paul, 1962.

Muir, Percy. *Victorian Illustrated Books.* New York: Praeger, 1971.

Munich, Adrienne. *Queen Victoria's Secrets.* New York: Columbia University Press, 1996.

Murray, Lindley. *English Grammar.* 1795. Menston, England: Scolar, 1968.

Murray, Peter, and Linda. *The Art of the Renaissance.* New York: Frederick A. Praeger, 1963.

Newsom, Robert. *Dickens on the Romantic Side of Familiar Things.* New York: Columbia University Press, 1977.

Owst, G. R. *Literature and Pulpit in Medieval England.* Oxford: Basil Blackwell, 1966.

Panofsky, Erwin. *Meaning in the Visual Arts.* Garden City, N.Y.: Doubleday Anchor, 1955.

———. *Studies in Iconology.* New York: Harper Torchbooks, 1962.

Parish, Charles. "A Boy Brought Up 'By Hand.'" *Nineteenth-Century Fiction* 17 (1962): 286–88.

Patch, Howard R. *The Goddess Fortuna in Mediaeval Literature.* New York: Octagon, 1974.

Patten, Robert. "Dickens Time and Again." *Dickens Studies Annual* 2 (1972): 163–96.

Paulson, Ronald. *Emblem and Expression.* Cambridge: Harvard University Press, 1975.

———. *Hogarth: His Life, Art, and Times.* 2 vols. New Haven: Yale University Press, 1971.

———. *Popular and Polite Art in the Age of Hogarth and Fielding.* Notre Dame: University of Notre Dame Press, 1977.

Pearlman, E. "Inversion in *Great Expectations.*" *Dickens Studies Annual* 7 (1978): 190–202.

Pitkin, Hanna. *Fortune Is a Woman.* Berkeley and Los Angeles: University of California Press, 1984.

Plato. *Works.* Trans. B. Jowett. New York: Dial, n.d.

Praz, Mario. *Studies in Seventeenth-Century Imagery.* Rome: Edizioni di Storia e Letteratura, 1964.

Pritchett, V. S. *The Living Novel and Later Appreciations.* New York: Random House, 1964.

Propp, V. *Morphology of the Folktale.* Trans. Lawrence Scott. Austin: University of Texas Press, 1968.

Qualls, Barry V. *The Secular Pilgrims of Victorian Fiction.* Cambridge: Cambridge University Press, 1982.

Quarles, Francis. *Emblems, Divine and Moral.* 1635. Reprint, New York: Robert Carter & Brothers, 1854.

Reynolds, Kimberley, and Nicola Humble. *Victorian Heroines: Representations of Femininity in Nineteenth-Century Literature and Art.* New York: New York University Press, 1993.

Roopnaraine, R. Rupert. "Time and the Circle in *Little Dorrit.*" *Dickens Studies Annual* 3 (1974): 54–76.

Ruskin, John. *Works.* 10 vols. Ed. E. T. Cook and A. Wedderburn. London: George Allen, 1902–12.

Seznec, Jean. *The Survival of the Pagan Gods: The Mythological Tradition and Its Place in Renaissance Humanism and Art.* Princeton, N.J.: Princeton University Press, 1981.

Shakespeare, William. *The Complete Pelican Shakespeare.* Ed. Alfred Harbage. New York: Viking, 1969.

Shepard, Leslie. *The History of Street Literature.* Detroit: Singing Tree, 1973.

Silver, Carole G. *Strange and Secret Peoples: Fairies and Victorian Consciousness.* Oxford: Oxford University Press, 1999.

Slater, Michael. *Dickens and Women.* London: J. M. Dent, 1983.

Smith, Adam. *An Inquiry into the Nature and Causes of the Wealth of Nations.* Ed. Edwin Cannan. New York: Modern Library, 1937.

Southey, Robert. *History of Brazil.* 1822. Reprint, New York: Burt Franklin, 1970.

Stang, Richard. "*Little Dorrit:* A World in Reverse." In *Dickens the Craftsman: Strategies of Presentation,* ed. Robert Partlow Jr., 140–64. Carbondale: Southern Illinois University Press, 1970.

Steig, Michael. *Dickens and Phiz.* Bloomington: Indiana University Press, 1978.

Stein, Richard L. "Street Figures: Victorian Urban Iconography." In *Victorian Literature and the Victorian Visual Imagination,* ed. Carol T. Christ and John O. Jordan, 236-40. Berkeley and Los Angeles: University of California Press, 1995.

Stevens, Joan. "Woodcuts Dropped into the Text." *Studies in Bibliography* 20 (1967): 113–33.

Stoehr, Taylor. *Dickens: The Dreamer's Stance.* Ithaca, N.Y.: Cornell University Press, 1965.

Stone, Harry. *Dickens and the Invisible World: Fairy Tales, Fantasy, and Novel-Making.* Bloomington: Indiana University Press, 1979.

———. *Dickens' Working Notes for His Novels.* Chicago: University of Chicago Press, 1987.

Taplin, Gardner. *The Life of Elizabeth Barrett Browning.* New Haven: Yale University Press, 1957.

Tennyson, Alfred, Lord. *Idylls of the King.* Ed. J. M. Gray. New York: Penguin, 1983.

———. *In Memoriam.* Ed. Robert H. Ross. New York: W. W. Norton, 1973.

———. *The Poetic and Dramatic Works of Alfred Lord Tennyson.* Ed. W. J. Rolfe. Boston: Houghton Mifflin, 1898.

Thomas, Keith. *Religion and the Decline of Magic.* New York: Oxford University Press, 1971.

Thompson, E. P. *The Making of the English Working Class.* Harmondsworth, England: Penguin, 1968.

———. "Time, Work-Discipline and Industrial Capitalism." In *Essays in Social History,* ed. M. W. Flinn and T. C. Smout, 39–77. Oxford: Clarendon, 1974.

Thompson, Roger, ed. *Samuel Pepys' Penny Merriments.* New York: Columbia University Press, 1977.

Thomson, Leslie. *Fortune: "All Is But Fortune."* Washington, D.C.: Folger Shakespeare Library, 2000.

Tillotson, Kathleen. *Novels of the Eighteen-Forties.* Oxford: Oxford University Press, 1956.

Trotter, David. *Circulation: Defoe, Dickens, and the Economies of the Novel.* London: Macmillan, 1988.

Van Ghent, Dorothy. *The English Novel: Form and Function.* New York: Harper & Row, 1953.

Vann, J. Don. *Victorian Novels in Serial.* New York: Modern Language Association of America, 1985.

Vargish, Thomas. *The Providential Aesthetic in Victorian Fiction.* Charlottesville: University of Virginia Press, 1985.

Vicinus, Martha, ed. *Suffer and Be Still: Women in the Victorian Age.* Bloomington and London: Indiana University Press, 1972.

Wall, Stephen. "Dickens's Plot of Fortune." *Review of English Literature* 6 (1965): 56–67.

Warner, Marina. *Alone of All Her Sex.* New York: Knopf, 1976.

———. *From the Beast to the Blonde: On Fairy Tales and Their Tellers.* New York: Farrar, Straus & Giroux, 1994.

Watt, Ian. *The Rise of the Novel.* Berkeley and Los Angeles: University of California Press, 1957.

Welsh, Alexander. *The City of Dickens.* Cambridge: Harvard University Press, 1971.

Whitney, Geffrey. *A Choice of Emblems.* 1586. Reprint, ed. Henry Green, 1866. Reissued with introduction by Frank b. Fieler, New York: Benjamin Blom, 1967.

Williams, Merryn. *Women in the English Novel, 1800–1950.* New York: St. Martin's, 1984.

Williams, Raymond. *The English Novel from Dickens to Lawrence.* New York: Oxford University Press, 1970.

Woolf, Rosemary. *The English Religious Lyric in the Middle Ages.* Oxford: Clarendon, 1968.

Wordsworth, William. *The Complete Poetical Works.* Cambridge Edition. Ed. Andrew J. George. Boston: Houghton Mifflin, 1904.

Wright, Thomas, and R. H. Evans. *Historical and Descriptive Account of the Caricatures of James Gillray.* 2 vols. New York: Benjamin Blom, 1968.

Zadkiel. *The Grammar of Astrology.* 2nd ed. London: Sherwood, Gilbert, and Piper, Paternoster Row, 1840. British Library.

Zwerdling, Alex. "Esther Summerson Rehabilitated." *Publications of the Modern Language Association* 88 (1973): 429–39.

INDEX